# Introduction to Intellectual Property (2025)

SENIOR CONTRIBUTING AUTHORS

**DAVID KLINE, PULITZER PRIZE-NOMINATED JOURNALIST**

**DAVID KAPPOS, FORMER DIRECTOR, UNITED STATES PATENT AND TRADEMARK OFFICE**

**PRESENTED BY GARY MICHELSON, M.D.**

# CONTENTS

# 1 Patent Basics

**Figure 1.1** (credit: modification of work "Float Glass Unloading" by ICAPlants/wikimedia.org, CC BY 3.0)

## Chapter Outline



## Introduction

## 1.1 The Foundations of Patent Protection

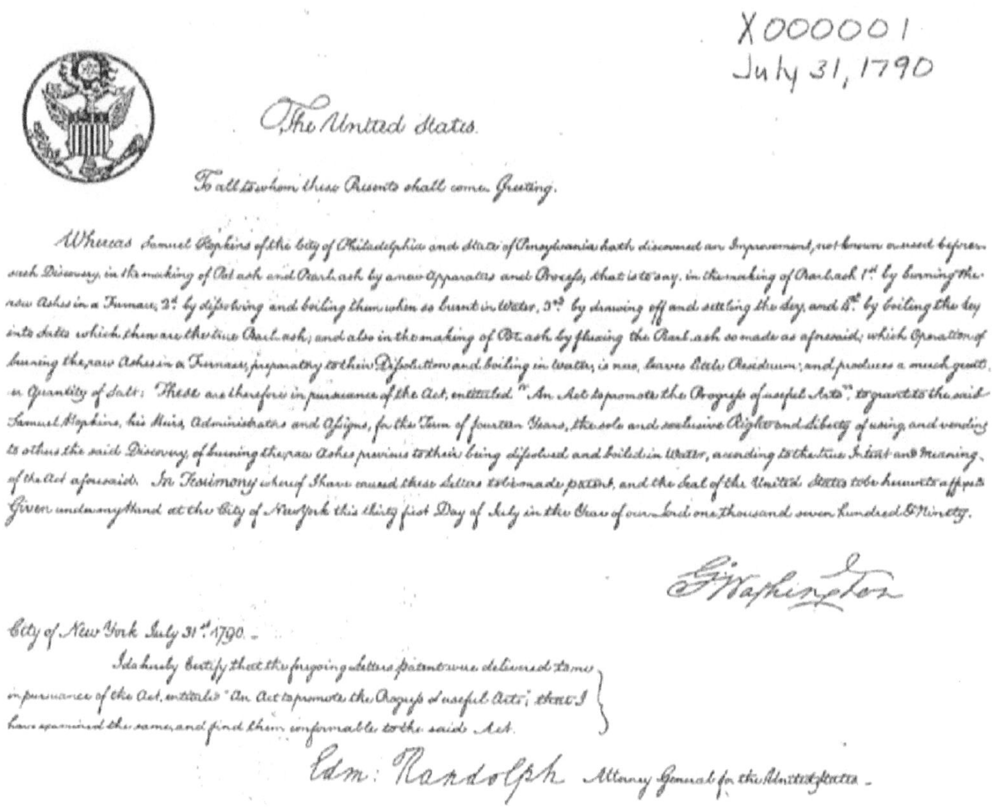
X000001
July 31, 1790

The United States.

To all to whom these Presents shall come. Greeting.

Whereas Samuel Hopkins of the City of Philadelphia and State of Pensylvania hath discovered an Improvement, not known or used before such Discovery, in the making of Pot ash and Pearl ash by a new Apparatus and Process; that is to say, in the making of Pearl ash 1st by burning the raw Ashes in a Furnace, 2d by dissolving and boiling them when so burnt in Water, 3d by drawing off and settling the Ley, and 4th by boiling the Ley into Salts which then are the true Pearl ash; and also in the making of Pot ash by fluxing the Pearl ash so made as aforesaid; which Operation of burning the raw Ashes in a Furnace, preparatory to their Dissolution and boiling in Water, is new, leaves little Residuum, and produces a much greater Quantity of Salt: These are therefore in pursuance of the Act, entituled "An Act to promote the Progress of useful Arts", to grant to the said Samuel Hopkins, his Heirs, Administrators and Assigns, for the Term of fourteen Years, the sole and exclusive Right and Liberty of using and vending to others the said Discovery, of burning the raw Ashes previous to their being dissolved and boiled in Water, according to the true Intent and Meaning of the Act aforesaid. In Testimony whereof I have caused these Letters to be made patent, and the Seal of the United States to be hereunto affixed. Given under my Hand at the City of New York this thirty first Day of July in the Year of our Lord one thousand seven hundred & Ninety.

G. Washington

City of New York July 31st 1790.

I do hereby Certify that the foregoing Letters patent were delivered to me in pursuance of the Act, entituled "An Act to promote the Progress of useful Arts"; that I have examined the same, and find them conformable to the said Act.

Edm: Randolph Attorney General for the United States.

Figure 1.2 The first U.S. Patent (credit: US Patent Office via Wikimedia Commons / Public Domain)

### Learning Objectives

After completing this section, you will be able to

- Describe the philosophical logic behind granting patents.
- Describe the role of patents in fostering invention.

## Do Patents Really Promote Innovation?

Before reading this section, please watch this overview video (https://openstax.org/l/DoPatentsPromoteInnovation) covering the usefulness of patents - how ironic that a system for granting exclusive rights to inventors is the greatest vehicle for knowledge-sharing and technology transfer ever devised by human beings.

## What Is a Patent?

A **patent** is an **intellectual property** right granted by the government of a nation to an inventor that gives them the exclusive right to the invention for up to 20 years, in exchange for disclosing the details of the new technology to society for its ultimate benefit.

In the United States, a **patent** is a legal instrument in the form of a document issued by the United States Patent and Trademark Office (USPTO). It gives the inventor of any new, useful, and non-obvious machine, process, manufacture, or composition of matter the right "to exclude others from making, using, offering for sale, or selling the invention throughout the United States or importing the invention into the United States" for a limited time in exchange for public disclosure of the invention.[i] A U.S. patent is only recognized domestically, and cannot be enforced in another country.

## History of Patents in the United States

The legal foundation for U.S. intellectual property rights was laid by the Founders in 1787, in the very first Article of the U.S. Constitution, which outlined the precepts of our democratic society. In Article 1, Section 8, Clause 8 of the Constitution, Congress was given the authority to "promote the progress of Science and useful Arts, by securing for limited times to authors and inventors the exclusive right to their respective writings and discoveries".[ii]

America was the first country in the world to enshrine intellectual property rights in its national constitution. And the Founders did this quite deliberately, says B. Zorina Khan, an economic historian at Bowdoin College whose book, *The Democratization of Invention: Patents and Copyrights in American Economic Development*, was awarded the Alice Hanson Jones Prize for an outstanding work in economic history.[iii] "To the men who gathered in Philadelphia to 'promote the general welfare,'" Khan wrote, "it was self-evident that ideas, industrial and cultural inventions, and democratic values were integrally related. American democratic institutions would ensure that rewards accrued to the deserving based on [merit] rather than on the arbitrary basis of class, patronage, or privilege."

Indeed, the Founders viewed intellectual property rights as vital to the new nation's economic survival. As George Washington himself stated in his first annual address to Congress in 1790, "The advancement of agriculture, commerce, and manufactures by all proper means will not, I trust, need recommendation. But I cannot forbear intimating to you the expediency of giving effectual encouragement to the introduction of new and useful inventions."

The question is, with all the challenges they faced, why did the Founders think it so crucial to create a strong intellectual property system? Their reasons were both universal—i.e., applying to all societies—and also very particular to America's revolutionary experience.

## "Bargain" Theory vs. "Natural Rights" Theory

Every society that affirms intellectual property rights offers two justifications for doing so: the **bargain or contract theory** and the **natural rights theory**.

### "Bargain" Theory

The "bargain" theory starts with the commonsense premise that people will be encouraged to invent new products and services that benefit society if they are likely to profit by doing so. The U.S. Constitution thus offers inventors a bargain: If you invent something useful—e.g., a cotton gin in 1794 that boosted agricultural production a hundredfold, or a semiconductor 163 years later that sparked the creation of a trillion-dollar new industry and millions of jobs—then the Constitution and statutes say that, as a quid pro quo, you can have the exclusive right to that invention for a "limited time," after which it goes into the public domain and belongs to society.

---

i United States Patent and Trademark Office. (2012, January 26). Patents. Retrieved from www.uspto.gov/patents/index.jsp

ii U.S. Constitution Arr. 1, § 8

iii B. Zorina Khan, *The Democratization of Invention: Patents and Copyrights in American Economic Development*, 1790-1920, Cambridge University Press, 2005.

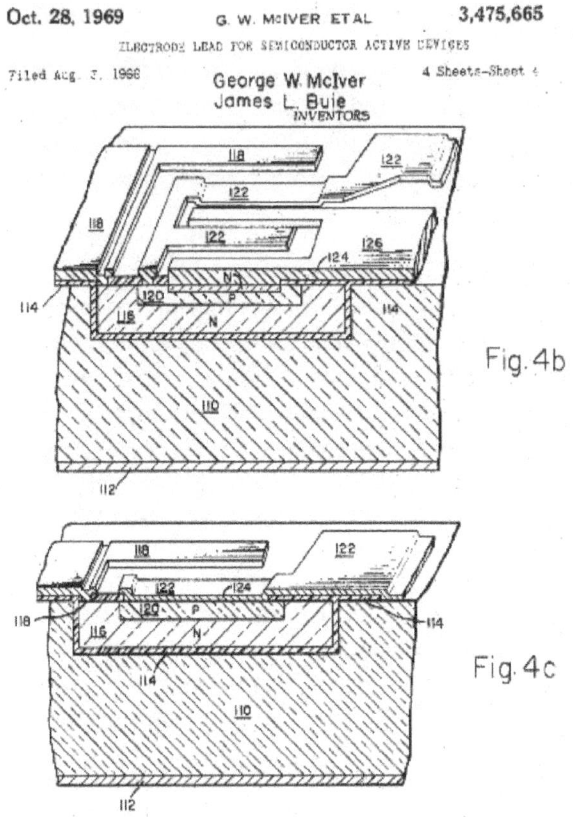


**Figure 1.3** Patent for an electrode lead for semiconductor devices(credit: US Patent Office via Wikimedia Commons / Public Domain)

There is something so simple yet economically potent about this concept. As Abraham Lincoln—America's only presidential patentee (No. 6469 (https://www.openstax.org/l/US6469) for a device to lift boats over shoals)—noted, the beauty of the patent system is that it "added the fuel of interest to the fire of genius."

### "Natural Rights" Theory

The "natural rights" theory, meanwhile, invokes another commonsense premise that most of us instinctively hold to be true: that the product of mental labor is by all rights the property of its creator, no less than the product of physical labor is the property of its creator (or of the person who purchases it from that creator). This is what Daniel Webster was referring to when he said, "The American Constitution does not attempt to give an inventor a right to their invention, or an author a right to his composition; it recognizes an original, pre-existing, inherent right of property in such invention or composition."

This right is not absolute, of course, and inventors' inherent rights may at times be circumscribed by national security or other concerns. But in exchange for disclosing to the public the nature and details of the invention, the Constitution authorizes the government to enforce the inventor's exclusive property right to that invention for a limited time.

**Figure 1.4** Daniel Webster, an American lawyer and statesman. (credit: Wikipedia / Public Domain)

Two important public policy goals are thus served. The inherent property rights of inventors and authors to their creations are protected, thereby helping to ensure that the wellsprings of creation and productivity do not dry up for lack of incentive. And yet the benefits derived from these inventions and creations are ultimately harnessed to the public good through disclosure, thus promoting the progress of the nation and "the general welfare" of its citizens.

### How Patents Foster Innovation

To help understand why patent rights not only encourage inventors but also promote the wider diffusion of new technology for the benefit of society, economic historians Naomi Lamoreaux and the late Kenneth Sokoloff suggested the following thought experiment:

Imagine a world in which there was no patent system to guarantee inventors property rights to their discoveries. In such a world, inventors would have every incentive to be secretive and to guard jealously their discoveries from competitors [because those discoveries] could, of course, be copied with impunity. "By contrast, in a world where property rights in invention were protected, the situation would be very different. Inventors would now feel free to promote their discoveries as widely as possible so as to maximize returns either from commercializing their ideas themselves or from [licensing] rights to the idea to others. The protections offered by the patent system would thus be an important stimulus to the exchange of technological information in and of themselves. Moreover, it is likely that the cross -fertilization that resulted from these information flows would be a potent stimulus to technological change. [iv]

iv Naomi R. Lamoreaux and Kenneth L. Sokoloff, *"Inventors, Firms, and the Market for Technology: U.S. Manufacturing in the Late Nineteenth and Early Twentieth Centuries,"* Historical Paper 98, National Bureau of Economic Research, Cambridge, Mass., 1997.

It's more than just "likely." Extensive research in the United States and other nations shows that patents have served as a powerful stimulant to technological knowledge sharing. A 2006 survey published by the French economists Francois Leveque and Yann Meniere, for example, found that 88 percent of U.S., European, and Japanese businesses rely upon the information disclosed in patents to keep up with technology advances and direct their own R&D efforts.[v]

### Patents Don't Block Innovation, They Promote It

From the earliest days of the United States, patent and legal records show how inventors (including Thomas Edison) regularly kept abreast of developments in their fields. They did this by studying patent descriptions published by both the USPTO as well as by industry publications such as Scientific American, which was founded in 1845 by Munn and Company, the leading patent agency of the nineteenth century, expressly to spread new technological knowledge and facilitate the buying and selling of patents. For example, Elias E. Reis—inventor of a number of devices to exploit the heat generated by electrical currents—reported that when he read in the Official Gazette in 1886 about a patent issued to Elihu Thomson for a new method of electric welding, "there immediately opened up to my mind a field of new applications to which I saw I could apply my system of producing heat in large quantities."[vi] In many industries, specialized journals kept readers informed about new patents of interest.

In fact, new research in 2012 discovered that rather than blocking development, Thomas Edison's seminal 1880 incandescent lamp patent (No. 223,898 (https://www.openstax.org/l/US223898A) ) actually "stimulated downstream development work" that resulted in "new technologies of commercial significance [including] the Tesla coil, hermetically sealed connectors, chemical vapor deposition process, tungsten lamp filaments and phosphorescent lighting that led to today's fluorescent lamps."[vii]

Even the word "patent" signifies its social purpose of disclosure. It is derived from the Latin patent meaning "open," and is the present participle of "pate-re," meaning "to stand wide open."

This explains the origin of the term "letters patent" ("letters that lie open"), which refer to the patent documents issued by the English Crown. These were not closed with a seal but were instead kept open, with the seal hanging at the bottom, notifying all not to infringe upon the patent.

v Francois Leveque and Yann Meniere, "Patents and Innovation: Friends or Foes?" CERNA (Centre d'economie industrielle Ecole Nationale Superieure des Mines de Paris), December, 2006.

vi See "Record of Elias E. Reis," 8, *Thomson v. Reis*, case 13,971, box 1,845, Interference Case Files, 1836-1905, Records of the Patent Office, Record Group 241, National Archives, courtesy of B. Zorina Khan.

vii Ron D. Katznelson, "Inventing Around Edison's Incandescent Lamp Patent: Evidence of Patents' Role in Stimulating Downstream Development," May, 2012, derived from: http://works.bepress.com/cgi/viewcontent.cgi?article=1073&context=rkatznelson

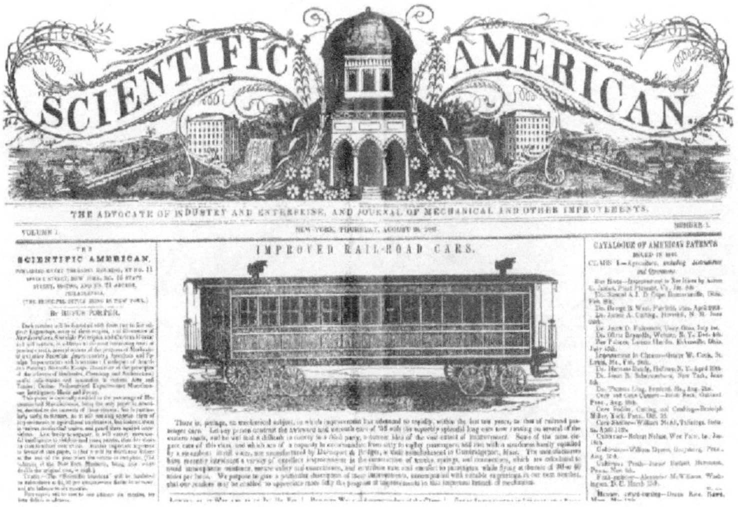
SCIENTIFIC AMERICAN.

THE ADVOCATE OF INDUSTRY AND ENTERPRISE, AND JOURNAL OF MECHANICAL AND OTHER IMPROVEMENTS.

IMPROVED RAIL-ROAD CARS.

**Figure 1.5** Front page of the first "Scientific American" issue, August 8, 1845. (credit: modification of work by Scientific American via Wikimedia Commons / Public Domain)

As with any economic and legal instrument, patents have the potential to slow innovation if their grant of exclusive rights is too broad. But the overwhelming preponderance of economic research and real-world experience demonstrate that, on balance, intellectual property rights tend to stimulate invention, economic growth, and the diffusion of new technological knowledge in every country where they exist.

This fact by itself, however, does not explain why the U.S. patent system became a model for much of the world. To understand why it did—and how it helped build the most successful economy in the history of the world—we must examine the revolutionary design of the U.S. patent system itself and the ways in which it overcame the weaknesses of earlier patent systems.

## 1.2 The Weakness of Early Patent Systems

**Figure 1.6** (credit: modification of work "Ink Jar and Quills" by Student of Rhythm via flickr / CC BY 2.0)

### Learning Objectives

After completing this section, you will be able to

- Outline the history of patents from antiquity through the 1700s.
- Identify flaws in early European patent systems.

### History of Patents: 500 BC to the 1700s

Given the commonsense logic of granting patents to stimulate invention, it comes as no surprise that patent-like incentives date all the way back to antiquity. In the ancient Greek city of Sybaris (located in what is now southern Italy) in 500 BC, "encouragement was held out to all who should discover any new refinement in luxury, the profits arising from which were secured to the inventor by patent for the space of a year."[viii]

The first formal patent legal institutions were developed in the Republic of Venice in the mid-1400s. The Venetian Statute of 1474 decreed that the inventors of new and useful devices would be protected from infringers and copiers for ten years so long as they disclosed the details of their inventions. Most Venetian patents were granted in the field of glass making, and when a large number of these glass makers emigrated to other countries in Europe, they sought similar protections from the local authorities. This is how the notion of patent rights, and their expression in patent legal systems, began to spread and gain acceptance throughout Europe.

Initially, however, English and French monarchs used patents not simply to stimulate invention, but also to grant exclusive trade monopolies to those favored by the court. In the reign of Elizabeth I in the latter 1500s, some 50 patent monopolies were granted over the trade in such staples as salt, soap, starch, iron, and paper. Critics said these "enriched the monopolist and robbed the community" while doing absolutely nothing to stimulate new technology or industry.

A growing public outcry ultimately forced Elizabeth's successor James I to revoke these grants of trade monopolies in 1610. In 1624, the Statute of Monopolies formally repealed the practice and henceforth restricted patent rights solely to new inventions.

viii Charles Anthon, "*A Classical Dictionary,*" Harper & Bros, 1841.

**Figure 1.7** Portrait depicting Queen Anne of Great Britain by John Closterman, circa 1702. (credit: Workshop of John Closterman via Wikimedia Commons / Public domain)

European countries made several other important innovations in their early patent systems. In the mid-1500s, France became the first to publish patent descriptions from inventors who chose to submit them. England under the reign of Queen Anne (1702–1714) was the first to require inventors to submit a written description of their patent to "describe and ascertain the nature of the invention and the manner in which it is to be performed." And in 1729, France began to publish abbreviated digests of patent descriptions, but these were intermittent and subject to delays of up to 60 years after the patents were originally granted. As might be expected, this lack of regularity limited the technological knowledge sharing that is one of the great benefits of a patent system.

## Flaws of Early Patent Systems

Old World patent systems suffered from other major weaknesses as well. Patents for inventions imported from other countries were regularly granted, increasing the incentive for would-be patentees to copy the creative work of others rather than invent for themselves. And there was generally no systematic examination of patents by technical experts, in part because this was viewed as an intrusion upon the prerogatives of the Crown.

But the biggest problem with early patent systems was that they all shared a tendency to reinforce the wealth and prerogatives of elites, not the welfare and productive capacity of the whole of society. In Britain, patents were favors granted "by grace of the Crown" and were often only secured through court connections. They were also "subject to any restrictions the government cared to impose, including the expropriation of the patent without compensation."[ix]

What's more, patent application fees were prohibitively high—more than 11 times the per capita annual income of the average British citizen—which put the system out of reach of all but the wealthy. Yet ironically, in

ix Op. cit., Khan.

the parliamentary debates over the patent system, the exclusion of the "working classes" was regarded as one of the chief virtues of the British patent system.

British patent law also severely limited the ability of inventors to sell or license the rights to their discoveries, as noted in a contemporary 1832 book entitled *A Practical Treatise on the Law of Patents for Inventions.* [x] This restriction, along with "working requirements"—these were regulations that forced patentees to manufacture products based on their patents within two or three years of issuance or lose their patent rights—limited innovation activity mainly to those who had the factories (or the ready capital to build them) needed to produce such products.

These rules had two significant effects upon the British economy. They restricted innovation to only a small sector of the population rather than unleashing the creativity and productivity of the whole people. And they created a bias toward inventions that enhanced the market dominance of incumbent, capital-intensive industries rather than opening up new markets for the sorts of disruptive new industries that usually drive economic progress.

"European societies were organized in ways that concentrated power in the hands of elites and facilitated [parasitic] rent-seeking by favored producers," notes historian B. Zorina Khan. "The organization of invention was no exception. A society that restricts [invention] to elites can generate exceptional gains early on, but the initial spurt is unlikely to be maintained."

Indeed, the result in Britain was unbalanced and narrowly focused economic growth. Inventors faced high transaction and monetary costs, a limited market for their inventions, and a great deal of uncertainty. Diffusion of new technological knowledge was severely inhibited, and the rate of technological change was adversely affected as a result. Eventually, Britain's initial leadership of the Industrial Revolution had more to do with its large existing commercial holdings and manufacturing base, and its vast stores of amassed capital, than with systemic or broad-based encouragement of innovation within British society.

### The Changing Tide

The elitist nature of early patent systems reflected the feudal economic relations that dominated that era. But by the late eighteenth century, capitalist economies were beginning to emerge across Europe, and in Britain, nationwide lobbies of manufacturers and patentees called for an overhaul of the patent system to bring it in line with this new economy. The needed reinvention would come not from Britain, however, nor even from France, which had its own democratic revolution soon after America's. Instead, it took place in the newly liberated United States, where a vibrant capitalism unburdened by centuries of entrenched feudalism was developing.

This, then, is the story of one of the most admired of all American inventions—the modern democratized patent system, now used widely throughout the world.

## 1.3 America's Uniquely Democratic Patent System

#### Learning Objectives

After completing this section, you will be able to

- Explain the role of the Founding Fathers in developing the U.S. patent system.
- Explain the six unique features of the U.S. patent system. Never mind that intellectual capital accounts

### A Patent System For Everyone

Before reading this section, please watch this overview video (https://openstax.org/l/PatentSystemForEveryone) covering why America developed the world's first patent system for the common

x Richard. Godson, A Practical Treatise on the Law of Patents for Inventions and of Copyright, Saunders and Benning, 1832. Retrieved from Google books, at bit.ly/QmPhaZ man, and what we got out of it as a result (hint: the strongest economy on the face of the earth).

Never mind that intellectual capital accounts for 55 percent of total U.S. GDP today.[xi] Or that it represents up to 80 percent of the market value of all public companies in the U.S.[xii] To most citizens today, patents and other intellectual property are inscrutable mysteries. But to America's Founding Fathers, they were matters of the highest national importance.

## The Challenge Facing the Founders

The people who led the revolution and were later tasked with writing a Constitution were not concerned simply with creating lasting political structures that could defend the hard-won freedom and sovereignty of the newly liberated colonies. They also struggled to stimulate the rapid growth of industry to ensure the new nation's economic survival.

The survival of the United States of America was far from certain in those days. It was a backward agrarian economy, dependent on imports and lacking major domestic industry, with a population of barely three million inhabitants. Britain, meanwhile, with whom the United States had just fought a war and would soon fight another, had three times the U.S. population, boasted the most powerful economy on Earth, and was the unrivaled leader of the emerging Industrial Revolution.

**Figure 1.8** Political cartoon circa 1780 titled "The English Lion Dismember'd or the Voice of the Public for an Enquiry into the Public Expenditure" (credit: modification of work by BPL via Wikimedia Commons / CC BY 2.0)

It was, therefore, a critical task of the leaders of the new American nation to design institutions—including a patent system—that would encourage economic activity and investments to spur the growth of America's primitive economy.

It's important to note that although the Founders deeply believed in democratic ideals of government, they were not wild-eyed idealists. They were very practical people who faced an overwhelming challenge: How do you build a national economy from scratch, one that can prosper without British imports? To do that, they needed to mobilize every asset they had.

---

xi Kevin A. Hassett and Robert J. Shapiro, "*What Ideas Are Worth: The Value of Intellectual Capital and Intangible Assets in the American Economy*," Sonecon, 2012.

xii "Intangible Asset Market Value," Ocean Tomo, derived from http://bit.ly/bAPJVH

Unlike Britain, however, America had no significant capital or commercial assets. In fact, the American standard of living at that time was actually lower than in many of their South American neighbors.[xiii] All America had was abundant, but still untapped, natural resources, and a population widely regarded in the world as uniquely enterprising and independent minded.

Ours was the world's fastest-growing population, doubling in size every 20 years. Americans were also widely literate (albeit mostly lacking in higher education) and informed by what Washington Irving called "the general diffusion of knowledge."

Most important, unlike the tenant farmers and laborers who made up the bulk of England's rigid class society, the vast majority of Americans were free-holding small farmers, merchants, shopkeepers, artisans, and mechanics—the forerunners of what we today call the middle class—who were possessed with what publisher Hezekiah Niles called "a universal ambition to go forward."

This was America's principal asset, their ace in the hole. And men such as George Washington, Thomas Jefferson, and James Madison knew they had to find a way to unleash the creative and productive potential of these independent citizens if the country was to industrialize and survive.

## Incentives Needed to Spur Economic Growth

As Jefferson wrote to his daughter Martha in 1787, it was precisely because America was bereft of Europe's vast resources and left to its own devices that "we are obliged to invent and execute; to find means within ourselves, and not to lean on others."

But how to do that? From the historical record, it appears that the Founders quite consciously sought to construct a patent system that would do what no other patent system in the world had ever done before—namely, stimulate the inventive genius and entrepreneurial energy of the common man.

As noted earlier, the first thing they did was to affirm inventors' and authors' rights in the U.S.Constitution itself. Although the intellectual property clause was ultimately adopted by unanimous consent of the delegates on September 5, 1787, there had been some debate about the issue. Thomas Jefferson in particular had expressed reservations about the wisdom of granting "temporary monopolies" (i.e., patent rights), given that Americans had just waged a bloody war of independence to overthrow the British monopoly of trade and political power. But as other delegates noted, and Jefferson eventually came to realize, a monopoly of trade is a far cry from the temporary incentives granted to inventors in return for the benefits they provide society.

"How can the exclusive right of an invention be compared with a monopoly in trade?" D.P. Holloway, a Commissioner of Patents, would later argue in his 1863 annual report to Congress. "How can the exclusive privilege to sell salt in Elizabeth's time, which added not one bushel to the production, but which enriched the monopolist and robbed the community, and the exclusive right of Whitney to his cotton gin, which has added hundreds of millions [of dollars] to the products and exports of the country, be both branded, with equal justice, with the odious name of monopoly?"[xiv]

---

xiii Stanley Engerman and Kenneth Sokoloff,"*Factor Endowments, Institutions, and Differential Paths of Growth Among New World Economies*," in Stephen Haber (ed), How Latin America Fell Behind, Stanford University Press, Palo Alto, California, 1997.

xiv United States Patent Office, Annual Report of the Commissioner of Patents 1863. Retrieved from Google Books at http:// bit.ly/ MehOPv

**Figure 1.9** Portrait of Thomas Jefferson by Rembrandt Peale, circa 1805 (credit: Rembrandt Peale via Wikimedia Commons / Public domain)

In the words of Louis Wolowski, Chair of Industrial Economics at the Conservatoire des Arts et Métiers: "[Inventors'] rights under patents, are called 'monopolies' only from the poverty of language, which has failed to express in words a distinction which no less clearly exists."

The Founders understood this distinction clearly. "Rather than monopolists," says historian Khan, "patentees were viewed as beneficent contributors to progress, and the consistent goal of those who shaped the system was to encourage domestic ingenuity, whatever the social class of the inventor."[xv]

Or as James Madison put it in Federalist Paper 43, "The public good fully coincides with the [patent rights] of individuals."

## Creating a New Type of Patent System

The real genius of the Founders, however, lay in the way they consciously integrated democratic principles into the design of the world's first modern patent system—principles that had a profound impact on the pace and direction of U.S. economic growth. These were reflected in six fundamental innovations in our patent system that departed from European practice.

## Low Fees: Making Patents Affordable

The original patent law passed by Congress on April 10, 1790, deliberately set patent fees to a level any ordinary citizen could afford—initially $3.70, but three years later raised to $30. This was still less than 5 percent of the rate in Britain. Patent fees remained $30 for the next 70 years, ensuring that virtually any citizen could participate in the Industrial Revolution.

The results were dramatic. Whereas most of Britain's handful of inventors came from privilege, the vast

xv Opt. cit., Khan.

majority of America's thousands of inventors came from humble beginnings. They included farmers, factory workers, merchants, mechanics, and other artisans.

Of the 160 so-called "great inventors" of nineteenth-century America, over 70 percent had only a primary or secondary school education. Many had no formal schooling at all. And some of the most famous names in American invention—Matthias Baldwin (locomotive), George Eastman (roll film), Elias Howe (sewing machine), and Thomas Edison (electric light and phonograph)—had to leave school early to support their families.

**Figure 1.10** One of Matthias Baldwin's early locomotives, the Memnon. (credit: Internet Archive Book Images via Wikimedia Commons / No restrictions)

What's more, in another sign of economic democratization, most U.S. inventors had no formal scientific or technical training. They had only the general knowledge common to citizens of the day, plus whatever they taught themselves. What distinguished them was their ingenuity in applying that general knowledge to the practical problems of daily existence, and then exploiting the commercial opportunities that arose as a result. In short, they were entrepreneurial.

The rapid growth of inventive activity during early American industrialization was characterized by a disproportionate increase in the involvement of segments of the population with relatively common sets of skills and knowledge," note Sokoloff and Khan. "Rather than being accounted for by an elite who possessed rare technical knowledge or commanded large amounts of financial resources, the rise in patenting coincided with a broadening of the ranks of patentees to encompass many individuals, occupations, and geographic districts."[xvi]

Making the patent system inexpensive invited everyone's participation. In the words of Englishman John Standfield, quoted in an 1880 issue of *Scientific American*, "The cheap patent law of the United States has been and still is the secret of the great success of that country."

xvi Kenneth Sokoloff and B. Zorina Khan, "*The Democratization of Invention During Early Industrialization, 1790O1846,*" Working Paper No. 578, Department of Economics, University of California, Los Angeles, December, 1989.

## Simplifying Application Procedures

The Founders greatly simplified administrative procedures in applying for a patent. This was no small thing when you consider that British applicants were forced to seek approval from seven different offices, and then twice—twice!—obtain the signature of the King. If they wanted a patent that covered Scotland and Ireland as well, they needed approval from ten more offices. British patent procedures were so Byzantine, in fact, that author Charles Dickens wrote a spoof of them entitled *A Poor Man's Tale of a Patent*, in which his main character, an inventor, is forced to seek approvals from 34 offices, some of which had been abolished years before and no longer existed. Obviously, few inventors could hope to run this gauntlet successfully unless they had the wherewithal to hire very expensive patent agents to assist them.

In the United States, on the other hand, applications only needed the approval of a single patent office, which created repositories throughout the country where inventors could drop off their applications and models and have them forwarded to the patent office at government expense. Rural inventors could even apply for a patent through the mail—postage free!

This last perk for rural inventors turned out to have a big impact on the course of U.S. economic development. While most British industrial breakthroughs were confined to London or other big cities, U.S. inventions were widely distributed across the country, in urban and rural areas both. The result was broader- based economic growth and less income inequality in the United States.

## Spreading New Technological Knowledge

Another unique feature of the U.S. patent system was its systematic effort to spread new technological knowledge throughout society, thereby creating a virtuous circle of innovation begetting more innovation. In Britain, patents were only open to public inspection after paying a fee, and until 1852 were not even officially printed, published, or indexed. In France, printed information about patents was limited to brief titles in patent indexes, intermittently published and only available in the office in which these had been originally filed.

By contrast, the first U.S. patent law explicitly stated that "copies of patent Specification together with similar Models [are] to be made at the public Expence and lodged in each state."[xvii] In addition, as noted in the previous section, a plethora of publications by government and industry enabled any citizen with an interest to keep abreast of the latest patented technologies.

## Examining Patents for Validity

In a very crucial departure from Old World practice, the Founders created the world's first examination system for patents to ensure their **novelty**, **non-obviousness**, and **utility**. The examinations were initially conducted by a committee composed of the Secretary of State (Thomas Jefferson), Secretary of War (Henry Knox), and Attorney General (Edmund Randolph). But this was found to be cumbersome, so in 1793 a simple registration system was established. It turned out, however, that without the examination of applications for novelty, non-obviousness, and utility, the validity of issued patents began to be questioned. So the reforms of the 1836 Patent Act (https://www.openstax.org/l/1836PatentAct) specified that henceforth applications would be scrutinized by technically trained examiners to ensure that the invention represented a genuine advance in the state of the art.

For the first time anywhere in the world, the criteria for granting a patent depended solely upon the merits of the application rather than the identity or the mere say-so of the inventor.

The situation was very different in Europe. In France, the following caveat was printed on each patent: "The government, in granting a patent without prior examination, does not in any manner guarantee either the priority, merit or success of an invention." Imagine trying to interest a group of investors in your new invention with that kind of warning label attached to it!

---

xvii Patent Act of 1790, HR-41,

In Britain, meanwhile, the lack of any examination of patent validity made the purchase of a patent right highly speculative and costly, thereby limiting investment in new technology.

By contrast, says Khan, "the U.S. examination system reduced uncertainty about the validity of patents, and provided [interested parties] with a signal of [their] potential value." This proved to be crucial in facilitating the growth of an extensive market in the sale and licensing of valuable patent rights—the first large-scale market of this type in the world.

## No "Working Requirements" Reduced Monopoly Control

The fifth distinguishing feature of the U.S. patent system was the lack of any sort of "**working requirements**." In the debate over HR-41, the bill that became the first U.S. patent law in 1790, "the Senate suggested requiring patentees to make products based on the patent or license others to do so. But the House rejected this as an infringement of patentees' rights."[xviii]

Indeed, the Founders believed working requirements would only strengthen monopoly power and skew invention toward incumbent industry by limiting patents to those with the factories (or the capital to build them) needed to manufacture products from their inventions. [xix]

In short, the Founding Fathers of this nation deliberately and quite consciously created what we now call "**non-practicing entities**" (NPEs) in order to expand the pool of inventors in their then backward economy to include ordinary citizens without the wealth or resources to commercialize their own inventions. And it worked, leading to a dramatic surge in innovation in nineteenth-century America as large numbers of ordinary citizens started inventing and then licensing their discoveries to enterprises for commercialization.

By 1865, the U.S. per capita patenting rate was more than triple that of Britain's, according to the annual reports from the commissioners of patents in both countries, and by 1885, it was more than quadruple that of Britain. Each U.S. patentee was also far more prolific than their British counterpart, so by mid-century, the United States was patenting five times the number of inventions as Britain each year, even though the populations were then equal in size.

## Creating a Market for New Technology

The sixth unique feature of the U.S. patent system—and along with the refusal to impose working requirements, the one that had the greatest impact on future U.S. economic growth—was "an explicit provision for the sale of patent rights [that] both the courts and the U.S. Patent Office acted to facilitate."[xx]

Why facilitate the buying and selling of patents? Because doing so enabled ordinary worker or farmer inventors without the capital to commercialize their own discoveries to still participate in inventive activity and earn income by licensing or selling their patents to enterprises that could. This ability to license patent rights (along with the low application fees) turned inventing into a new career path for thousands of poor but technically creative citizens.[xxi] It also proved to be a powerful means of mobilizing capital for investment in new technologies and their commercialization into new products and services for society.

That patents could be used as tradable assets by non-practicing entities without the wealth to commercialize their own discoveries was a wholly unique feature of the American patent system. By 1880, 85 percent of all U.S. patents were licensed by their inventors, compared with 30 percent of British patents.[xxii]

---

xviii Op. cit., Khan.

xix B. Zorina Khan, "*Antitrust and Innovation Before the Sherman Act,*" Antitrust Law Journal, No. 3, 2011.

xx Naomi R. Lamoreaux and Kenneth L. Sokoloff, "*Inventive Activity and the Market for Technology in the United States: 1840O1920,*" Working Paper 7107, National Bureau of Economic Research, Cambridge, Mass. 1999.

xxi B. Zorina Khan, "*Institutions and Technological Innovation During Early Economic Growth: Evidence From the Great Inventors of the United States, 1790-1930,*" Working Paper 10966, National Bureau of Economic Research, Cambridge, Mass., 2004.

Patent licensing, in fact, was the principal means by which new discoveries were commercialized in the decades before the early twentieth- century emergence of in-house corporate R&D departments. Publications such as *Scientific American* were founded specifically to facilitate the trade in patents, and it regularly featured lists of new and interesting patents, which commercial enterprises then licensed or purchased to use in their product development efforts.

American Bell Telephone's new product pipeline, for example, operated like most others at the time. According to its 1894 annual report, the company's R&D department licensed 73 patents from outside inventors, while developing only 12 from its own employees.

Thomas Blanchard was a typical inventor-licensor. He was the son of a small farmer who invented and patented a mechanical tack-maker in 1806 that could fabricate five hundred tacks per minute, each superior to tacks made by hand. He sold the rights to his machine for $5,000, quite a sum in those days. He then invented a lathe to produce uniform gun stocks, and the patent he received for it enabled him to attract investors for the production of those gun stocks for the local Boston market. Blanchard also leased his patent rights to gun producers nationwide, as well as to manufacturers of tool handles and wheel spokes. The income he generated from patent licensing enabled him to make inventing his full-time career. He went on to invent a wood-bending machine, an upriver steamboat, and a steam wagon that was used until the introduction of railroads in the United States, and received a total of 25 patents during his career.

**Figure 1.11** Portrait of Thomas Blanchard, circa 1912 (credit: modification of work by George Iles via Wikimedia Commons / Public domain)

According to a 2013 Congressionally mandated Government Accountability Office (GAO) report on NPEs, "History is filled with examples of successful inventors who did not develop products based on the technologies they patented." It specifically cited the case of Elias Howe, who patented a method of making a lockstitch but did not produce sewing machines. Instead, Howe licensed his patents to the Singer Company, which then deployed Howe's invention in its sewing machines.[xxiii]

xxii B.Zorina Khan, *The Democratization of Invention Patents and Copyrights in American Economic Development, 1790-1920*, Cambridge University Press, 2005.

Patent licensing, scholars have found, was facilitated by an array of intermediaries—lawyers, venture financiers, and patent licensing agents—who "lowered the transaction costs and improved the efficiency" of the trade in and commercialization of patented technology. "By enabling, indeed encouraging, inventors to focus on what they did best [i.e., invention], this division of labor gave rise to the most technologically fertile period in American history."[xxiv]

## The Positive Effects of Licensing

The Founders' decision to foster NPEs and patent licensing proved crucial to America's rapid technological progress and economic growth. Indeed, patent records from the nineteenth century reveal that more than two-thirds of the "great inventors" of the Industrial Revolution, including Thomas Edison and Elias Howe, were NPEs who specialized in invention and licensed some or all of their patents to outside enterprises for development into new products.[xxv]

Had the United States followed the approach of older European patent systems and limited patent rights solely to inventors who made or sold products—or prevented them from licensing their patents—America might not have even had an Industrial Revolution.

In any event, the result of this division of labor between invention and production was exactly as Adam Smith predicted:

> "The growth of market trade in patents raised the returns to invention and encouraged a division of labor whereby technologically-creative individuals increasingly specialized in their comparative advantage—invention," noted Lamoreaux and Sokoloff. "It was the expanded opportunities to trade in patented technologies that enabled the independent inventors of this golden age to flourish—and that stimulated the growth of inventive activity generally."

The benefits of that division of labor remain visible today, embodied in the thousands of university and other NPE patents licensed by companies large and small each year, as well as by the positive U.S. balance of trade in patent licensing, estimated to be worth at least $150 billion annually as of 2006. More than 5,000 new products and 7,000 new companies have been created with the help of university NPE patents alone in the last 30 years.[xxvi] And licensors of patented technology help the United States maintain its technology leadership in critical economic sectors.

## A New Species called "Patent Trolls"

To be sure, there is new a species of NPE known as "patent trolls" who use low-quality patents to extort so-called "license fees" from small businesses unable to pay the cost of standing up to them in court. But their activities have nothing in common with real patent licensing.

Typically, these patent owners send form letters to hundreds, or in some cases thousands, of random small businesses, claiming with little or no evidence that they are "infringing" their patents. These letters then demand so-called "licensing fees" ranging from one to several thousands of dollars to avoid a patent infringement lawsuit that could cost those businesses far more to defend against in court—even if the business owner is innocent of any infringement.

---

xxiii *"Intellectual Property: Assessing Factors that Affect Patent Infringement Litigation Could Improve Patent Quality,"* U.S. GAO, August 2013.

xxiv Naomi Lamoreayx and Kenneth Sokoloff, *"Intermediaries in the U.S. Market for Technology, 1870-1920,"* Working Paper No. 9017, National Bureau of Economic Research, Cambridge, MA. June, 2002.

xxv B.Zorina Khan and Kenneth L.Sokoloff, *"Intellectual Property Institutions in the United States: Early Development and Comparative Perspective,"* World Bank Research Workshop, July 17-19, 2000

xxvi Joseph Hornett and David Johnson, Purdue Research Foundation. Derived from: bit.ly/O7iA18

Beginning in mid-2013, a torrent of bad faith demand letters began targeting small businesses, sparking wide protest. The National Federation of Independent Businesses (NFIB) and many other business groups and trade associations demanded action, and Washington responded in 2014 with several pieces of proposed reform legislation. By early 2015, the Federal Trade Commission (FTC) had acted against one sender of bad faith demand letters, and federal legislation to rein in such abuses seemed likely to pass.

At the state level, meanwhile, by early 2015, 15 states had enacted laws to curb abusive patent demand letters, and 11 others were actively considering similar bills. In addition, the attorneys general of several states have used consumer protection laws against making false claims to force these "patent trolls" to stop sending their extortionist demand letters.

These abusive patent litigants should not be confused with legitimate NPEs, however, whose primary business is invention and technology licensing, not extorting so-called "license fees" from innocent businesses. Patent licensing facilitates the transfer and commercialization of technology into new products and services and promotes U.S. economic growth.

### A Patent System for Everyone

In sum, these six unique features of the U.S. patent system—low fees, simplified procedures, examination of applications by trained experts, systematic disclosure of new technological knowledge, lack of "working requirements," and encouragement of robust trade in patent rights—all had a powerfully beneficial impact on the nation's economic growth.

But none of that would have been possible were it not for the broad-based democratic rule of law in the United States and the critical role played by the U.S. legal system in interpreting and enforcing America's revolutionary patent laws.

## 1.4 The Role of the U.S. Legal System

#### Learning Objectives

After completing this section, you will be able to

- Describe the differences between U.S. and European patent laws.
- Describe the history of patent litigation in the United States.

### U.S. Patent Law vs. European Patent Law

Just as with any other property right, patent rights would be meaningless without the ability to enforce them in court. And from the earliest days of the patent system, says Khan, "Our legal system remained true to the Constitution in the belief that the defense of rights in patented invention was important in fostering industrial and economic development."

In Britain and other European countries, patents were viewed as "pernicious monopolies that restricted community rights and [Had] to be carefully monitored and narrowly construed."[xxvii] The enforcement and interpretation of patent laws by the courts in Europe also tended to be highly variable and dependent upon the whims of each individual judge.

In the United States, however, early courts treated inventors' patent rights with deference, just as they did the rights of other property owners. Famed Supreme Court Justice Joseph Story repeatedly declared that patent rights were "sacred" and were the just reward for inventive ingenuity. As he noted in *Lowell v. Lewis* (https://openstax.org/l/Lowell_v_Lewis) (1817), "the proper duty of the court" is to ensure that "wrongdoers may not reap the fruits of the labor and genius of other men."

The relative uniformity and certainty of enforcement of patent rights by the courts also proved critical in

xxvii B.Zorina Khan, *The Democratization of Invention: Patents and Copyrights in American Economic Development, 1790-1920*, Cambridge University Press, 2005.

encouraging capital to invest in commercializing those patent rights.

Contrasting the patent laws and policies of the United States and Britain, Supreme Court Justice Henry Baldwin went to some lengths in *Whitney v. Emmett* (https://openstax.org/l/Whitney_v_Emmett) (1831) to show how English courts saw patents as a zero-sum trade-off between private rights and the public good. The explicit intention of U.S. patent law, however, was "to benefit the inventor, in the belief that maximizing individual welfare leads to maximum social welfare."

Nonetheless, U.S. intellectual property laws did try to strike a balance between the needs of the many and the few. "Patent laws ensured the security of private property rights in invention. However, it was also necessary to balance the just claims of inventors against the dangers of exclusive monopolies that might restrict the scope of current and future invention."[xxviii]

## Changes in U.S. Patent Law Through the Years

Over the years, of course, that balance has moved back and forth between relatively stronger versus weaker enforcement of patent rights. With the rise of the robber barons in the late nineteenth century, government and the courts increasingly viewed patents through the prism of antitrust, in some cases even compelling large firms like IBM to license their patents to competitors. Then with the advent of the high-tech revolution in the 1980s, antitrust concerns faded and the courts began once again to view stronger patent rights as helpful in fostering innovation.

Interestingly, the U.S. legal system has always operated on the theory that the best way to achieve the proper balance between private rights and public interest was not through government decree, centralized management, or compulsory licensing but rather through the decentralized decision making and market interactions of inventors themselves. The court's role was to resolve the inevitable conflicts that arose, on a case by case basis.

Throughout all the twists and turns in patent enforcement over the centuries, however, the federal courts have remained unwavering on four key principles of U.S. patent law.

## An "Explosion" of Patent Litigation?

Patent litigation, of course, has always been an integral feature of the U.S. patent system. The first patent case on record was that of Benjamin Folger, whose patent for the production of candles was invalidated by the district federal court for New York in 1792. This was merely the first of many hundreds (and eventually thousands) of cases in which patent litigation served the important function of settling either the validity or the disputed ownership of the rights to critical new technologies—the litigation between telephone inventors Alexander Graham Bell and Elisha Gray being perhaps the most famous case in point. By doing so, the courts provided greater certainty regarding the value of such rights to entrepreneurs and investors alike.

Today, some critics contend that an "explosion of patent litigation" unlike any in history is harming business and diverting resources better spent on innovation. No responsible observer would deny that the courts have seen an increase in patent infringement suits in recent years, just as they have seen a rise in personal injury claims and product liability suits. But that said, the evidence shows that the rate of patent litigation today is actually below historical norms.

According to USCourts.gov (https://www.USCourts.gov) figures, the number of patent infringement suits filed in the United States increased 59 percent between 2001 and 2011—from 2,520 cases in 2001 to 4,015 cases in 2011. Meanwhile, the number of patents granted in that same period increased by only 35 percent, which supports the view that patent litigation has become more frequent over the last decade as the role and value of intellectual property has increased in the Knowledge Economy.

---

xxviii Op. cit., Khan.

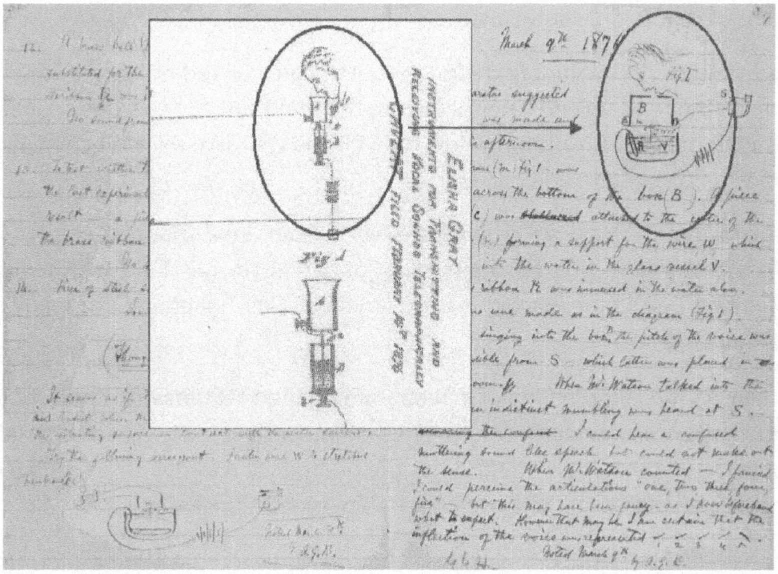

**Figure 1.12** A comparison of the illustration of the telephone in Alexander Graham Bell's diaries and Elisha Gray's patent application. (credit: modification of work by Elisha Gray and Alexander Graham Bell via Wikimedia Commons / Public domain)

Statistics from USCourts.gov (https://www.USCourts.gov) show an even sharper rise in the number of patent suits filed in 2012, to 5,189 cases. But analysts attribute most of this increase to the anti-joinder provisions of the Patent Act of 2011, which curtailed the practice of naming multiple defendants in a single infringement suit. According to Carla Rydholm of the patent analytics firm Lex Machina, "Plaintiffs must [now] meet more stringent requirements to file a case against multiple defendants. So instead of Plaintiff X filing one case naming 20 defendants, Plaintiff X might file 20 lawsuits (one per defendant) each with unique civil action numbers."

When looked at over the longer term, however, it turns out that 96 percent of all the increase in patent infringement suits since 1991 can be explained by a corresponding increase in patents granted, reports the PricewaterhouseCoopers's 2013 Patent Litigation Study.[xxix]

In case you're wondering if the increase in patents granted is itself a sign of a patent system being increasingly gamed by speculators wanting to cash in on the new "patent gold rush," note that the average number of patents issued per billion dollars of GDP has remained at or below the same level—13 patents per billion dollars of GDP—since 1963.[xxx]

Interestingly, although the number of suits filed has increased in rough correlation to patent grants, the number that actually go to trial has remained fairly constant over the last 30 years. About 90 percent of the suits filed each year are abandoned or settled. Of the three hundred that remain, two-thirds never go to trial, and are adjudicated on summary judgment (of noninfringement in most cases).

The nation is thus left with, at most, between 90 and 112 patent infringement trials per year—exactly the same number that went to trial 10, 20, and even 30 years ago.[xxxi]

To be sure, there can be significant costs to business even in litigating and settling patent suits that never go to trial. But no one has shown that the relative cost of patent litigation today is higher than it was historically, or that the cost of patent litigation is more burdensome than other customary legal costs in business,

---

xxix Http://www.pwc.com/en_US/us/forensic-services/publications/assets/2012-patent- litigation-study.pdf

xxx Sean Connolly, "Patent Litigation Rates: What They Tell Us and What They Don't," derived from: http://connollyip.com/patent-litigation-rates-what-they-tell-us-and-what-they-dont/

xxxi Gene Quinn, "Patent Litigation Statistics: 1980- 2010, *IP Watchdog*, derived from: http://www.ipwatchdog.com/2011/08/02/patent-litigation-statistics-1980-2010/id=17995/

especially the huge cost of regulatory compliance.

The evidence does not suggest that patent litigation is "out of control" today. As retired Chief Judge Paul Michel of the U.S. Court of Appeals for the Federal Circuit, the main court for patent appeals since 1982, notes, "The level of patent litigation today is rather modest for a nation with two million active patents and hundreds of thousands of businesses competing against each other."

History supports Judge Michel on this point. The estimated 124-plus smartphone patent suits filed between 2009 and 2012[xxxii] are less than one- quarter the number of patent suits filed during the first "Telephone Wars" of Alexander Graham Bell's time. Back then, the American Bell Telephone Company and its successor, AT&T, litigated 587 patent cases alone.[xxxiii]

Even more surprising, given the common belief in a patent litigation "explosion" today, patent and legal records from the golden age of invention during the mid-nineteenth century U.S. Industrial Revolution show that the patent litigation rate at that time—defined as the number of patent suits filed in a decade divided by the number of patents issued in that decade—reached 3.6 percent.[xxxiv]

In contrast, USCourts.gov (https://www.USCourts.gov) figures show the patent litigation rate during the decade 2001 to 2011 was less than half that—only 1.52 percent. From 2002 to 2012, reflecting the increased suits but also the increased (276,788) patents issued, the litigation rate was 1.57 percent.

Over the entire period from 1790 to 1860, the patent litigation rate averaged 1.65 percent.

Today's smartphone wars, then, are simply "back to the future" when it comes to the ways in which disruptive new industries are developed. Historians have noted that every major industrial breakthrough of the last 150 years—from the development of the sewing machine, telephone, automobile, radio, aircraft, medical stent, and even disposable diaper industries, to the birth of the semiconductor and Internet e-commerce industries—witnessed exactly the same surge in patenting and patent litigation that we see in today's smartphone field.[xxxv]

And just as with smartphones today, the most competitive technology arenas have always been the most litigious. In Edison's time, the inventors of electrical discoveries were four times more likely than other inventors to be involved in patent litigation, and accounted for 41 percent of all patent suits filed during that period.[xxxvi]

In any event, by early 2015, it had already become clear that a noticeable decline in patent litigation was under way. Most analysts attributed the decline to a series of U.S. Supreme Court rulings in 2014 limiting the patentability of software and increasing the ability of the courts to impose sanctions on abusive litigants, which will be discussed later in this chapter. Also driving this decline in litigation was the availability of new post-grant review proceedings under the new America Invents Act, which allow third parties to challenge patents and, if the evidence so warrants, have their claims invalidated by the USPTO's Patent Trial and Appeal Board.

Although patent litigation is costly, the historical record suggests that it serves a vital function by settling the validity and disputed ownership of patent rights so these can be commercialized into new products, new

---

xxxii http://en.wikipedia.org/wiki/Smartphone_wars.

xxxiii "The Telephone Cases," Wikipedia, http://en.wikipedia.org/wiki/The_T elephone_Cases.

xxxiv B. Zorina Khan, "*Property Rights and Patent Litigation in Early Nineteenth-Century America*," Journal of Economic History, 1995, vol. 55, issue 01, pages 58-97.

xxxv Adam Mossoff, "The Rise and Fall of the First American Patent Thicket: The Sewing Machine War of the 1850s, "*Arizona Law Review*, Vol. 53, pp.165-211,2011.

xxxvi B.Zorina Khan,*The Democratization of Invention: Patents and Copyrights in American Economic Development, 1790-1920*, Cambridge University Press, 2005.

services, and new medical treatments.

This is, in fact, the proper role of the courts.

## 1.5 What the U.S. Patent System Wrought

### Learning Objectives

After completing this section, you will be able to

- Explain the effects of the U.S. patent system on American economic development.
- Describe trends in U.S. patenting over the years.

### Creating the World's Most Successful Economy

In 1630, the puritan John Winthrop, future governor of Massachusetts colony, declared that "We shall be as a city upon a hill, the eyes of all people are upon us."

One hundred and fifty years later, the Founders of the United States of America proved Winthrop right, offering the world a vision of liberty and democratic governance that continues to inspire people to this day. As noted previously, the men who led the Revolution and wrote the Constitution were not wild-eyed revolutionaries. They were eminently practical people who managed to create the longest- living modern democratic political and economic system on the planet.

In other words, they must have done something right. And one of those things was surely the patent system they created. Because almost from the moment of its inception, it began to spark innovation and economic growth on a scope and scale never before seen in the world.

Only two months after America's first patent law was signed in 1790, in fact, Thomas Jefferson himself noted that it had "given a spring to invention beyond my conception." Within 13 years, America surpassed Britain—until then, the unrivaled leader of the industrial revolution—in the number of new inventions patented, even though Britain still had more than twice America's population. By 1870, as noted earlier, the United States was patenting more than five times the number of inventions as Britain, although their populations were by then roughly equal in size.

At first, most British observers were dismissive of American innovation efforts, declaring that the former colony would never be able to progress beyond the simple imitation of superior European technologies. But eventually Britain and other nations took note of the way the U.S. patent system seemed to be stimulating invention and economic growth at an unheard-of pace.

**Figure 1.13** Photograph of William Thompson, Lord Kelvin. (credit: modification of "Photo by Messrs. Dickinson, London, New Bond Street" (according to http://www.sil.si.edu/DigitalCollections/hst/scientific-identity/fullsize/SIL14-T002-07a.jpg) via Wikimedia Commons / Public domain)

Sir William Thompson (pictured above), a British inventor and scientist attending the 1876 Centennial Exhibition in Philadelphia, looked at the amazing array of American inventions—including Bell's telephone, the Westinghouse airbrake, Singer's sewing machines, and Edison's improved telegraph—and had this to say: "If Europe does not amend its patent laws, America will speedily become the nursery of useful inventions for the world."[xxxvii]

Meanwhile, the Swiss Commissioner in attendance, the shoe manufacturer Edward Bally, offered a similar warning to his Old World countrymen: "American industry has taken a lead which in a few years may cause Europe to feel its consequences in a very marked degree."

Then, there's Japan's Assistant Secretary of State Korekiyo Takahashi, who visited the U.S. Patent Office. Upon his return home, he said, "What is it that makes the United States such a great nation? We investigated, and we found it was patents. And we will have patents."

Even the British jurist Sir Henry Sumner Maine, who had once argued that "the establishment of the masses in power is the blackest omen" for the future of invention, later changed his tune. He conceded that the U.S. patent system was "one of the provisions of the Constitution that have most influenced the destinies of the American people" and that it had made the United States "the first in the world for the number and ingenuity of [its] inventors".[xxxviii]

As historians Lamoreaux and Sokoloff noted, "[Foreign] observers attributed much of the country's rapid technological progress to its distinctive patent system. Quite revolutionary in design at inception, the U.S. patent system came to be much admired for providing broad access to property rights in new technological knowledge and for facilitating trade in patented technologies. These features attracted the technologically creative, even those who lacked the capital to directly exploit [i.e., commercialize] their inventions . . . and also fostered a division of labor between the conduct of inventive activity and the application of technical discoveries to actual production. It is no coincidence that Britain and many other European countries [later] began to modify their patent institutions to make them more like those of the Americans."[xxxix]

---

xxxvii *Scientific American*, October 21, 1876, courtesy of B. Zorina Khan.

xxxviii Henry Sumner Maine, *Popular Government*, courtesy of B. Zorina Khan.

xxxix Naomi R. Lamoreaux and Kenneth L. Sokoloff, "*Financing Innovation in the United States: 1870 to Present*," MIT Press,

## Every Breakthrough Spurs Patenting Spikes

The patent system's central role in fostering innovation can be seen in the patenting spikes that occur with every major industrial breakthrough. A major surge in patenting took place in the 1880s, for example, when the number of new patents issued each year jumped 56 percent to about 20,000, compared with the 12,000 issued yearly during the previous decade. This patent boom corresponded with rapid advances in the emerging railroad, telegraph, telephone, and electric light and power industries that signaled the industrialization of the U.S. economy.

The next sharp surge in patent issuances began around 1902 and lasted until 1916 or so, when the number of patents granted doubled from 20,000 per year to around 40,000 per year. This was the period of the newborn automobile and aircraft industries' most rapid early-stage growth. Patenting levels then remained relatively stable at about 40,000 per year until around 1960 or so, when the revolution in plastics and other synthetic materials along with boom-time growth in the aerospace and computer industries pushed patenting levels to 60,000 per year. There they remained until the mid- 1980s, when the personal computer and emerging high-tech industries of Silicon Valley began to power the whole of the U.S. economy and propel us toward the age of the Internet. Patenting levels then rose to around 80,000 to 100,000 yearly

With the rise of the Internet, social media, mobile telephony, and smartphones over the last two decades, the number of patent applications filed each year with the U.S. Patent and Trademark Office (USPTO) has surged fourfold. In 2014, the USPTO received 578,802 applications, finding 300,678 of these applications worthy of receiving a patent. This is but the latest spike in innovation and patenting.

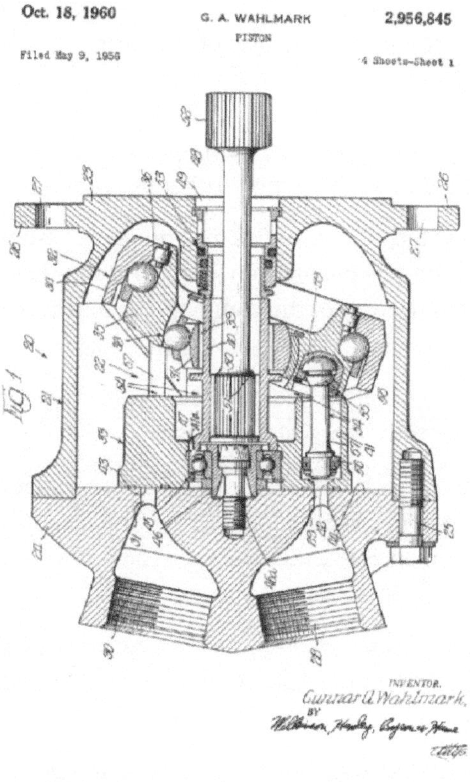


**Figure 1.14** USPTO Patent No. 2956845 for an axial piston pump. (credit: modification of work by Gunnar A. Wahlmark, Rockford, Illinois USA. via Wikimedia Commons / Public domain)

Cambridge, Mass. 2007.

Clearly, whenever the United States has undergone a major industrial renaissance during which technology advances lead not only to the birth of new industries, but also to the reshaping of existing ones, patenting levels rise dramatically. It is no surprise, therefore, that Silicon Valley, midwife of many of the new Knowledge Economy industries of the past 60 years, is home to less than 1 percent of the nation's population but earns 12 percent of its patents each year. The Valley is now the site of a new USPTO satellite office serving high-tech innovators there.[xl]

The patent system has also been crucial in facilitating the growth of new start-up businesses, with 67 percent of entrepreneurs reporting that they find patents valuable in obtaining venture financing.[xli] This is important because although large companies contribute enormously to American innovation and industrial growth through their in-house research and development operations as well as via their partnerships with research universities, start-up companies play a particularly strong role in the creation of entirely new industries. Indeed, virtually every innovative new industry of the last 150 years—From the telegraph, telephone, and electric power industries of the 1800s, to the auto, aircraft, materials, and aerospace industries of the twentieth century, to the semiconductor, personal computer, software, biotech and Internet e-commerce industries of the last 60 years—was launched by an entrepreneurial start-up company.

The Founders would not be surprised by this. They created the world's first democratized patent system, after all, for a reason: to stimulate the ingenuity of the common man. They had asked themselves a question—the same question reiterated two generations later by Supreme Court Justice Joseph Story when he spoke before an audience of ordinary mechanics: "Ask yourselves, what would be the result of one hundred thousand minds ... urged on by the daily motives of interest, to acquire new skill, or invent new improvements."[xlii]

The result was the most successful economy on the face of the earth.

## Patents and the American Dream

It's not only the economy that the patent system helped shape, but the culture and consciousness as well. As the eminent historian Gordon S. Wood observed in his 2010 book *Empire of Liberty*,

> "By the early nineteenth century, technology and prosperity were assuming for Americans the same sublime and moral significance that the enlightenment had reserved for the classical state and the Newtonian universe. Eli Whitney, inventor of the cotton gin, and Robert Fulton, creator of the steamboat, became national heroes."

And for the first time in human history, a nation had come to see its greatness not in empire or military might or royal lineage, but in its capacity for technological progress.

There was nothing preordained about America's economic success, no special "Yankee ingenuity" gene in their hereditary stock. As *Scientific American* noted in 1876, the United States advanced "not because we are by nature more inventive than other men. Every nationality becomes inventive the moment it comes under our laws."

Rather, the secret of America's success was a uniquely democratic patent system that "added the fuel of interest to the fire of genius" in generations of ordinary citizens—and in so doing, helped in a very real way to give birth to the American Dream itself.

Ironically, few people today even know the origin of the term "the American Dream." In fact, it was coined in 1931, by the historian James Truslow Adams in his book *Epic of America*, and it is instructive to read what Adams meant by it:

> "The American Dream, that has lured tens of millions of all nations to our shores in the past century,

xl "*Silicon Valley wins in securing U.S. patent office,*" San Francisco Chronicle, July 3, 2012.

xli "*Patenting by Entrepreneurs: The Berkeley Patent Survey Part III of III,*" PatentlyO, July 21, 2010.

xlii Reported in *American Jurist and Law Magazine*, vol. 1 (1829), courtesy of B. Zorina Khan.

> has not been a dream merely of material plenty, though that has doubtless counted heavily. It has been much more than that. It has been a dream of being able to grow to fullest development as a man and woman, unhampered by the barriers which had slowly been erected in the older civilizations, unrepressed by social orders which had developed for the benefit of classes rather than for the simple human being of any and every class."

Only in America could a working class youth named Thomas Edison with less than three years of schooling develop himself into the world's greatest inventor—a visionary who gave the world some of the most important technologies of late nineteenth- and early twentieth-century life.

This is exactly what the Founders had in mind when they created the U.S. patent system.

## 1.6 Patent-Eligible Inventions

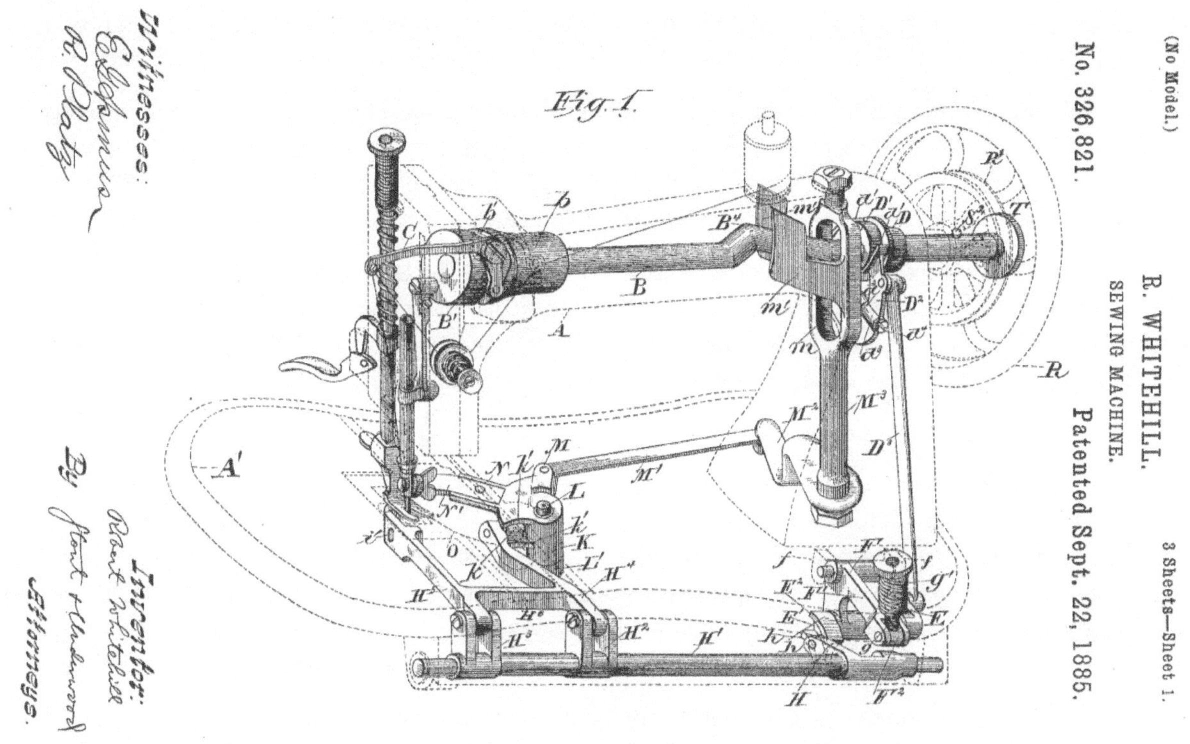


**Figure 1.15** USPTO Patent No. 326821 for a sewing machine. (credit: USPTO via Wikimedia Commons / Public domain)

### Learning Objectives

After completing this section, you will be able to

- Identify the characteristics of a patentable invention.
- Understand what is not patentable and why.

### What, Exactly, Can You Patent?

Title 35 of the United States Code (the Patent Act) allows anyone who invents or discovers any new, non-obvious, and useful machine, manufacture, process, or composition of matter—or who makes an improvement of any of the above—to obtain a patent.[xliii]

These four kinds of patentable inventions fall into one of two categories: They are products or processes.[xliv]

---

xliii 35 U.S.C § 101.

xliv Arthur R. Millerand Michael H. Davis, *Intellectual Property: Patents, Trademarks, and Copyright in a Nutshell.* (5th ed., p. 25). St. Paul MN: West Publishing Co., 2007.

## Product or Process?

Products are physical things—whether they be machines (a new type of robotic welder), manufactures (an artificial knee made of titanium), or compositions of matter (a new chemical "superglue" for binding materials together). In this photo, Elon Musk observes the robotic arms in the Tesla Motors factory. Specialized manufacturing equipment like this are patentable products.

Processes (or methods), on the other hand, are a means to an end—either a means of doing something new (being able to pay for purchases directly from your smartphone), or a new way of doing something old (using "pinch, swipe, and zoom" gestures on a touchscreen, rather than clicking drop-down menus, to manipulate text, music, and images on a smartphone).

## You Cannot Patent Ideas

All patented inventions fit into one of these four categories: machine, manufacture, process, or composition of matter. But not everything that fits in one of these four categories can be patented. And the most important reason why one thing is patentable and another is not lies in the difference between ideas and applications.

You cannot patent an idea for a better mousetrap—not unless it can be developed into a new, non-obvious, and useful machine, manufacture, process, or composition of matter that can actually accomplish the task. You may have a genius idea for faster-than-light travel, but that will not get you a patent unless you can outline how to develop a tangible process or device for actually doing so, in which case you can seek to patent it.

Put another way, "talk is cheap" when it comes to securing a patent. The U.S. Patent and Trademark Office offers no judgment as to the wisdom or desirability of any particular invention—patent No. 2,882,858 for a bird diaper is certainly proof of that. But it absolutely will insist that every invention include a tangible device or process for achieving its intended purpose before it deems the invention worthy of a patent.

## Mathematical Formulas Not Patentable

There are other discoveries that fall into the broad category of abstract ideas and are thus unpatentable. You cannot patent a mathematical formula. You cannot patent a law of nature, such as Einstein's $E=MC^2$. And you cannot patent natural phenomena like electricity (discovered by William Gilbert in 1600) or the Higgs particle that gives all matter its mass (discovered by researchers at the Large Hadron Collider on July 4, 2012). These all exist independently of human intervention, whether we have discovered them or formulated their rules yet or not, and must be freely available to all of humanity for its understanding and betterment.

To restate the distinction, you cannot patent electromagnetism but you can patent a telegraph that uses electromagnetism to communicate rapidly over great distances, as Samuel Morse did in 1840 with patent no. 1647. And although you cannot patent light waves, you can patent a fiber optic wire that employs light waves to communicate even more rapidly and over greater distances, as Corning Glass researchers did in 1970 with patent no. 3,711,262.

**Figure 1.16** Portion of the Large Hadron Collider. (credit: Photograph by Luigi Selmi via flickr / CC BY 2.0)

## Can You Patent Computer Software?

The boundary between ideas and applications might seem clear, but it has become blurred since the advent of computer technology 40 years ago, especially regarding the patentability of software.

To learn more, watch this video from PBS Digital Studios (https://openstax.org/l/PBSFirstPatent) about the first software patent ever awarded and to learn a bit about the debate around software patentability.

## Mixed Verdicts on Software Patentability

The federal courts and the U.S. Supreme Court have tried to clarify the limits of patentability in the computer age. Three Supreme Court cases in particular—often called the "patent-eligibility trilogy"—reveal the evolution of its thinking about software patentability.

In 1972, the Supreme Court held in *Gottschalk v. Benson* (https://openstax.org/l/Gottschalk_v_Benson) that an algorithm in a computer program—in this case, a mathematical procedure executed electronically that was similar to long division with paper and pencil—was in and of itself not patentable. Phenomena of nature, mental processes, and abstract intellectual concepts are the basic tools of scientific and technical research, the court noted, and therefore could not be patented lest it foreclose others from using the algorithm and thereby stifle rather than promote technological progress. Granting a patent in this case, the court said, would be analogous to having granted Samuel Morse a patent covering all possible uses of electromagnetism in communications, rather than for the specific method and apparatus he actually invented.

The court made a point of saying, however, that its decision did not mean that computer software could not be patented—only that software whose only useful characteristic was an abstract algorithm could not be patented.

The Supreme Court further refined its thinking on software patentability in the 1978 case *Parker v. Flook* (https://openstax.org/l/Parker_v_Flook). Unlike the attempt to patent all uses of an algorithm in the *Benson* case, here the use of a software algorithm was limited to a specific application—setting off an alarm during the catalytic chemical conversion of hydrocarbons. This was a specific and tangible use of an algorithm, but the Court still ruled the software unpatentable because it felt the application itself was not inventive.

But once again, the Court left the door open: "Even though a phenomenon of nature or mathematical formula may be well known, an inventive application ... may be patented."

Three years later, the Supreme Court made its third attempt to define the patent-eligibility of software. In *Diamond v. Diehr* (https://openstax.org/l/Diamond_v_Diehr), the Court ruled that although algorithms by themselves are not patentable, a software program that used algorithms to govern the molding of raw synthetic rubber into cured precision products was in fact patentable because it involved "transforming or reducing an article to a different state or thing."

## The Software Picture Blurs Even More

Taken together, the three rulings appeared for a time to arrive finally at a coherent definition of software patentability—namely, that although algorithms by themselves are abstract concepts and therefore unpatentable, software programs may be patented if they employ algorithms to produce a tangible and inventive or transformative result. This view was further augmented by a 1998 U.S. Court of Appeals for the Federal Circuit decision in *State Street Bank v. Signature Financial Group* (https://openstax.org/l/StateStreet_v_Signature), which extended software patentability to software-enabled methods of doing business so long as these produced a "useful, concrete, and tangible result."

But this definitional equilibrium was not to last. The "useful, concrete, and tangible result" test in *State Street Bank* was rejected ten years later by the same court in *In re Bilski* (https://openstax.org/l/InreBilski), which upheld the USPTO's denial of a patent for a method of hedging risk in commodities trading. The court instead offered a "machine or transformation" test, which allows a software program or business method to be patented only if it is implemented on a specific machine to achieve a special purpose that is novel, non-obvious, and useful; it transforms an article from one thing or state to another.

But in its review of *Bilski v. Kappos* (https://openstax.org/l/Bilski_v_Kappos), the Supreme Court ruled that while the "machine or transformation" test was useful, it was not the only test for patentability. In addition to the "machine or transformation" test, the court decreed (rather vaguely) that any future test should be "grounded in the examples and concepts" expressed in its original "patent-eligibility trilogy" of opinions. They thus reaffirmed that business methods may indeed be patentable.

## Finally, a "Pretty Clear" Message

While businesses and the courts were trying to figure out what the other tests for patentability might be, the Supreme Court provided further input with its March 2012 decision in *Mayo Collaborative Services v. Prometheus Laboratories* (https://openstax.org/l/Mayo_v_Prometheus). Here, the court ruled that a process enabling physicians to correlate blood test results with medication levels to achieve the most appropriate dosages was ineligible for patent protection."

But then in June of 2014, The Supreme Court issued what may prove to be its most consequential decision on the patentability of software in the 33 years since *Diamond v. Diehr*. In *Alice v. CLS Bank*, the Court ruled that taking some activity that people have been doing for centuries—in this case, holding funds in escrow until a transaction is completed—and then merely "doing it through a computer" did not turn this age-old activity into a patentable new invention.

At first, many observers believed that the effects of the *Alice v. CLS Bank* ruling would be very limited. Only the patent in the suit was invalidated, after all, not all software patents. What's more, the abstract reasoning of the court in its decision did not provide clarity on how the ruling may or may not apply to other kinds of software patents—for example, the sort of software used in manufacturing that was ruled patentable in the 1981 *Diamond v. Diehr* case.

But by October of 2014, a series of lower court decisions applying the new *Alice v. CLS Bank* standard had invalidated 13 additional software patents. As technology policy journalist Timothy B. Lee noted, "The courts are sending a pretty clear message: you can't take a commonplace human activity, do it with a computer, and call that a patentable invention."

> *"The courts are sending a pretty clear message: you can't take a commonplace human activity, do it with a computer, and call that a patentable invention."*
>
> -Timothy B. Lee, technology policy journalist

How far reaching will the impact of *Alice v. CLS Bank* be? "This doesn't necessarily mean that all software patents are in danger," Lee noted, because the patents involved "were particularly vulnerable to challenge under the new *Alice* precedent. But it does mean that the pendulum of patent law is clearly swinging in an anti-[software] patent direction."

## Overcoming the Alice Paradox

By late 2015, however, it was clear that the *Alice* ruling was having an impact not only on patent law, but also on the innovation process itself within corporate America.

As John Cronin, a former top inventor at IBM and now the CEO of the innovation-on-demand firm ipCreate, observes: "The highest-value products and services today—the ones that increasingly drive margins in business—involve cloud computing, Big Data, machine learning, connectivity, mobility and location-based services, and on-demand and anything-as-a-service software applications and business processes. But ironically, these high-value innovations are also the most difficult to patent nowadays as a result of the Supreme Court's *Alice* decision."

Cronin calls this the "*Alice* Paradox," and it has left many in-house patent groups struggling for a solution. One thing is clear: To be patentable nowadays, software has to take a genuinely-inventive step and either trigger an action, employ a device, or in some other way produce a tangible transformative result.

In addition, smart companies are trying to address patentability issues involving software and business processes much earlier in the innovation cycle, before huge investments are made in R&D that may turn out to be not patentable.

Overall, addressing the "*Alice* Paradox" will be critical for many companies because patenting clearly adds value to a new product or service. In a groundbreaking joint study from Carnegie Mellon University, Georgia Institute of Technology, and Duke University entitled "R&D and the Patent Premium," economists found that "the patent premium for innovations that were patented is substantial. Firms earn on average a 50% premium over the no patenting case, ranging from 60% in the health-related industries to 40% in electronics."[xlv]

## The Debate on Software Continues

The debate over the dividing line between patentable versus unpatentable computer software-related inventions continues—in corporate R&D labs and in the courts.

However, there are some who don't believe that software and business methods should be patented under any conditions. They argue first of all that software is different from other industries—more iterative and more incremental, with each advance building upon thousands of previous advances. Therefore, their thinking goes, software should not be entitled to patents that ought to be more properly reserved for truly breakthrough or revolutionary inventions.

There are two problems with this argument. First, as anyone in the semiconductor, chemical, or medical device

---

xlv Ashish Arora, Marco Ceccagnoli, and Wesley M. Cohen, "*R&D and the Patent Premium,*" Science Direct, International Journal of Industrial Organization Issue 26, 2008.

industries can attest, innovation is no more iterative, incremental, or cumulative in software than is innovation in many other industries. Indeed, there are probably just as many or more patents for incremental semiconductor inventions that build modestly upon earlier work as there are patents for incremental software inventions that do the same.

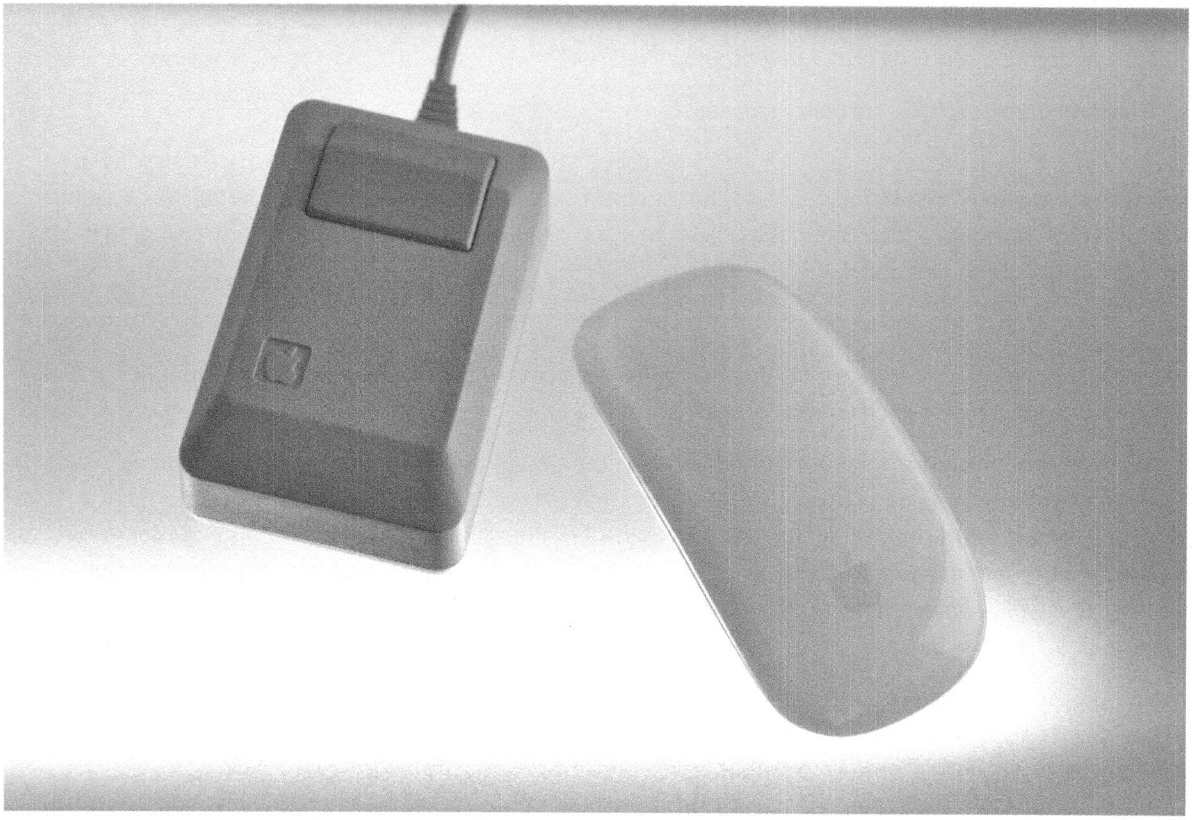

**Figure 1.17** An Apple Macintosh Mouse M0100 Beige from 1984 (left), and an Apple Magic Mouse from 2009 (right) (credit: Photograph by reneko via flickr / CC BY 2.0)

As patent scholar and veteran practitioner Paul Janicke of the University of Houston put it, "There really are no breakthrough inventions—at least not in the sense imagined by these critics. Everything moves one step at a time. In fact, every time I thought I encountered a large leap, it turned out that I didn't know the full extent of the prior art."

The second problem with their logic is that the Founding Fathers specifically designed the patent system to encourage precisely this kind of incremental invention, so that ordinary people—using only the basic technical skills possessed by most citizens—could participate in rapidly developing the economy from the ground up. This was a very different approach than that of elitist European patent systems of the day, and it produced results that the rest of the world very soon came to envy (see "Section 1.5: What the U.S. Patent System Wrought").

As the October 21, 1876, issue of Scientific American noted, "In the aggregate the little things—which in England or the continent would not or could not be patented—probably add more to the wealth and wellbeing of the community ... than the great things do." Or to quote Thomas Jefferson himself: "A smaller [invention], applicable to our daily concerns, is infinitely more valuable than the greatest which can only be used for great objects."[xlvi] Any uncertainty over the validity of incremental patenting was removed once and for all by the Patent Act of 1952. Consistent with the Founders' intentions, U.S. law now explicitly holds that patent eligibility is not restricted solely to revolutionary inventions or "flash of genius" discoveries, but also includes more iterative advances in the state of the technological art so long as these meet the requisite novelty, non-obviousness, and utility criteria.

## Evidence Shows Software Patents Don't Hinder Innovation

Another argument made by critics of software patenting is that patents stifle innovation and foster monopolization in the software industry. Research, however, suggests that this is decidedly not the case.[xlvii] If anything, in fact, the software industry has become even more innovative, more diversified, and more start-up friendly since patenting became common in the 1990s. You need only look at the huge proliferation of highly innovative start-ups in today's social media and apps software fields to see just how erroneous the claim is that software patents stifle innovation. Or consider for a moment the fate of the Blackberry, once dominant but within the space of a couple of years superseded by more innovative competing smartphone makers.

Finally, some critics insist that the intangible nature of software ought to disqualify it from patentability. But as noted earlier, the Supreme Court has affirmed repeatedly that although abstract concepts cannot be patented, software that employs algorithms to produce a tangible and inventive result—e.g., software that governs the molding of raw synthetic rubber into cured precision products—may be patented.

It's also helpful to view this issue in a larger context. Forty years ago, 80 percent of the market value of all public companies resided in their tangible physical assets—their plant, equipment, and raw materials. In today's Knowledge Economy, however, it is intangible assets—intellectual property—that make up 80 percent of the market value of public companies.[xlviii]

Indeed, the entire history of economic progress on our planet may be described as one long climb by humanity up the ladder of abstraction—from brute force to the subtle use of energy, from wealth derived from tangible resources and industrial machinery to wealth derived from ever-more ingenious ways to deploy that energy and those resources. It seems only logical, therefore, to expect that invention itself should follow a similar trajectory—from the realm of the tangible to the realm of the intangible.

Ironically, the debate over patents for software, business methods, and other intangible inventions is nowhere more heated than on the Internet, itself an intangible realm in which "virtual" businesses launched with little more than hope and electrons (e.g., Facebook) are creating real and substantial wealth in the form of new products, new services, new jobs, and new economic growth for society. Yet strangely, those who have no trouble accepting the Internet as the intangible fruit of information age invention seem to get stuck in industrial age conceptions of what should and should not be patentable.

Odd perhaps, but not surprising. The expansion of patentable subject matter into new and more intangible realms has always met with resistance. Patents involving the use of electricity were condemned 140 years ago, as were biotechnology patents 30 years ago, and of course software patents when they began to appear in large numbers 20 years ago. In each case, critics warned that these new kinds of patents would hold back further scientific discovery and innovation. Yet in each case, innovation and discovery actually intensified and their benefits to society multiplied.

## When Gene-Related Inventions Are Patentable

A similar resistance is also developing toward gene-related patents. These began to be issued in significant numbers after the Supreme Court's 1980 ruling in *Diamond v. Chakrabarty*, which upheld the first patent on a newly-created living organism—a bacterium for digesting crude oil in oil spills. Since then, patents have been granted for isolated gene sequences, but so far only on those with known functions and not on naturally-occurring genes in humans or other organisms. Patents have also been granted for gene sequences used in diagnostic testing, and on gene sequences that have been altered to make them more useful in a specific

---

xlvi From Jefferson's letter to George Fleming in 1815, excerpt from *The Jefferson Cyclopedia*, courtesy of B. Zorina Khan.

xlvii Robert Merges, "*Patents, Entry and Growth in The Software Industry*," University of California at Berkeley School of Law, Berkeley, California, 2006. Retrieved from: http://papers.ssrn.com/sol3/papers.cfm?abstract_id=926204

xlviii Op. cit., Ocean Tomo.

application.

In March of 2010, however, a federal district court judge ruled in the case of *Myriad Genetics* that even isolated DNA is fundamentally the same as naturally- occurring DNA and is therefore ineligible for patenting. His ruling was reversed by the U.S. Court of Appeals for the Federal Circuit in July, 2011. But the Supreme Court then set aside that decision and directed the appeals court to once again review the case in light of its March, 2012 *Prometheus* decision. On August 16, 2012, however, the U.S. Court of Appeals for the Federal Circuit once again reaffirmed Myriad's right to patent the isolated genes BCRA1 and BCRA2, which are involved in most inherited forms of breast and ovarian cancer.

On June 13, 2013, however, the U.S. Supreme Court finally determined in a unanimous decision that a naturally occurring DNA segment is a product of nature and cannot be patented merely because it has been isolated, thereby invalidating Myriad's patents on the BRCA1 and BRCA2 genes. The Court did rule, however, that the manipulation of a gene to create something not found in nature—such as a strand of synthetically-produced complementary DNA (cDNA)—could still be eligible for patent protection.

To the average citizen—and perhaps to many patent lawyers as well—all this legal hairsplitting over the limits of patentability in the computer age must seem a bit like the debates in medieval times over how many angels can dance on the head of a pin. But two critical points must be borne in mind regarding these debates.

First, no matter what anyone thinks the limits of patentability in an ideal world ought to be, out in the real world where we actually live, software, business method, and gene patents are multi- billion-dollar facts of life that businesses ignore only at their peril.

Second, whatever confusion may exist today, the debates over patentability in the computer age will almost certainly be resolved eventually to most people's satisfaction, just as all previous debates over patentability have. For if nothing else, the two hundred year-plus history of the courts and the patent office demonstrate a remarkable ability on the part of these institutions to adapt to the challenges posed by new technologies and new economic conditions.

## 1.7 Criteria for Patenting

### Learning Objectives

After completing this section, you will be able to

- Identify the criteria that an invention must meet to earn a patent.
- Understand why non-obviousness is the most difficult hurdle to overcome.

### Can I Patent That?

Before reading this section, please watch this overview video (https://openstax.org/l/CanIPatent) covering what you can and cannot patent. You can't patent an idea (like an idea for a better mousetrap), only an application of that idea in a practical invention. Novelty, utility, and non-obviousness—the holy trinity of patents.

Now that you've learned what can be patented and what cannot, we will next examine the criteria for determining if a patent-eligible invention actually merits one. These criteria center around three concepts mentioned in the previous section and enumerated in the Patent Act: novelty, utility, and non- obviousness.[xlix]

Let's discuss these three concepts in greater detail.

### Novelty

The requirement in Sections 101 and 102 of the Patent Act for novelty in an invention means that to qualify for a patent, a machine, manufacture, process, or composition of matter must not have been previously described

xlix 35 U.S.C.§101, §102, and §103

or known. Specifically, it must not have been patented, described in an unpublished or published patent application, explained in a printed publication such as an article or technical paper, or publicly known prior to the filing date of the new patent application. In addition, it must not have been published, used in public, or offered for sale by the applicant or their colleagues more than 12 months prior to the filing of a patent application.

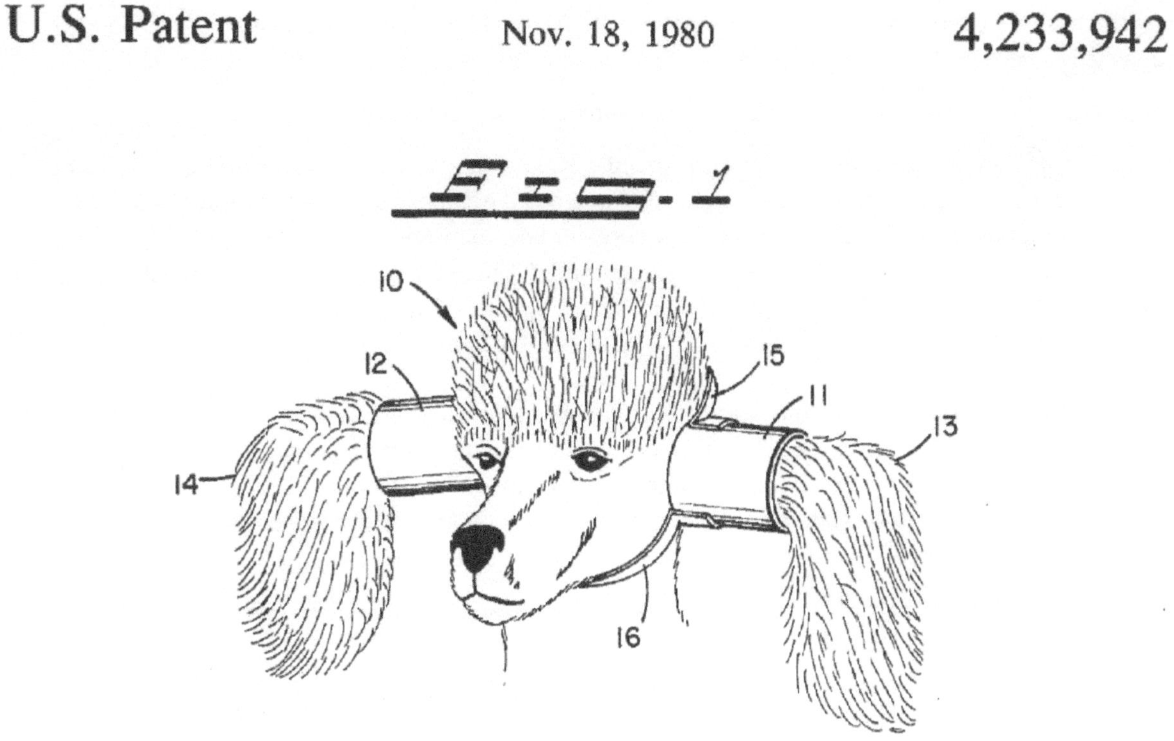


**Figure 1.18** Patent for dog ear protectors designed to keep a dog's hair clean while eating. (creadit: USPTO via uspto.gov / Public domain)

If any of the above is true of an invention, it is said to have been "anticipated" and cannot be patented. These novelty requirements exist whether the "prior art"—the catchall term for any previous patent, publication, or use—is domestic or foreign.

This does not mean, of course, that your faster-than-light warp drive is unpatentable simply because it was envisioned in a general way in episodes of *Star Trek* and its successors' television shows, and in many *Star Trek* books.

"It is not enough that an invention be suggested by the literature," explains the eminent New York University scholar Arthur R. Miller and his coauthor Michael H. Davis' in their textbook for law students.[1] "Nor is it sufficient that the literature made the invention inevitable—that bears on the question of non-obviousness. The test, with one major exception, is whether enough of the invention has been disclosed to enable a person skilled in the applicable art to duplicate the product or process."

That one exception, writes Miller and Davis, is public use of the invention. In that case, even a limited disclosure that does not reveal the secrets of the invention can still foreclose a patent if the public use of it "discloses the invention's benefits."

## Prior Art Must Be Enabling

In the era of social media, the previously mentioned requirements could pose a novelty barrier if not handled

1 Op. cit., Miller & Davis.

properly.

For instance, if you develop a new watch that displays information from an iPhone, and then disclose it on the crowdsourced funding site Kickstarter in order to raise capital from thousands of small-time investors, then you will probably want to file a patent application prior to, or certainly no later than a year after, your disclosure of the benefits of your watch to the public.

But in the absence of such public use, disclosure in prior art must be substantial and enabling to be disqualifying.

As patent attorney and writer of the widely read *IP Watchdog* blog Gene Quinn explains:

> "What *Star Trek* teaches is the idea of warp speed wit some suggested articulation of how it could be achieved. But that's not informing enough. Someone could not make and use the device based on what is taught in *Star Trek*. So if you actually figure out how to make a faster-than-light warp drive work—and can describe it sufficiently so that someone skilled in the science of space propulsion could build it—then yes, it would be patentable." Take heart, *Star Trek* fans!

## Utility

As the *Star Trek* example suggests, the novelty issue can also touch on the question of utility—the second patentability criteria. Utility has a special meaning in patent law, which is simply that an invention must function and be of some benefit qualitatively—although no minimum quantum of benefit is necessary. The landscape of business is littered with companies that have invented not very useful or necessary products. But these may satisfy the requirement for utility if at least someone would find them useful.

But snake oil medicines and other products that do not work in any meaningful way will not meet the requirement for utility. "The inventor of an ineffective drug may not obtain a patent merely because he convinces gullible patients that it has a non-existent curative effect," Miller and Davis note. "It is not so much that it lacks a minimum quantum of benefit (the patients may find it subjectively useful), but it is, instead, that it has an impermissible fraudulent quality."

**Figure 1.19** An ad for Worner's Famous Rattlesnake Oil, circa 1914. (credit: Wormer's Famous Rattlesnake Oil via Wikimedia Commons / Public domain)

Even when no fraud is intended, the utility of a product or process must be demonstrate in a patent application—not presumed, but affirmatively demonstrated. Simply put, the thing or the method you have invented must actually work as it is intended and claimed to work.

"Forget *Star Trek* for a moment," says Quinn. "On a more mundane level, the USPTO used to deny patents for methods and compositions for re-growing hair. These were seen as lacking utility because re-growing hair was believed to be impossible. Finally, someone was able to prove that his method and composition actually re-grew hair on a bald scalp. The patent examiners withdrew their rejection, and patents for such products have issued ever since."

Interestingly, Quinn explains, since the earlier patent applications on hair-growing products didn't describe anything that actually worked, they could not be used under the novelty bar to block later patent applications for hair-growing products that did work.

### Non-Obviousness

An invention may be new. It may also have utility. But to meet the criteria for a patent, it must also be non-obvious under Section 103 of the Patent Act.

Let's now dig deeper into the requirements of the concept of non-obviousness.

### Requirements

The requirement for non-obviousness may be illustrated with a fanciful example. If the number 4 were an invented product rather than a mathematical symbol, then even though the number 4 had never been invented before and was thus novel, it would still not be patentable. That's because someone skilled in the art could have put 2 and 2 together to come up with it.

But to offer a more practical example, say you invent a wheeled cart to move office supplies more easily between departments. If this is the first such wheeled office cart in history, you can get a patent for it. But if you then decide, "Hey, why not put those wheels on a chair?" you won't get a patent for it. That's because combining two such widely-known and available elements would be obvious to anyone skilled in the art of office furniture design.

But things are not so obvious when it comes to inventing a camera phone. Even though it's composed of well-known and widely-available components, combining the two did satisfy the requirement for non-obviousness because it became more than the sum of its parts and met a large and previously-unfilled need in the marketplace. The millions of people who take selfies everyday is certainly proof of that.

There are various ways of presenting evidence that your invention satisfies the non-obvious requirement for patentability. You can demonstrate that the existing elements of your invention, although individually already known, yield an unexpected or hidden result. Or you can show that your invention, although composed of well- known and widely available components, when combined satisfies a long-felt but previously unfilled need in the marketplace, thus indicating its non-obviousness. Both of these demonstrations of non-obviousness apply to the camera phone example above.

### The One-Click Patent

Some people criticized the so-called "one-click" patent granted by the USPTO to Amazon.com in 1999 for Amazon's system enabling customers to buy an item with a single click of the mouse—with the payment information needed to complete the purchase already having been entered by the user previously.

They contended that although Amazon might have been the first company to employ the process, it was an obvious and inevitable iteration of already- existing mouse-clicking procedures for making a purchase online. The patent office reexamined the patent, however, and in 2007 upheld the validity and the bulk of its major claims.

It is important to note that it's an invention's function that is often examined to determine obviousness. "Even though it may be obvious that a certain object can be constructed in a certain way, its utility and novelty may lie in its functional use, not its construction," write Miller and Davis. "Therefore, the prior art must be used to determine whether the invention's new and useful function, not its construction, is non-obvious."

During the first half of the twentieth century, the courts often saw an invention as obvious when it lacked a "flash of genius" and was merely an incremental advance over the state of the art as opposed to what they imagined would be a "revolutionary" breakthrough discovery. But that subjective interpretation of inventiveness was overturned by the 1952 Patent Act, which codified a more objective standard—namely, that whether an invention is developed through laborious trial and error or through a eureka flash-of-genius moment has no bearing on its obviousness or non-obviousness.

## Overcoming Patent Hurdles

Taken together, the three patenting criteria—novelty, utility, and non-obviousness—function like the obstacles in an Olympic hurdles race. The utility hurdle is easiest to overcome. The novelty hurdle less so. But by far, the highest hurdle facing inventors is non-obviousness.

"The vast majority of all rejections at the patent office are for obviousness reasons," explains retired Chief Judge Paul Michel of the U.S. Court of Appeals for the Federal Circuit, the main court that handles patent appeals. "And it's not very difficult to see why. Given the millions of patented inventions over the decades, the tens of millions of past and current products on the market, it's not all that easy to come up with an invention that is not only novel but also truly non-obvious to someone with ordinary skill in the state of the art."

Many believe that the criteria for patenting weakened in the late 1990s and early 2000s, and that as a result, too many poor-quality patents were issued. To the extent this problem exists, one of its likeliest causes is the fivefold increase in patent applications that has taken place over the last 30 years without a commensurate increase in USPTO funding, resources, and capabilities.

Despite these challenges, the USPTO has made substantial progress in the last five years in improving examiner training and tools, reducing the backlog of pending applications, and strengthening the quality of the examination process for patent applications. This progress has been made despite oftentimes-unclear or contradictory patentability rulings from the courts.

Patent quality is essential to the maintenance of public confidence in the patent system. After all, when property rights (either real or intellectual) are seen as overbroad, ill-defined, or illegitimate, individuals and businesses are more willing to trespass on them.

# 1.8 Other Types of Patents

**Figure 1.20** (credit: Photograph by Brian Boucheron via flickr / CC BY 2.0)

## Learning Objectives

After completing this section, you will be able to

- Explain the diff ences among utility, plant, and design patents.
- Describe common patent misconceptions.

Up to this point, we have focused only on the most common types of patents, called **utility patents**, which preclude others from making, using, or selling the invention during the term of the patent, which begins on the grant date and ends 20 years from the filing date (for an average of 17 to 18 years). But in addition to these, the Patent Act also provides for two other types of patents—**plant patents** and **design patents**.

## Plant Patents

Plant patents were first created by the Patent Act of 1930 (https://www.openstax.org/l/PatentAct1930), which had been proposed by Luther Burbank to protect new species of asexually reproduced plants, mostly flowers. These are different than the utility patents granted to bioengineered plants used in agriculture. The United States was the first country in the world to grant plant patents, and even today many countries continue to deny protection for plants. Indeed, even some signatories to the Agreement on Trade-Related Aspects of Intellectual Property Rights (TRIPS) administered by the World Trade Organization (WTO) reserve the right to deny patents for plants.

Although the requirements for plant and design patents are substantially the same as those for utility patents, there are some crucial differences. The most important of these is the substitution of a different test for one of the three criteria for patentability discussed in the previous section.

Instead of novelty, utility, and non-obviousness, the criteria for plant patentability are novelty, **distinctiveness**, and non-obviousness. To be patentable, plants must be cultivated rather than found in the wild, and plant patents are granted only to protect a new, distinct, and non-obvious variety of asexually reproduced plant—i.e., those grown not with seeds but by grafting, budding, or cutting. A plant need not be useful to qualify for a patent, but it must be distinctive in its color, habit, soil, flavor, productivity, form, or other aspects.

## Design Patents

Design patents are granted to protect new, original, and non-obvious ornamental designs for articles of manufacture. Examples include Apple's 2009 and 2010 patents—No. D593087 (https://www.openstax.org/l/USD593087) and No. D618677 (https://www.openstax.org/l/USD618677) —which covered among other things the unique, rounded-corner design of the iPhone, as well as its 2005 design patent No. D504889 (https://www.openstax.org/l/USD504889) for the look and feel of the iPad. Design patents can be just as valuable as utility patents, as Apple discovered when a jury awarded it $1 billion in damages against Samsung in August 2012, for the latter's infringement of Apple's utility and design patents. The case is currently on appeal.

Like plant patents, design patents also substitute a different test than utility in their requirements for patentability. Instead of the novelty, utility, and non-obvious requirements for utility patents, the criteria for design patents are novelty, **ornamentality**, and non-obviousness.

It was on the subject of design patents that one example of media confusion appeared. The *New York Times* published an article November 16, 2012, declaring in a sensational headline that "Apple Now Owns the Page Turn (https://www.openstax.org/l/ApplePageTurn) ." The article claimed that a new Apple design patent "gives Apple the exclusive rights to the page turn in an e-reader application." According to the article's author, this showed "just how broken the patent system is."

Had the author of the article even read an obvious and easily-available source as the Wikipedia entry on design patents, however, he would have learned that design patents are granted only for nonfunctional ornamental designs. In fact, says Wikipedia, "design patents can be invalidated if the design has practical utility."

What Apple actually "owns," therefore, is not the "page turn" function itself but merely the particular ornamental design of the way a page turn is executed in their devices.

Another example of confused media reporting on patent matters was the February 6, 2013, *Forbes* article headlined: "Is the Patent System Broken? Well, Amazon's Just Patented the Sale of Second Hand Goods (http://www.forbes.com/#/62ee8b9728c2) ." Amazon actually did no such thing, but the author of that article probably made this assumption after reading the abstract of the patent describing its general subject matter. Like many reporters new to patent issues, the author didn't realize that the abstract tells you literally nothing about the exclusive rights conferred by a patent. Only the claims of the patent detail the specific exclusionary rights of the patent holder.

Indeed, when you read the claims of the Amazon patent in question, you discover that Amazon hasn't claimed ownership of the idea of a "market in second-hand digital goods" at all. Instead, the claims involve merely a very specific and novel method of conducting such a market. Meanwhile, Apple, ReDigi, and other firms have patented their own alternative methods of conducting a secondary digital market.

# 1.9 The Patenting Process

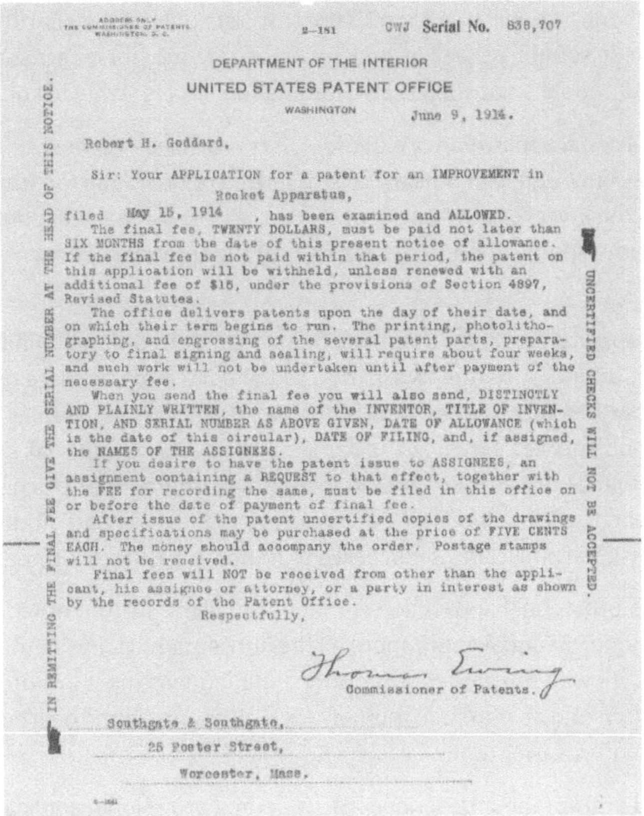

ADDRESS ONLY THE COMMISSIONER OF PATENTS WASHINGTON, D. C.

2—181 CWJ **Serial No.** 838,707

DEPARTMENT OF THE INTERIOR

UNITED STATES PATENT OFFICE

WASHINGTON June 9, 1914.

Robert H. Goddard,

Sir: Your APPLICATION for a patent for an IMPROVEMENT in

Rocket Apparatus,

filed May 15, 1914, has been examined and ALLOWED.

The final fee, TWENTY DOLLARS, must be paid not later than SIX MONTHS from the date of this present notice of allowance. If the final fee be not paid within that period, the patent on this application will be withheld, unless renewed with an additional fee of $15, under the provisions of Section 4897, Revised Statutes.

The office delivers patents upon the day of their date, and on which their term begins to run. The printing, photolithographing, and engrossing of the several patent parts, preparatory to final signing and sealing, will require about four weeks, and such work will not be undertaken until after payment of the necessary fee.

When you send the final fee you will also send, DISTINCTLY AND PLAINLY WRITTEN, the name of the INVENTOR, TITLE OF INVENTION, AND SERIAL NUMBER AS ABOVE GIVEN, DATE OF ALLOWANCE (which is the date of this circular), DATE OF FILING, and, if assigned, the NAMES OF THE ASSIGNEES.

If you desire to have the patent issue to ASSIGNEES, an assignment containing a REQUEST to that effect, together with the FEE for recording the same, must be filed in this office on or before the date of payment of final fee.

After issue of the patent uncertified copies of the drawings and specifications may be purchased at the price of FIVE CENTS EACH. The money should accompany the order. Postage stamps will not be received.

Final fees will NOT be received from other than the applicant, his assignee or attorney, or a party in interest as shown by the records of the Patent Office.

Respectfully,

Thomas Ewing

Commissioner of Patents.

Southgate & Southgate,

25 Foster Street,

Worcester, Mass.

IN REMITTING THE FINAL FEE GIVE THE SERIAL NUMBER AT THE HEAD OF THIS NOTICE.

UNCERTIFIED CHECKS WILL NOT BE ACCEPTED.

**Figure 1.21** Notice of Examination and Approval of Patent Application. (credit: National Archives and Records Administration via Wikimedia Commons / Public domain)

## Learning Objectives

After completing this section, you will be able to

- Describe the steps in the patent application process.
- Discuss the importance of proper claims drafting.

## Applying for a Patent

Much is at stake in the process of applying for a patent. Depending upon how you draft the claims and write the specification of your application, you could win or lose patent rights at any point in the examination process. In addition, any patent rights you win can be worth a considerable amount of money, and can be enforced by the U.S. federal courts.

An applicant must first determine whether to file an application for a utility, design, or plant patent. Then, the applicant must determine their filing status: large entity, small entity, or the new category of micro entity created by the America Invents Act of 2011 (AIA) (https://www.openstax.org/l/AmericaInventsAct) . Small entities, which are universities, non-profits, and small businesses with fewer than 500 employees who also meet certain other criteria, receive a 50 percent discount on the application fees paid by large entities. Micro entities, which are small entities who have a gross income less than three times U.S. median household income or meet certain other criteria, receive a 75 percent discount. These discounts on USPTO fees for small and micro entities do not apply to the attorneys' fees often involved in applying for a patent, which can be significant.

## Provisional vs. Nonprovisional Patent Application

Finally, the applicant must decide whether to file an abbreviated, "provisional" patent application or a complete, "nonprovisional" one. A provisional application consists only of the specification describing the invention for which a patent is sought, as well as any drawings that might be necessary to understand the invention. A provisional application is not subject to examination, and is viable for one year.

The chief benefits of a provisional application are twofold. It is much less expensive to file than a regular nonprovisional application—only $1,000 in official fees for large entities, $500 for small entities, and $250 for micro entities. It also gives the inventor the benefit of the earlier provisional filing date of the nonprovisional application based on the same specification, while measuring the term of the patent from the nonprovisional application's filing date.

In a sense, the provisional application serves as a placeholder for up to one year while the inventor does all the prior art searching, claims drafting, and other work required of a full and complete nonprovisional application. This priority date placeholder function can be important given that many companies and inventors are working on new products and services aimed at the same markets. This is especially so under the United States' new "first inventor to file" rather than "first to invent" priority regime, which some fear may give an edge to large companies with the legal and financial resources to file early and often. To the extent this concern may be valid, provisional applications can serve to mitigate any large company filing advantage.

The main disadvantage of a provisional application is that because the written description cannot be changed when filing the follow-on, nonprovisional application, all the subsequent claims in that follow-on application must be completely consistent with the earlier description language. As most inventors can attest, the understanding of an invention and its potential market—as well as the claims best suited to protect it—inevitably evolves and matures over time.

Here's how an experienced entrepreneur describes the value of a provisional application in the "first inventor to file" environment:

> "What I recommend to every entrepreneur is that if you write a new, non-obvious, and useful line of code, put it in the specification of a provisional patent application and file it. It only costs $1,000 at most. You then have a year in which to honestly evaluate where the industry is going, where the market is going, and whether your invention is truly valuable enough to pursue a patent for it."

A year might not seem very long. But a lot can happen to markets and to technology in that amount of time. Thanks to the rapid rise of smartphones, for example, it took merely a year for netbooks to go from the "next big thing" to "who cares?"

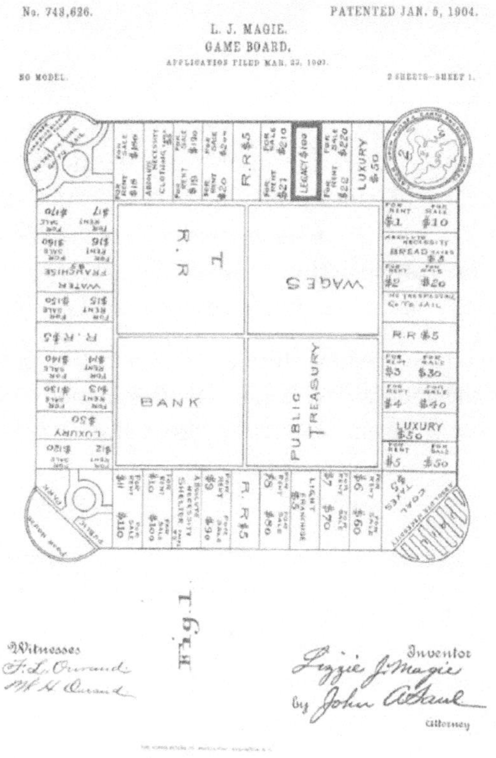


**Figure 1.22** The first patent drawing for Lizzie Magie's board game, The Landlord Game. (credit: U.S. National Archives via Wikimedia Commons / Public domain)

## The Critical Importance of the Claims

When it comes to filing a full nonprovisional application, the most critical task of the inventor (and patent attorney) is to draft the claims. This is an art in and of itself, one that will determine the inventor's rights and an infringer's liability.

Each claim serves as a stand-alone definition of the patent coverage—as a sort of mini-patent unto itself. After a patent is granted, a claim is the only thing that someone can be accused of infringing. Accordingly, broad claim language is essential if a commercially meaningful patent is to be obtained.

On the other hand, the broader the claim, the more likely it is that prior art may exist somewhere that anticipates the claim or renders it obvious and, therefore, invalidates the claim. So the competent draftsperson submits a dozen or more claims, typically moving from broader to narrower scope, in case the broader claims turn out to be disallowed by the USPTO or later invalidated by a court.

Some applicants make the opposite mistake and draft claims that are too narrow—"a programmable multifunction computer in the shape of a metal clamshell," for example. Such a claim is of little value because others can easily design around it simply by using plastic or other nonmetal materials in the design. Some claims are so narrow they are even referred to as "picture claims" because they paint a literal and limiting picture of the invention. You may get a patent with such picture claims, but it probably won't be worth the paper it's printed on.

The strongest claims usually define powerful functionality. They capture something fundamental or seminal in the functioning of the invention.

A good example is the claims in the aforementioned Amazon one-click patent. The algorithms for "one-click" shopping are not very complicated. Yet the claims capture a very profound functionality—the idea that a user should not have to type in credit card and shipping information every time he or she wants to buy something. The consumer-friendly functionality captured in that patent's claims has won Amazon a lot of customers and made it a lot of money.

## Reviewing the Patent Application

Once the patent application with all necessary forms is filed and all fees are paid, the **patent examiner** will review the patent application to determine if the invention meets the statutory requirements for patentability. The examiner will also conduct a search of patent and other databases to determine if the invention appears to be truly novel and non-obvious. Once a determination has been made, the patent examiner will send the applicant a document known as a **first office action**, in which the patent examiner approves, rejects, or requires additional information about the claims and/or other elements of the application.

If all the claims are allowed, which is rare in a first office action, the patent prosecution process is complete. A more common next step requires the applicant to respond to the patent examiner's rejections and requests for more information. In this response, the applicant will address all of the examiner's concerns and either rebut them or amend the application, typically by revising some or all of the claims.

But according to the Manual of Patenting Examination Procedure (MPEP) Section 1.121, "No amendment may introduce new matter into the disclosure of an application."[li] Thus, an applicant cannot file an application disclosing a new compound and how to make it, and then later, after discovering that the compound's structure and method are incorrect, amend the description.

After responding to the office action by perhaps amending the application, the examination process continues until the patent examiner either allows all of the claims or finally rejects them. If all claims are allowed, then the patent prosecution process is complete. If some claims are finally rejected, then the applicant's options at this point are more limited.

According to MPEP Section 706.07, "In the second or any subsequent examination or consideration by the examiner, the rejection can be made final."[lii] At that point, the applicant must usually choose one of three approaches: Cancel the rejected claims, leaving only allowed claims to issue as a patent; continue the fight by filing what is called a "continuation application" and drafting new claims; or appeal to the Patent Trial and Appeals Board arguing that the patent examiner erred in not allowing the claims.[liii] Any appeal to the Patent Trial and Appeals Board, as with any other office action, must occur within six months.[liv]

Finally, if the patent has been vetted through the patent prosecution process and is ready for issuance, the patent holder must pay the applicable fee. If the applicant pays the issue fee, the USPTO will issue the patent in due course. Additionally, utility patents are subject to maintenance fees. These fees are due 3 years and 6 months, 7 years and 6 months, and 11 years and 6 months from the date of the original patent grant. Plant and design patents are also required to pay maintenance fees.[lv]

---

li United States Patent and Trademark Office. (2010, July 21). *Manual of Patent Examining Procedure* § 1.121. Retrieved from http://www.uspto.gov/web/offices/pac/mpep/documents/appxr_1_121.htm

lii United States Patent and Trademark Office. (2010, July 21). *Manual of Patent Examining Procedure* §.0 Retrieved from http://www.uspto.gov/web/offices/pac/mpep/documents/0700_706_07.htm#sect706.07

liii 37 CFR Part 41. Department of Commerce, United States Patent and Trademark Office. (2008). *Rules of practice before the board of patent appeals and interferences in ex parte appeals.* Retrieved from website: http://www.gpo.gov/fdsys/pkg/FR-2008-06-10/pdf/E8-12451.pdf

liv 37 CFR § 1.134

lv 37 CFR § 1.362

## Assessment Questions

1. A patent gives an inventor the exclusive right to which of the following?
   A. The ability to profit from their invention.
   B. The ability to prevent others from making, using, offering for sale, or selling the invention.
   C. The ability to prevent others from learning the secrets of the invention.
   D. All of the above.

2. The "bargain" theory, a theoretical justification for patents, argues which of the following?
   A. In exchange for inventing something useful, society gives the inventor the exclusive right to their invention for a limited time.
   B. The product of mental labor should be the property of its creator.
   C. Government negotiates with inventors to determine the value of an invention.
   D. None of the above.

3. Which *two* public policy goals are served by granting patent rights?
   A. By protecting the property rights of inventors, the wellsprings of creation do not dry up for lack of incentive.
   B. Patent rights ensure equal treatment for all.
   C. From each according to their ability, to each according to their need.
   D. The public interest is served by disclosing the details of the invention and thereby promoting the progress of the nation.

4. Through which of the following means do patents also promote knowledge sharing?
   A. To get a patent, inventors must disclose the secrets of their inventions.
   B. Patents represent the world's greatest library of technical knowledge.
   C. Innovators keep up with technical trends by reading other inventors' patents.
   D. All of the above.

5. The Statute of Monopolies in 1624 ended the practice of granting patents for which of the following?
   A. Inventions that were not truly novel.
   B. The Crown's favored inventors.
   C. Trade in staples such as salt or soap rather than for actual inventions.
   D. Inventions that helped industrialists monopolize whole industries.

6. Which of the following practices were common in early patent systems?
   A. Exorbitantly high patent fees.
   B. Limited or no disclosure of the details of the invention.
   C. No examination for patent validity.
   D. All of the above.

7. Early patent systems tended to have which of the following effects on the overall economy?
   A. Innovation was limited to a small sector of the population.
   B. Biased toward incumbent industries, early patent systems did not encourage disruptive change.
   C. Early patent systems reinforced the wealth of elites, not the productive capacity of society.
   D. All of the above.

**8.** The Founding Fathers created the U.S. patent system with which overarching goal in mind?

A. To defend America's newly won independence.
B. To rapidly stimulate the growth of domestic industry.
C. To create advanced new weapons for America's young army.
D. None of the above.

**9.** The U.S. patent system was designed to tap the creative and productive potential of which of the following?

A. Their abundant natural resources.
B. Their large stock of imported goods and machinery.
C. Rich agricultural lands.
D. An enterprising population with a "universal ambition to go forward"

**10.** Which of the following was NOT a unique feature of the U.S. patent system?

A. It was affordable by the common person.
B. It had an examination system to determine patent validity.
C. Patentees were required to make or sell products based on their inventions.
D. It had simplified application procedures.
E. It required full disclosure of the details of the invention.
F. It allowed for the sale and licensing of patent rights.

**11.** Which of the following is NOT true of the U.S. patent system?

A. Novelty, non-obviousness, and utility determine patent validity, not the identity or business model of the inventor.
B. Patents are freely transferable and tradable property rights.
C. You can't infringe a patent if you honestly don't know that it exists.
D. Patent holders are not required to make or sell products based on their inventions.

**12.** Compared with the Industrial Revolution, what is the overall patent litigation rate today?

A. It is twice what it used to be.
B. It is about the same as it used to be.
C. It is less than half what it used to be.

**13.** Historically speaking, patent litigation has served to which of the following?

A. Slow innovation and R&D.
B. Settle disputed rights to new technology so commercialization can proceed.
C. Block others from designing around patents.

**14.** How many years after the first patent law was signed in 1790 did it take for the United States to surpass Britain in the number of new inventions being patented?

A. 13 years.
B. 75 years.
C. 40 years.
D. 100 years.

**15.** Historically, in the United States, there have been major surges in new patent filings after which of the following?

A. A sharp increase in patent litigation.
B. New technological advances leading to the birth of new industries.
C. A Supreme Court decision on a major patent case.
D. None of the above.

**16.** What percentage of entrepreneurs say that patents are vital to securing venture funding?
   A. 20 percent.
   B. 40 percent.
   C. 67 percent.

**17.** The United States was the only nation to define its greatness in its capacity for which of the following?
   A. Economic growth.
   B. Military superiority.
   C. Bringing freedom to oppressed elsewhere in the world.
   D. Technological progress.

**18.** A patentable invention is a new, novel, and non-obvious machine, manufacture, process, or composition of matter. Which of the four types of inventions categories do these hypothetical mousetrap inventions represent?
   A. A mouse ray gun.
   B. Exploding mouse glue.
   C. A new way to catch mice using sound waves.
   D. A mouse-destroying missile.

**19.** All patentable inventions fall into two broad categories—they are products or processes. Which category do the following fall into?
   A. A machine.
   B. A means to an end.
   C. A composition of matter.
   D. A manufacture.

**20.** Can an idea for a better mousetrap be patented?
   A. Yes, so long as you outline the idea in detail.
   B. No, you can't patent a mere idea.

**21.** Which of the following is NOT patentable?
   A. Electricity.
   B. A random number generator.
   C. A device that uses electricity to communicate.

**22.** When might a software be patentable?
   A. If it contains a new, non-obvious, and useful algorithm.
   B. If it takes a genuinely-inventive step to either trigger an action, employ a device, or in some other way produce a tangible transformative result.
   C. If it records the sale of T-shirts over the Internet.
   D. None of the above.

**23.** Which of the following cases was NOT one of the Supreme Court's "software-eligibility trilogy" of cases?
   A. *Gottschalk v. Benson*
   B. *Williams & Wilkins v. United States*
   C. *Parker v. Flook*
   D. *Diamond v. Diehr*

**24.** Which court case most severely limited software patentability?
- A. *State Street Bank v. Signature Financial Group*
- B. *In re Bilski*
- C. *Mayo Collaborative Services v. Prometheus Laboratories*
- D. *Alice v. CLS Bank*

**25.** What is the so-called "*Alice* paradox"?
- A. The highest-value new software products and services are also hardest to patent.
- B. You can get software patents, but you can't enforce them.
- C. You can only patent software that replicates human activity.
- D. None of the above.

**26.** Patents should only be granted for big revolutionary breakthroughs. True or False?
- A. True.
- B. False.

**27.** Which of the following Supreme Court cases held that a naturally occurring DNA segment CANNOT be patented?
- A. *Mayo Collaborative Services v. Prometheus Labs., Inc.*
- B. *Association for Molecular Pathology v. Myriad Genetics, Inc.*
- C. *Nautilus, Inc. v. Biosig Instruments, Inc.*

**28.** Which of the following is NOT a requirement for patent eligibility?
- A. Novel.
- B. Revolutionary.
- C. Non-obvious.
- D. Useful.

**29.** What does the term "prior art" refer to?
- A. Any previous private discussions of an invention or its components.
- B. Any previous patent, publication, or public use of an invention.
- C. Any previous speculation about an invention.
- D. None of the above.

**30.** If you invent a functioning starship warp drive, *Star Trek* would be considered prior art and your invention would be ineligible for a patent. True or False?
- A. True.
- B. False.

**31.** To meet the requirement for utility, which of the following must an invention do?
- A. Work or function as intended.
- B. Be of some benefit to society.
- C. Be a worthwhile product, process, or composition of matter.
- D. All of the above.

**32.** Why would combining a camera with a cell phone in a smartphone pass the test for non-obviousness, whereas putting wheels from a chair onto an office cart would not?
- A. The technology in a smartphone is much more complicated.
- B. Putting wheels from a chair onto a cart is less difficult.
- C. Combining a camera and a cell phone produced an unexpected result.

**33.** Of the three criteria for patenting, which is the most difficult to surmount?
- A. Utility.
- B. Novelty.
- C. Non-obviousness.

**34.** For which of the following are plant patents granted?
- A. Bioengineered plants.
- B. Naturally grown plants that are distinctively different.
- C. Plants that are asexually cultivated, not grown from seeds.
- D. All of the above.

**35.** What are the three patentability criteria for plant patents?
- A. Novelty, utility, and non-obviousness.
- B. Novelty, distinctiveness, and non-obviousness.
- C. Novelty, beauty, and non-obviousness.

**36.** What are design patents granted for?
- A. Functional designs for manufactured items, like the shape of a chair.
- B. Ornamental designs for items of manufacture, like the fabric design of a chair.
- C. All of the above.

**37.** What are the three patentability criteria for a design patent?
- A. Novelty, utility, and non-obviousness.
- B. Novelty, beauty, and non-obviousness.
- C. Novelty, ornamentality, and non-obviousness.

**38.** By what percentage are filing fees reduced if the applicant is on of the following:
- A. Universities, non-profits, and small businesses with fewer than 500 employees.
- B. Those with gross income less than three times U.S. median household income or meet other certain critera.

**39.** What is the advantage of a provisional patent application, which lasts only one year?
- A. It is less expensive.
- B. It is not subject to examination.
- C. It grants an early filing date while the inventor continues working on the invention.
- D. All of the above.

**40.** What is the main disadvantage of a provisional patent application?
- A. It reserves an early filing date for a later, nonprovisional application.
- B. The claims in a later, nonprovisional application must be completely consistent with the early description contained in the provisional application.
- C. The provisional patent only contains the specifications, and drawings, if any.
- D. All of the above.

**41.** What is the most critical part of a patent application that determines both the inventor's rights and an infringer's liability?
- A. The claims.
- B. The specification.
- C. The drawings.
- D. The abstract.

**42.** Which of the following is the best strategy in drafting claims in a patent application?
   A. Draft them as broadly as possible, to cover every possible use of the invention.
   B. Draft them as narrowly as possible, so the examiner won't reject them.
   C. Draft them as broadly as the specifications and the prior art allows, then back up those broad claims with successively narrower claims as backup.

**43.** In a "first office action," the examiner usually does which of the following?
   A. Allows all the claims in the patent application.
   B. Rejects some claims and/or requests further information.
   C. Rejects the entire application.

**44.** In a second or subsequent examination, if the examiner finally rejects some or all of the claims, what can the applicant do at that point?
   A. Cancel the rejected claims, leaving only allowed claims.
   B. File what's called a "continuation application."
   C. Appeal to the Patent Trial and Appeal Board.
   D. All of the above.

# 2 Patent Enforcement

**Figure 2.1** (credit: modification of work "Lee County Courthouse, Giddings, Texas 1805081201" by Patrick Feller/rights holder/flikr.com, CC BY 2.0)

## Chapter Outline



## Introduction

## 2.1 The Right to Enforce Patents

**Figure 2.2** The statue of Blind Justice in front of the Albert V. Bryan United States Courthouse in Alexandria, Virginia. (credit: Tim Evanson via flickr / CC BY 2.0)

### Learning Objectives

After completing this section, you will be able to

- Understand the basic rights of patent owners.
- Gain an appreciation of the complex process of patent litigation.

Patents issued by the United States Patent and Trademark Office (USPTO) can be enforced by their owners in U.S. federal courts. The USPTO is responsible only for examining and issuing patents—it does not enforce them. It is up to the owner of the patent to enforce it against infringers by filing a civil case in federal court for patent infringement.

A patent owner is called the "patentee." The patentee has the statutory right to exclude others from making, using, offering for sale, selling, or importing the invention covered by the patent throughout the United States.[i] ecall that these are rights to exclude others from using the patentee's invention. The Patent Act does not grant the patent owner the right to practice the invention covered by the patent. Indeed, it may be that the invention, if practiced in the United States, could infringe someone else's patent! For example, if you obtain a patent on an improvement to a patented product (e.g., a faster-acting version of a patented painkiller), you might not be able to sell the improved product unless you obtain a license under the patent for the underlying product.

i 35 U.S.C. §154(a)(1).

Infringement is a **strict liability violation**—you do not need to know that you are infringing a patent, or that a patent even exists, to be liable for patent infringement. If someone makes, uses, offers for sale, sells, or imports what is covered by a claim of a valid patent, that person is an infringer. Neither lack of knowledge of the patent, nor lack of intent to infringe it, is a defense to patent infringement. [ii]

Enforcing a patent is almost invariably a long and expensive process. The first step is to decide whether someone is infringing your patent—i.e., making, using, selling, offering to sell, or importing your invention without your permission. To decide whether someone is infringing your patent, the elements of each claim of the patent must be compared with the elements of the potential infringer's device or process. If the elements of a patent claim match (or "read on") the elements of the device or process, an infringement has occurred.

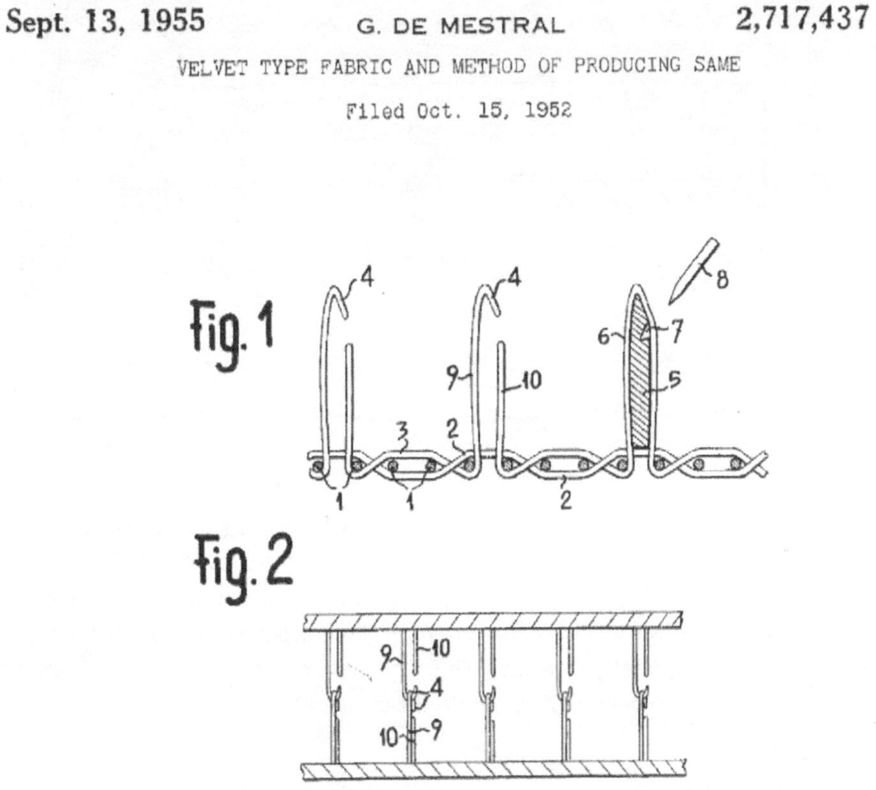


**Figure 2.3** Patent for velvet type fabric and method of producing same (credit: USPTO doc ID 02717437 / )

Even if some elements of a claim do not literally read on the infringing device, but are sufficiently equivalent in what the device does and how the device does it, they may nevertheless be infringed under the legal rule called the "**doctrine of equivalents.**"This doctrine prevents an infringer from copying the essence of the invention, but making insignificant modifications in an effort to avoid infringement. If the accused device or process performs substantially the same function in substantially the same way and yields substantially the same result, infringement exists so long as any differences between the claim elements and the accused device are not substantial. A patent calling for an "adhesive" connection (describing glue as the preferred adhesive) could be infringed by a device using a hook-and-loop fastener(e.g.,Velcro). That's because the hook-and-loop fastener arguably performs substantially the same adhesive function in substantially the same way and with substantially the same result as the glue adhesive.

ii 35 U.S.C. §271(a). An exception, where lack of knowledge may be a defense, is indirect infringement, of which there are two principal types: (1) actively inducing someone else to infringe, which requires knowledge of the patent and an intent to cause the infringement (35 U.S.C. §271(b)), and (2) contributing to someone else's infringement, which requires selling or offering for sale a component to a patented combination knowing that it is specially made or adapted for use as a material part of an infringing combination and that it is not suitable for substantial noninfringing use. 35 U.S.C. §271(c).

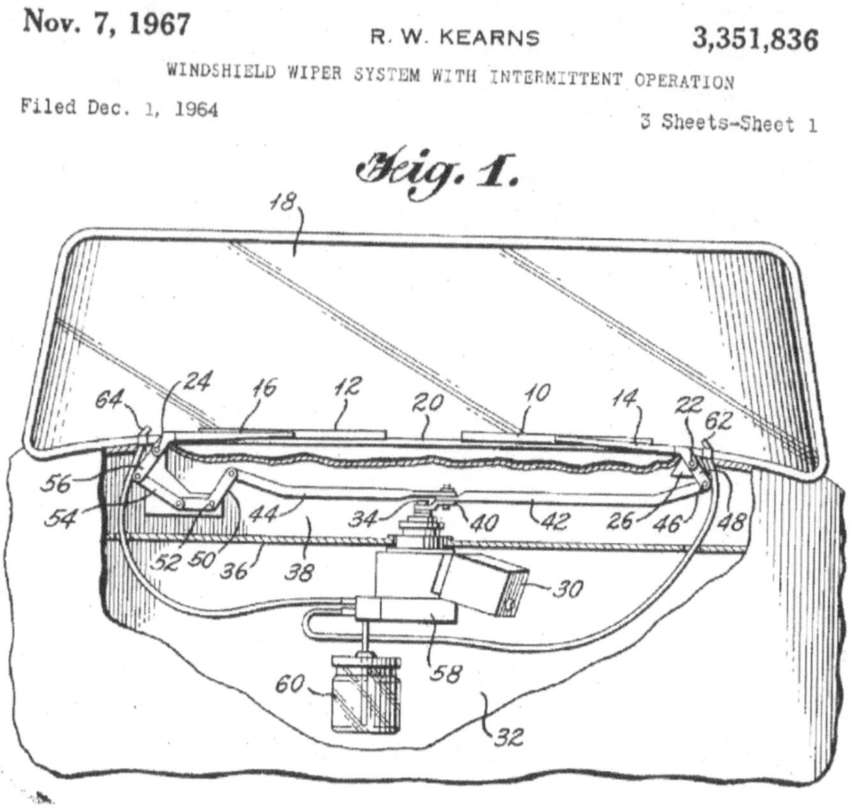


**Figure 2.4** Patent for windshield wiper system with intermittent operation. (credit: USPTO doc ID 03351836 / )

If a patent owner believes their patents are being infringed, the person typically hires a patent trial lawyer who specializes in enforcing patents. Often, but not always, this is a different person at a different law firm than the lawyer or agent who previously assisted the inventor(s) in obtaining a patent from the USPTO. Once the patent trial lawyer is retained, that lawyer will evaluate the patent and the accused device or process, and will provide the patentee a legal opinion about whether or not an infringement exists. If an infringement is found, the patentee then must decide how to proceed. Several options exist.

Options for Pursuing a Patent Infringement Claim

- Demand that the alleged infringer stop infringing, and pay damages for past infringement.
- Offer the alleged infringer a license to practice your invention for money, called a "**royalty**."
- Ignore the infringement, or postpone any action for a time.
- File a patent infringement lawsuit in federal court against the alleged infringer.

Each option has benefits and risks, which should be carefully considered before proceeding.

## 2.2 Deciding Whether and How to Enforce a Patent

**Figure 2.5** (credit: Phtograph by Kārlis Dambrāns via flickr / CC BY 2.0)

### Learning Objectives

After completing this section, you will be able to

- Understand the variety of options one has in enforcing patent rights.
- Appreciate the time and expense involved in doing so.

The decision of how to proceed depends on the patentee's objectives and a clear understanding of the risks and rewards of each potential course of action. If you do not know your objectives, you cannot decide on a course of action to achieve them.

For example, if your goal is to stop a competitor from offering a competing product that infringes your patent, you have little choice but to file a lawsuit and pursue it to completion. This can easily cost from $1 million to over $10 million, depending upon the complexity of the case and the intensity of the defense. If you do not have the resources to pursue such expensive litigation on your own, there are contingency fee lawyers, who may be willing to take your case in return for a share of any damages (typically 30 to 40+ percent) that are collected from the infringer. As of 2014, a wide variety of litigation finance firms exist that may be willing to fund your litigation in return for a share of any damage award or settlement payment you receive.[iii]

However, if your goal is to obtain a royalty for the use of your invention, you may be able to negotiate a license agreement without the need for litigation. Even if the infringer balks at an agreement unless you initiate a lawsuit, often the lawsuit can be settled via a license agreement short of trial. About 95 percent of patent lawsuits settle before trial, many with the defendant(s) taking a license for which they pay a royalty.[iv]

---

iii See, e.g., http://www.tennessean.com/story/money/2014/05/20/lawsuit-financingcarves-niche/9306059/ and http://www.patentlitigationfunding.com/litigation-funding.

Even small entities and individuals can successfully license a patent without filing a lawsuit if they have a good patent and a reasonable licensing plan. Most prospective licensees know that lawsuits are very expensive and would prefer to settle a dispute with a license rather than fight a lawsuit and end up taking a license later. The key is to have a plan, and implement it diligently, with good counsel supporting the effort.

Thus, the first step in deciding if and how you will enforce your patent is deciding what you want to achieve and how much effort, and money, you are willing to devote to the endeavor. The "costs" of enforcement are not limited to the out-of-pocket expenses for lawyers and litigation expenses. Any enforcement effort requires the time and attention of the patentee, whether an individual or company, which disrupts normal business activities. The time and attention required includes providing information and documents, reviewing pleadings prepared by your lawyers, analyzing information received from your opponent during the litigation, appearing for depositions and other pretrial proceedings, and appearing at trial. Just the information and document gathering can consume hundreds, even thousands, of person hours and disrupt the normal operations of virtually every part of an organization.

Enforcing a patent also takes time. Lawsuits typically take two to four years to reach trial. Post-trial proceedings can take another six months to a year, and appeals take several additional years before the lawsuit is "finished."

On the positive side, successful patentees can reap huge monetary damages for another's patent infringement, including lost profits, treble damages (i.e., triple the amount of money damages found), and, in exceptional cases, an award of the patentee's attorneys' fees. Awards of tens to hundreds of millions, and occasionally even billions, of dollars can be achieved, even if they are not typical. If you sell a product or service and are asserting your patent against a competitor, you can also obtain an injunction barring your competitor from continuing its infringement. This can reap huge additional rewards, measured in increased market share and pricing power.

Patents not only offer patentees the opportunity to play offense in the marketplace, but also provide a very potent defense against charges of infringement (or other claims) by others. Competitors are wary of attacking businesses with extensive patent portfolios. The recent "smartphone wars" are a timely example. After becoming embroiled in patent litigation with Apple and Oracle over its Android operating system and the phones that use it, Google spent $12.5 billion to acquire Motorola Mobility in August 2011 to gain access to its extensive patent portfolio so that it would have patent weapons of its own.[v] Google also acquired 1,023 more patents from IBM for an undisclosed amount around the same time.[vi] Perhaps this was also partly in response to Apple joining with BlackBerry maker Research In Motion (RIM), Microsoft, Ericsson, Sony, and EMC to buy 6,000 patents owned by Nortel for $4.5 billion in July 2011, largely to keep them from falling into the hands of competitors like Google and Samsung.[vii]

Expert assistance in making the decision to enforce your patent, and to map out the "who, what, where, when, and how" of doing so, is critically important. A variety of lawyers and law firms specialize in patent trials, from solo practitioners to multinational law firms. The choice depends on your needs, means, and objectives.

---

iv Jay P. Kesan and Gwendolyn G. Ball, How Are Patent Cases Resolved? An Empirical Examination of the Adjudication and Settlement of Patent Disputes, 84 Wash. U. L. Rev. 237, 254 (2006). Available at: http://digitalcommons.law.wustl.edu/lawreview/vol84/iss2/1

v http://techcrunch.com/2011/08/15/breakinggoogle-buys-motorola-for-12-5-billion/

vi http://www.bloomberg.com/news/2011-09-14/google-purchases-1-023-patents-from-ibm-tobolster-portfolio.html.

vii http://gadgets.ndtv.com/apple/news/apple-ledgroup-buys-nortel-patents-for-4-5-bn-225830.

# 2.3 Patent Litigation

**Figure 2.6** (credit: Photograph by Karen Neoh via flickr / CC BY 2.0)

## Learning Objectives

After completing this section, you will be able to

- Understand the pros and cons in deciding who, what, where, when, and how to sue an infringer.

Once a decision is made to enforce a patent via litigation, a complex series of steps begins that determine the "who, what, where, when, and how" of events that will unfold.

### Who

First you decide whom to sue. Many options may exist. If the infringer is a corporation, you can sue it. But you can also sue its owners and/or officers if it is a closely held company or is dominated by a single shareholder or manager. If the infringer has subsidiaries, you must choose which of them to include as defendants. Recall that your patent gives you the right to exclude others from making, using, selling, offering for sale, or importing your invention in the territory the patent covers. (We will assume for simplicity that you own a U.S. patent; foreign patents can be obtained in other countries and enforcement of those foreign patents is subject to their local laws.) Any person or entity that violates one of these exclusive rights is a potential defendant.

Strategic issues should be considered in deciding whom to sue. For example, the location of one or more defendants may make it hard to include them in a lawsuit filed in a place ("forum") convenient to you. Although the infringer's customers are also infringers (i.e., they "use" the infringing product or service), most patentees disfavor suing customers because these are also the patentee's customers or potential customers—and suing them may be bad for business. Often, the manufacturer or seller of the infringing product or service indemnifies and defends its customers. In other words, in many cases the manufacturer or seller of a product will agree to "cover" its customers in the event of a patent infringement claim. So, if the infringing manufacturer and/or seller is already a defendant, you gain little by suing customers, except their ire! Thus, select your defendants carefully, with your desired end result in mind.

Another strategic decision, when more than one infringer exists, is whether to sue them one at a time or collectively.[viii] Common sense might suggest suing them one at a time, to avoid having them gang up on you. But experience shows that suing multiple defendants simultaneously is often a better strategy. It turns out that, in many cases, rather than encouraging them to gang up on you, they spend most of their energy trying to sort out differences among themselves and trying to present a united front.

Although the America Invents Act narrowed the joinder rule in patent cases beginning in September, 2011 to cases where a plaintiff can show a "common question of law or fact" as well as a true "transaction or occurrence" between the defendants (which must be more than infringement of the same patent), judges still typically consolidate separate cases involving the same patent for their own convenience in handling discovery and pre-trial issues. Thus, proceeding simultaneously against multiple defendants can still be an effective strategy.

### What

Which patents (if you have more than one) and which claims of those patents you assert in a lawsuit is another important decision you must make. Twenty years ago, you could simply file a lawsuit against an alleged infringer, listing your patent(s) and little more. You could defer deciding which claims to assert against which allegedly infringing products or services until after you received information from the defendant(s) through discovery in the litigation. However, courts now routinely require that you provide details in the **complaint** you file, or shortly after, about which patent claims are asserted against which product or service, and also that you provide a "claim chart" that details those assertions precisely. Although it is possible to revise these assertions after receiving more information during the discovery process, your initial assertions remain in the court's record and can come back to haunt you if they are not consistent with your revised assertions. Therefore, careful pre-filing investigation and analysis is crucial to a successful pursuit of the infringers.

Ideally, hire not only an experienced patent trial lawyer to guide this effort, but also the experts you will rely on in the litigation, and who will testify during the trial on how and why the accused products or services infringe your patent(s). Experts can provide essential evidence of the infringement during the trial. Good experts are critical to success in litigation, as much as experienced trial lawyers, but are sometimes surprisingly hard to find. First, you must find an expert who is neutral, or at least appears so. Most experts are employed in the same field as the patentee and the alleged infringer, making them potentially unsuitable candidates because they have allegiances to existing companies that suggest the possibility of bias. Second, a good expert must not only know their subject thoroughly, but also be able to communicate it to a lay audience (i.e., the nonexpert judge and jury). Such communication skills are not always found in experts with strong technical credentials. Finally, you want an expert who has the right skills, but not one who appears to be a hired gun (exemplified by someone who spends most of their time testifying for a fee).

Thus, prepare in advance, and hire experts early in the process, both to assist your preparations and to remain available during the progress of the lawsuit and for trial.

### Where

The selection of where to file is an important, perhaps determinative, decision. As we have noted, patent infringement cases seeking damages can only be filed in U.S. federal courts (as opposed to state courts). If your defendant is a private party, the proper location for the case (called "**venue**") is the federal district court in the geographic location where the defendant is incorporated or resides, or where the claim arose.[ix]

---

viii Prior to the America Invents Act (AIA) in 2011, joinder rules allowed you to sue multiple infringers in the same lawsuit, even if their products were different. The AIA limited this ability by restricting joinder. Nevertheless, you can still file a separate lawsuit against each alleged infringer, and ask the court to consolidate them for discovery and other pretrial purposes. Courts are usually eager to do this because it simplifies their work. The practical effect is almost the same as a single case with multiple defendants.

The first two criteria are usually easily determined—i.e., a company's state of incorporation is a matter of public record, as are the places where it has facilities. The place where the claim arose includes every place the infringing product or service is made, sold, offered for sale, used, or imported. If it is a low volume product or service, or is very new or lightly distributed, the proper venues may be quite limited. But typically products or services with enough sales to justify a multimillion dollar patent infringement lawsuit are broadly available throughout the country, opening up virtually any federal court as a possible venue.

Thus, you can, and should, select a venue that meets your objectives as closely as possible. Some venues (e.g., the Eastern District of Virginia and the Western District of Wisconsin) have reputations (and rules) for moving cases through to trial very quickly, often in less than a year. Speed is desirable in terms of reaching a conclusion quickly, but has its downsides in terms of accelerated costs and maximum disruption to the normal business operations of you and your opponent. Other districts exhibit much slower progress toward trial, which may be desirable or undesirable in meeting your particular objectives.

Another factor is experience. Some district courts have handled many complex patent cases, have detailed rules about what must be done to get the case ready for trial, and an excellent track record on appeal. Still other districts have reputations for being "plaintiff friendly" or "defendant friendly," although these reputations are often more "urban legend" than accurate. In any given case, the outcome is dependent on the parties, the facts, the lawyers, and the judge/jury assigned.

Experienced patent trial counsel can assist you in making an appropriate choice of venue for your case, taking into account the myriad factors pertinent to your case.

### When

The timing of filing suit is often dictated by when you discover the existence of the infringement and have gathered the required information for drafting a complaint and the necessary initial disclosures. But other considerations may be relevant also, such as the timing of industry trade shows, holiday sales pushes, or the financing activities of your opponent. Absent any other constraints or objectives, lawsuits should usually be filed as soon after the infringing activity is discovered as possible, given the need to investigate and prepare before filing a complaint.

At the outside, any suit filed more than six years after the infringement began and was reasonably capable of being discovered can give rise to a defense of "**laches**" and/or "**estoppel**"by your opponent. In other words,the accused infringer is arguing that you waited too long to bring your infringement claim. It may be necessary for you to prove that the defendant was not prejudiced by your delay. If laches applies, which simply means you waited an unreasonable time tomake your claim, prejudicing your opponent, your damages will be limited to those that arise after you filed your lawsuit. If estoppel applies, which means that you not only delayed, but affirmatively misled your opponent into believing you would not file suit, your claim is barred altogether.

---

ix If the alleged infringer is the federal government itself, or a government contractor, the proper venue is the Court of Federal Claims. 28 U.S.C. §1491 Another forum for enforcing a U.S. patent against imported goods exists at the U.S. International Trade Commission (ITC) in Washington, D.C. 19 U.S.C. §1330. The ITC has the power to investigate alleged infringement and bar goods found to infringe from entering the country. This can be a very effective tool against infringing imports, especially if all the sources of those imports are unknown. The ITC's jurisdiction is "quasi in rem" so that the infringing goods themselves provide the basis for jurisdiction, allowing their adjudication and prohibition even if the source of the goods is unknown. Proceedings before the ITC are extremely expedited, usually taking 18 months or less, and can be very expensive.

Another issue you face is whether to notify the alleged infringer before filing suit. This seems prudent—demand that the infringer cease the infringement before filing a lawsuit aimed at enforcing such cessation. But such a strategy is fraught with pitfalls. First, accusing someone of infringement allows them to sue you preemptively, asking the court for a quick decision that no infringement exists. This type of judicial decision is called a declaratory judgment of noninfringement.[x] If the accused infringer sues you before you sue them, the accused infringer becomes the plaintiff and can sue in a forum of their choice. Ceding to your opponent the initiative and the choice of forum for the litigation is a strategic blunder that could cost you not just that battle, but the war. Second, an old adage applies here: If you are going to kick someone, don't warn them, because they will prepare to deflect the blow. Patent litigation (like all litigation) is like war, albeit civilized war. Ceding to your opponent important strategic advantages, such as the choice of forum and the element of surprise, is costly and can be fatal.

So, do these considerations dictate that you ambush your opponent and appear to be unreasonable by suing without notice? No, a middle ground does exist. Consider filing the lawsuit simultaneously with, or immediately after, making a demand that the infringer cease the infringing activities. You can defer formally "serving" the lawsuit on your opponent (that is, providing notice by delivering the complaint) for at least 30 days, and as long as 90 days in some courts. This allows you to negotiate with your opponent from a position of strength and with your choice of forum firmly established, without appearing unreasonable.

### How

Once you choose to file suit in federal court, the how is largely dictated by the Federal Rules of Civil Procedure, the Federal Rules of Evidence, and the loal rules of the chosen venue. However, one important decision remains-judge or jury.[xi] Until the 1990s, almost all patent cases were tried to a judge because they were thought to be too complex for juries. but then some enterprising plaintiffs' lawyers decided to request that a jury decide their case, perhaps seeking to take advantage of the complexity of the cases and the belief that juries trust patents because they are issued by the federal government after examination by USPTO experts. That has led to the current reality, which is that almost all patent cases filed now request a jury trial. Interestingly, statistics show that this trend does not always benefit plaintiffs. Depending on the venue, plaintiffs only win 60 to 75 percent of the time, despite having the advantage of being able to pick what cases they file (presumably they self-select only the strongest cases) and where they file them (i.e., they can select what they think is the most favorable forum—often their own hometown).[xii] Of course, the outcome of a particular case depends on a myriad of factors unique to that case. No party can be assured victory when a jury is involved.

---

x 28 U.S.C. § 2201(a); See *MedImmune, Inc. v. Genentech, Inc.*, 127 S.Ct. 764 (2007) and *SanDisk Corp. v. STMicroelectronics, Inc.*, 480 F.3d 1372 (Fed. Cir. 2007).

xi See Rules 38-39, Fed. R. Civ. P.

xii PricewaterhouseCoopers, 2013 Patent Litigation Study, at 9; https://www.pwc.com/us/en/forensicservices/publications/assets/2012-patentlitigation-study.html.

# 2.4 Getting Started

**Figure 2.7** (credit: Photograph by Mark Fischer via flickr / CC BY 2.0)

## Learning Objectives

After completing this section, you will be able to

- Understand the various pretrial motions available to parties in a litigation.

Once the decision to file suit is made, and all the factors noted above are considered, the complaint is filed in the clerks' office of the selected federal court and served in due course on the defendant(s).[xiii] The defendant(s) must then decide whether to move to dismiss or transfer the case to a different venue, or file an answer (a response to the infringement claim).[xiv] The defendant(s) can also file a counterclaim, asserting claims back against the plaintiff.[xv] Motions to dismiss may be based on any number of issues—improper jurisdiction (e.g., the court does not have power over the defendant because it does not reside or do business within the geographic jurisdiction of that court), improper venue (e.g., the defendant does not reside or did not commit any act of infringement in the jurisdiction of the court), failure to state a proper claim, etc.[xvi] Such a motion must be accompanied by a legal brief explaining the reasons for the motion, to which the plaintiff can file an opposing brief. The defendant who filed the motion usually has an opportunity to file a reply brief. After the briefing is completed, which can take one to two months, the court will decide the motion with an order, either granting or denying it.

xiii See Rules 3-5, and 7-8, Fed. R. Civ. P.

xiv See Rules 7-8, and 12, Fed. R. Civ. P.

xv See Rule 13, Fed. R. Civ. P.

xvi See Rule 12(b), Fed. R. Civ. P.

Motions to transfer can be filed by a defendant who believes another court would be a "better" place to proceed with the case.[xvii] The factors considered by the court as to whether it or another court is "better" include which court is most convenient in terms of the location of necessary witnesses and/or documents, and whether another court already has experience with the subject matter because a related case is pending or was handled there and it can handle the new case more efficiently. Such motions usually fail, but can delay the progress of the case by several months, sometimes longer, while the court considers how to rule on the motion. The parties must present detailed arguments about why the case should be moved, or not, and often the court will order oral argument during which each party can present its position and answer questions the court may have.

If no motions are filed by the defendant(s), or if they are denied, the defendant(s) must file an answer, which responds to the allegations in the complaint and sets forth any defenses the defendant(s) may have.[xviii] Such defenses can include that the patent is not infringed, that the patent is invalid, that the defendant has a license, that the plaintiff waited too long to file suit (laches) or misled the defendant into believing he or she would not complain about the alleged infringement (estoppel), that the alleged infringer is entitled to prior user rights,[xix] or myriad other defenses that may be available.[xx]

The defendant(s) may also file one or more **counterclaims**, which are essentially new charges filed against the plaintiff.[xxi] If such counterclaims are related to the subject matter of the initial case, they may be tried at the same time. If not, they may be severed and tried separately, either before or after the initial case.

The plaintiff has an opportunity to file a reply to the answer and an answer to any counterclaim that the defendant(s) file.[xxii] If a counterclaim is filed, followed by an answer, then the defendant(s) can file a reply to the plaintiff's answer.[xxiii]

Once these initial pleadings are filed, which usually takes about 60 days from when the initial complaint is filed, the case is considered "at issue" and the pretrial proceedings commence.

Defendants in patent cases are increasingly turning to a strategy of filing requests for **post-grant review** in the PTO to derail a patentee's efforts to enforce the patent. Although beyond the scope of this chapter, a post-grant review essentially asks the PTO to take another look at whether the patent is valid, i.e., whether it should have been granted in the first place. The requestor of any post-grant review must present supporting evidence to show that some issue renders one or more of the patent's claims invalid. The post-grant review request can be either **ex parte reexamination** (meaning the patentee does not get to participate) or **inter partes review** (in which the patentee is allowed to participate), or **covered business methods review** (to review patents that claim a method or corresponding apparatus for performing data processing or other operations used in the practice, administration, or management of a financial product or service). Complex rules govern these proceedings, and they changed in 2011 under the **America Invents Act (AIA)**, which substantially revised the nation's patent laws in a number of important ways.[xxiv]

The significance to a patentee of an opponent requesting post-grant review is twofold. First, the patentee risks losing its patent if the PTO finds it is invalid, and this is exactly what has happened in a majority of *inter partes*

xvii See 28 U.S.C. §1404(a)

xviii See Rules 8-9, Fed. R. Civ. P.

xix 35 U.S.C §273, which provides a defense to patent infringement for someone who can prove, by clear and convincing evidence, that they acted in good faith and commercially used the subject matter of the patent in the U.S. at least one year before the effective filing date of the patent or the invention's first public disclosure.

xx See Rules 8-9, and 12, Fed. R. Civ. P.

xxi See Rule 13, Fed. R. Civ. P.

xxii See Rule 7, Fed. R. Civ. P.

xxiii See Rules 8 and 13, Fed. R. Civ. P.

xxiv See the PTO's discussion of the AIA at http://www.uspto.gov/aia_implementation/index.jsp.

*review* hearings as of March, 2016. Second, a defendant requesting post-grant review usually asks the court to **stay** (i.e., temporarily suspend) the patent case filed against it while the PTO evaluates the patent, arguing that the result of the PTO's actions may either invalidate or modify the patent such that the court should await the outcome before proceeding with the litigation. This strategy has been successful in many courts.

## 2.5 Pretrial Procedures

**Figure 2.8** (credit: Photograph by Nelson Runkle via flickr / CC BY 2.0)

### Learning Objectives

After completing this section, you will be able to

- Understand the multiple procedures involved in the pretrial phase of patent litigation.
- Appreciate the costs involved and the ways they affect the ultimate trial outcome.

The first steps in the pretrial procedure are the filing by the parties of their "initial disclosures" and the holding of the preliminary pretrial conference.[xxv] Initial disclosures must provide preliminary information about each party's positions in the case, and disclose the identity and location of witnesses and documents likely to be relevant to the issues in the case.[xxvi] These disclosures help frame the "discovery," or information that the parties can request of each other, which is one of the hallmarks of litigation in the United States and one of the drivers of the expense of litigation. The concept is laudable—require each party to disclose the information it has relevant to the case to preclude a "trial by ambush." But, in practice, discovery can become an endless game of cat and mouse, with costs escalating exponentially. We will talk more about discovery shortly.

The preliminary pretrial conference is usually the first time the parties appear in court before the judge, unless there has been a hearing on a pretrial motion (as discussed above). At this conference, the judge discusses with the parties the issues likely to arise in the case, the time that pretrial discovery is expected to take, and

xxv See Rules 12, 16, and 26, Fed. R. Civ. P.

xxvi See Rule 26(a), Fed. R. Civ. P.

any issues that make the case unique (such as witnesses in foreign countries that require extraordinary means to obtain their testimony for trial). Each party is usually required to submit a report to the court in advance of this conference, proposing what the timeline for the case should be and identifying any unique issues. The court typically issues a **scheduling order** at, or shortly after, the pretrial conference, specifying dates by which certain activities must be concluded. This order often "splits the baby" between the plaintiff's and defendant's proposed schedules (the plaintiff usually seeks speed while the defendant usually seeks delay). The figure below shows a typical scheduling order.

The scheduling order will also usually specify a length of the trial (e.g., 8 trial days), subject to revision at the final pretrial conference. A typical patent trial is scheduled to last from 5 to 20 trial days, but some can take much longer. Let's look at each step of this schedule to understand what is happening.

## Protective Order

Before information is shared between the parties, they usually agree on a protective order, which they will ask the court to enter, that specifies who has access to the confidential information produced during discovery in the litigation.[xxvii] This is important to all parties, and even third parties that may be asked to produce information during discovery, because sensitive business, technical, and financial information is routinely requested by and produced to each party during the lawsuit. The protective order proscribes that the disclosure of confidential information during discovery is limited to lawyers involved in handling the case, outside experts retained by the lawyers to assist them, and court reporters (who record testimony during the case), videographers (who videotape deposition testimony, as is now common), and court personnel. It is also typical that certain employees of each party (usually in-house lawyers and/or business people directly involved in the oversight of the case) are also permitted to review certain materials, but not financial information of a competitor or future business plans, which are usually excluded from being disclosed to any party employees.

Everyone authorized to see confidential information is under court order to restrict use of the information to the pending lawsuit, not to disclose it to anyone not authorized by the protective order to see it, and requiring that all copies be returned or destroyed at the end of the case.

## Discovery

After the preliminary pretrial conference, discovery begins, which results in the exchange of documents, written responses, and witness testimony.[xxviii]

A request for production allows a party to demand that another party turn over relevant documents and electronically stored information in its possession or control, as well as an inspection of property (such as a manufacturing facility) to take photographs, measurements, and the like.[xxix] Documents and other tangible items can also be requested from third parties (i.e., people and entities not named as a party in the lawsuit) via subpoena.[xxx]

xxvii See Rule 26(c), Fed. R. Civ. P.

xxviii See Rules 26-37, Fed. R. Civ. P.

xxix See Rule 34, Fed. R. Civ. P.

xxx See Rule 45, Fed. R. Civ. P.

Interrogatories are written questions that a party can ask of other parties in the litigation, but not of third parties. Such questions can request any nonprivileged information that is relevant to any party's claim or defense—including the existence, description, nature, custody, condition, and location of any documents or other tangible things and the identity and location of persons who know of any discoverable information that may be relevant to the subject matter of the litigation.[xxxi] Interrogatories may also ask for opinions or the legal contentions of another party. The initial limit on the number of interrogatories is 25, including subparts. However, upon a showing of good cause, courts routinely permit additional interrogatories in patent litigation because the issues are usually complex.[xxxii] Answers to interrogatories are binding on the party providing them and may be used as admissions in the litigation, including at trial.

Depositions are interviews used to elicit testimony from witnesses having relevant knowledge.[xxxiii] This is similar to eliciting testimony during a trial, but occurs in a conference room with a court reporter present to record what is said. The judge is not present at depositions, but may intervene if a controversy arises. Testimony can also be requested by written questions to a witness, which the witness then answers and returns to the requesting party, called a deposition by written questions.[xxxiv]

Although in the United States, it is usually required that testimony at trial be presented live, with the opportunity for the opposing party to cross-examine the witness and for the jury and/or judge to assess each witness's demeanor in person, testimony elicited via depositions during discovery may be used at trial under certain circumstances.[xxxv] For example, if a witness dies before trial, or is unavailable through no fault of the party seeking to use the deposition testimony, the deposition may be used as testimony at trial in lieu of live testimony from the witness. Also, the deposition testimony of an opposing party or an officer or manager of the opposing party corporation may be used at trial for any purpose. Usually, however, deposition testimony is used primarily to "impeach" a witness testifying live at trial—that is, to show that the witness at trial has changed prior testimony from when they gave the deposition. Videotaped deposition testimony is very effective to show to a judge or jury during trial that the witness has changed the testimony—such as from "No" to "Yes" or the equivalent!

The parties can also demand that another party admit, for purposes of the pending litigation only, the truth of any facts, opinions, or conclusions, or the genuineness of any documents relevant to any party's claim or defense. Such demands are called requests for admission.[xxxvi] The responses to these demands are binding on the responding party and can be used to conclusively establish the matters admitted in the litigation, including at trial.

## Amendments to the Pleadings

Once initial information is obtained via discovery, the parties may be permitted to amend or supplement their pleadings (i.e., the complaint, answer, counterclaim, etc.) to address information or issues uncovered during the initial discovery.[xxxvii] For example, the plaintiff may uncover information about other companies, products, or services involved in the infringement and seek to add them to the lawsuit. A defendant may uncover information about invalidity defenses not previously known to it and want to add those to its answer.

---

xxxi See Rules 26(b) and 33(a)(2), Fed. R. Civ. P.

xxxii See Rule 33(a), Fed, R. Civ. P.

xxxiii See Rules 27-30, Fed. R. Civ. P.

xxxiv See Rule 31, Fed. R. Civ. P.

xxxv See Rule 32, Fed. R. Civ. P.

xxxvi See Rule 36, Fed. R. Civ. P.

xxxvii See Rule 15, Fed. R. Civ. P.

## Close of Discovery

This is the date by which all requests for documents, information, and depositions must be complete. It is usually interpreted as requiring that all responses to requests for production, interrogatories, and requests for admissions be answered by the end date set by the court, which means that the actual requests must be made sufficiently in advance of this date (typically 31 days—because responses are due to most discovery requests within 30 days) to allow the responses to be due before the cutoff date. Any depositions must also be completed by the date for the close of discovery (although the parties usually agree to finish select depositions after this date in order to accommodate scheduling problems).

## Claim Construction Briefing and Hearing

In virtually every patent case, a dispute arises over the meaning of certain language used in the asserted claims of the patents at issue. These are called "claim construction" disputes, and must be resolved by the judge before trial. The parties are permitted to provide their competing arguments in briefs to the court, usually after discovery is completed, and make an oral argument on their respective positions to the court at a claim construction hearing. These hearings are often called **Markman hearings**, after the name of the case that established that the judge, and not the jury, must decide the proper meaning of disputed claim language.[xxxviii]

This is a critical juncture in every patent case because the opposing parties try to craft an interpretation of the claim language that supports their respective positions. Most patent claims are drafted using a range of language, from specific to general, in an effort by the patentee (and lawyer) to cover as much territory for the claim as possible. The PTO interprets proposed claims in the broadest reasonable way possible, and then compares their scope with the prior art, before allowing them. The goal of the patentee in dealing with the PTO is to get allowed the broadest claims possible, in order to get the broadest patent coverage possible. But the use of broad, general language in claims permits the parties in later litigation to argue for different interpretations, depending on their interests at the time of litigation. Thus, a plaintiff seeks an interpretation that is broad enough to encompass the defendant's products and services so that infringement can be proven. In contrast, the defendant proposes a narrow interpretation (or "construction") that excludes its products and services.

The court resolves the dispute over the meaning of the contested claim terms by referring to the language of the claims, the language and drawings in the patent, and the history of the proceedings in the PTO that led to the issuance of the patent. The written record of that history is preserved in what is call a "file wrapper," so named because all the written documents making up the history are contained in a three-part file folder, the two outer portions of which fold over and "wrap" the documents within it. The patentee is bound by what it told the PTO to secure allowance of the patent. The court interprets the language according to its ordinary meaning to someone of ordinary skill in the art to which the invention pertains, unless the patentee specially defined the language within the patent or its file wrapper.

Once the claim construction decision is made by the court, the scope of the patent(s) in the case is fixed, and the only remaining issue for trial is whether the claims of the patent(s) as interpreted by the court are broad enough to include the accused products and services of the defendant(s).

xxxviii *Markman, et al. v. Westview Instruments, Inc.*, 517 U.S. 370 (1996).

### Summary Judgment Briefing and Hearing

**Summary judgment** is a procedure that obviates a trial where one of the parties can show that its opponent cannot win—as a matter of law.[xxxix] That is, if one party can show that the evidence is so clear that no fact dispute exists (i.e., no reasonable fact finder, whether judge or jury, could decide otherwise) and that the law requires the case be decided in favor of the party moving for summary judgment, the court can decide the case without holding a trial. The judge must decide such motions based only on the applicable law (which the judge determines), the evidence (i.e., documents, interrogatory answers, admissions, and deposition testimony) developed during discovery, and the court's claim construction decision, giving the benefit of any doubt about the facts to the nonmoving party. If the court finds that a fact relevant to the outcome is in dispute, summary judgment must be denied and a trial held to resolve that factual dispute.

Understandably, these are hotly contested motions. The moving party hopes to avoid the need for a trial, and the uncertainty a jury introduces, by having the judge decide the case in its favor early on. The nonmoving party wants to go to trial, and hope that the fluid events that are the essence of a jury trial will convince the jury to decide the case in its favor.

In recent years, most patent cases are resolved on summary judgment and only a handful go to trial (about 100 per year throughout the country). The primary reason for this phenomenon is the advent of the claim construction (Markman) hearing and the decision by the court, before trial, about how the language of the asserted claims must be interpreted. The court's claim construction decision resolves most of the uncertainty in a patent case, because what the accused products or services are, and how they operate, is rarely in dispute by the time discovery concludes.

The end result is that the case is often either settled after the claim construction decision, or decided in favor of one side or the other at the summary judgment stage. If summary judgment is granted, the losing party can appeal the decision to the United States Court of Appeals for the Federal Circuit, which is the appellate court to which all decisions in patent cases are appealed.

### Final Pretrial Order and Conference

The final pretrial order is the document that sets forth the "ground rules" for the trial.[xl] It typically identifies all the positions of each party, every issue in dispute in the case that must be resolved by order of the court or at trial, all the documents the parties may seek to introduce into evidence at the trial, and each witness that is expected to be called to testify, either live or via their deposition. The judge issues the order based on a draft prepared by the parties and once issued, it defines the issues that may be raised at the trial. If there is to be a jury trial, the order can rarely be modified after the final pretrial conference. If the trial is before the judge only (referred to as a "bench trial"), the judge may be more lenient in allowing modifications to the final pretrial order because he is the person deciding the case and can adjust more readily than a jury.

---

xxxix See Rule 56, Fed. R. Civ. P.

xl See Rule 16(e), Fed. R. Civ. P.

## 2.6 Trial

**Figure 2.9** (credit: Photograph by Joe Gratz via flickr / CC BY 2.0)

### Learning Objectives

After completing this section, you will be able to

- Understand the importance of jury selection and opposing arguments.
- Grasp why patent trials are often called "morality plays."

The following describes a jury trial. A bench trial is essentially the same, but without the elements involving the jury.[xli]

### Jury Selection

The trial begins with the selection of the jury. The jury is selected (or "picked") from a group of prospective jurors called to court to serve in accordance with the laws and practices of the local jurisdiction.

Each judge has a procedure for picking a jury. Most involve a questionnaire that each prospective juror must complete and provide to the judge and the parties' lawyers. The answers are intended to reveal whether any reason exists why a prospective juror should not serve on the jury. Typical reasons for excluding a prospective juror include that the juror works for or knows one of the lawyers in the case, works for or does business with one of the parties, has a close relative that works for one of the parties, knows something about the subject matter of the case, or is unable to serve because of a disability or a previously planned vacation for which they have already purchased a nonrefundable ticket. The judge also typically asks the prospective jurors whether they have a bias or prejudice that would prevent them from making a fair decision.

xli See generally, Rules 40-63, Fed. R. Civ. P.

Once the judge has "excused" from serving any prospective jurors for "cause" (i.e., because of one of the reasons listed above or some other reason that court believes provides good cause for excusing that person), the clerk selects at random from the remaining prospective jurors the number that will be seated as the jury, plus six. The number of jurors seated in a case depends on the expected length of the trial and the practices of that judge. At least six and no more than twelve jurors must decide a case, but any number between six and twelve can be seated.[xlii] The reason a court usually seats more than six jurors is to assure that the trial will end with at least the minimum of six jurors necessary to decide the case even if one or more jurors need to be excused during the trial, such as for illness or emergency. Judges typically seat seven to nine jurors for this reason. Only rarely do judges in civil patent cases seat a full twelve jurors, because once seated a juror must participate in reaching the decision (unless excused for cause), and all jury decisions in federal cases, including patent cases, must be unanimous.[xliii] The general rule is, the more jurors there are, the longer it takes for them to reach a unanimous verdict, and the higher the likelihood that the case will result in a "hung" jury (i.e., an inability for the jury to reach a unanimous decision).

The clerk selects the designated number for the jury, plus six, because each party gets three "peremptory challenges" to the proposed jury panel, whereby a party can remove a juror without having to give a reason why. Thus, if the judge has decided the jury should begin with eight jurors, the clerk will select 14 so that the plaintiff and defendant (collectively if there is more than one plaintiff and/or defendant) are each able to strike or eliminate three prospective jurors, leaving eight to hear the case.

Once the jury is picked and sworn in, the judge will give the jury preliminary jury instructions. These explain what the case is about, how the trial will proceed, and a description of what a patent is and how the patent system works. Occasionally, judges opt to show the jury the video below, entitled "An Introduction to the Patent System," which was created by the Federal Judicial Center and is intended to be neutral.[xliv]

### Opening Statements

The next step is the opening statements by the opposing parties, starting with the plaintiff and followed by the defendant. If there are multiple plaintiffs or defendants, the judge will give equal time to each side and let the individual parties work out the allocation of time. The opening statement is intended to provide a road map for the jury about what the party intends to prove, and is expected to be devoid of argument. But lawyers rarely present an opening statement without some argument. The judge can intercede, and an opposing party may object, if a party crosses the "no argument" line too far.

The opening statements are where many believe the trial is won or lost because the jury forms initial opinions about who is right and who is wrong in the case based on what they hear at this beginning stage. Thus, each party's trial lawyer tries to craft a story to tell that casts their client in the best possible light. Trials can be likened to a morality play, in which each party tries to cast themselves as in the right, and the opponent as doing them wrong. In patent cases, plaintiffs often portray defendants as thieving freeloaders, attempting to benefit unfairly from the inventiveness of the plaintiff rather than invest in developing their own products. Defendants, on the other hand, often portray patentees as greedy monopolists, trying to stifle competition and deny consumers choice and less-expensive alternatives.

Whether or not the common wisdom is correct, it is with the opening statements that the jurors begin their struggle to find truth among the competing stories they will hear during the trial.

### The Evidence is Presented

The plaintiff then presents its case, calling witnesses and introducing exhibits that support its positions. Each opposing party has the opportunity to object to exhibits and testimony, and to cross-examine witnesses. The

---

xlii See Rule 48, Fed. R. Civ. P.

xliii See Rule 48(a) and (b), Fed. R. Civ. P.

xliv You can see this video at https://archive.org/details/gov.ntis.ava21157vnb1.

judge rules on all objections and generally oversees the proceedings to assure that the trial is conducted properly. After the plaintiff rests its case, the defendant presents its defense, again by introducing exhibits and offering testimony from witnesses. The trial concludes with the plaintiff calling rebuttal witnesses, who are limited to rebutting testimony from the defendant's witnesses. Each side usually calls one or more experts to testify on the issues of infringement and validity (or invalidity), as well as on damages.

## Closing Arguments

After the evidence has been presented, the parties make their closing arguments. Usually the plaintiff goes first, followed by the defendant. The plaintiff has the opportunity to reserve time for rebuttal if it chooses. In some jurisdictions, the defendant must go first and the plaintiff next. In this case, the plaintiff has the last word, and the defendant does not have any opportunity for rebuttal.

Closing arguments give each party the opportunity to highlight what they believe is the critical evidence in their favor, and attack the deficiencies in their opponent's case. It is here that an observer would see the greatest geographic diversity in style and practice. Quite apart from the different styles of trial lawyers and judges across the country, jurors in different parts of the country expect different things from trials, and especially from closing arguments. Thus, an observer would see a very different "show" during a closing argument in the Eastern District of Texas than in the District of Maine.

After closing arguments are concluded, the judge reads the final jury instructions. These set forth the law to which the jury must apply the facts they determine during their deliberations.[xlv]

Thereafter, the jury retires to the jury room, with copies of the exhibits admitted into evidence, to decide the case.

## Deliberation and Verdict

In most patent cases, the jury must answer detailed questions listed in a verdict form, called a special verdict.[xlvi] These questions typically list the accused product(s) and the asserted claim(s) and require the jury to decide infringement and validity for each claim and accused product separately. If appropriate, the jury may also be asked to decide what damages, if any, are to be awarded the plaintiff and whether any infringement they may have found to exist was willful or not.

The jury deliberates as long as it takes to reach a unanimous decision on each question. During their deliberations, the jury may ask questions of the judge in writing, which the judge answers after consulting with the parties. Should the jury tell the judge that it cannot reach a unanimous verdict, the judge may provide additional instructions and return the jury to its deliberations to "try harder." Most juries reach a unanimous decision, which is recorded on the verdict form and read by the clerk in open court with the parties present.

---

xlv See Rule 51, Fed. R. Civ. P.

xlvi See Rule 49, Fed. R. Civ. P.

# 2.7 Post-Trial Procedures

**Figure 2.10** (credit: Jim henderson via Wikimedia Commons / CC0)

## Learning Objectives

After completing this section, you will be able to

- Grasp the significance of equitable proceedings in the post-trial phase.

Following the jury's decision, the court will set a schedule for any equitable proceedings required and for post-trial motions. Equitable proceedings deal with matters to be decided by the judge, not the jury. In terms of post-trial motions, the winning party will ask for entry of judgment.[xlvii] The losing party will file a motion for judgment as a matter of law and usually also a motion for a new trial.[xlviii]

## Equitable Proceedings

Issues arise in most patent cases that must be decided by the judge and not the jury. Many of these are called "equitable" issues because they are left to the sound, equitable discretion of the court. The most common equitable issues are the defense of inequitable conduct and the affirmative claims of willfulness and exceptional case.

## Inequitable Conduct

Misconduct by the patentee in dealing with the Patent and Trademark Office, through which the patentee or its attorney deceives or misleads the patent examiner in an effort to persuade the examiner to grant the patent, was historically called "fraud on the Patent Office," but more recently has been renamed "inequitable conduct." A defendant can raise this issue as a defense, which if proven results in the patent being unenforceable—that is, the patentee is unable to enforce the patent or recover any damages for its

xlvii See Rule 54, Fed. R. Civ. P.

xlviii See Rule 50, Fed. R. Civ. P.

infringement. Many different types of inequitable conduct have been found to render patents unenforceable, from outright fabrications of alleged evidence of unexpected results in the development of the invention, to hiding relevant prior art showing prior solutions to the problem solved by the patent, to failing to tell the patent examiner that another patent examiner had rejected a related application.

Most district courts defer ruling on inequitable conduct defenses until after the liability trial addressing infringement, validity, and damages. This is a commonsense attempt at efficiency because if the patent is found invalid or not infringed at trial, the inequitable conduct issues became moot. Only if the patent is found valid and infringed does the court need to hold a separate hearing to adduce evidence of alleged inequitable conduct. The court then decides whether such conduct had been proven, which is exceedingly rare. Nevertheless, because the consequences of such a finding essentially kill the patent, defendants assert inequitable conduct whenever possible in a final effort to avoid liability.

By 1988, the Federal Circuit Court of Appeals stated: "the habit of charging inequitable conduct in almost every major patent case has become an absolute plague."[xlix] In an effort to stem the spread of this plague, the Federal Circuit sought to restrict its use by holding that inequitable conduct must be established by clear and convincing evidence of deceptive intent. Gross negligence does not suffice and "does not of itself justify an inference of an intent to deceive."[l]

Nevertheless, the plague continued, leading a Federal Circuit judge to write:

> "'Inequitable conduct' in patent practice means misconduct by the patent applicant in dealings with the patent examiner, whereby the applicant or its attorney is found to have engaged in practices intended to deceive or mislead the examiner into granting the patent. It is a serious charge, and the effect is that an otherwise valid and invariably valuable patent is rendered unenforceable, for the charge arises only as a defense to patent infringement. As this litigation-driven issue evolved, the law came to demand a perfection that few could attain in the complexities of patent practice. The result was not simply the elimination of fraudulently obtained patents, when such situations existed. The consequences were disproportionately pernicious, for they went far beyond punishing improper practice. The defense was grossly misused, and with inequitable conduct charged in almost every case in litigation, judges came to believe that every inventor and every patent attorney wallowed in sharp practice."[li]

Still the plague continued, leading Federal Circuit Judge Gajarsa in 2010 to then refer to it as a "pandemic."[lii] Research showed that the percentage of patent cases in which inequitable conduct was charged grew from less than 5 percent in 2000 to 40 percent by 2009.[liii]

Finally, on May 25, 2011, the Federal Circuit restricted the doctrine of inequitable conduct by changing the standard for materiality and clarifying the requirements for finding intent to deceive.[liv] To find inequitable conduct, the court held that the party alleging unenforceability must prove a specific intent to deceive the USPTO by clear and convincing evidence. Moreover, the decision to deceive the USPTO must be knowing and deliberate. The court also clarified that district courts may not use a "sliding scale" to find intent. In other words, the Federal Circuit held it improper to find that a weak showing of intent was sufficient based on a strong showing that the information was material, or that a weak showing of materiality was sufficient based on a strong showing of intent. Although intent can be inferred to meet the clear and convincing evidence standard, specific intent to deceive must be "the single most reasonable inference able to be drawn from the evidence."

xlix *Burlington Indus., Inc. v. Dayco Corp.*, 849 F.2d 1418, 1422 (Fed. Cir.1988).

l *Kingsdown Medical Consultants, Ltd. v. Hollister, Inc.*, 863 F.2d 867, 872 (Fed.Cir. 1988).

li *Ferring B.V. v. Barr Laboratories, Inc.* 437 F.3d 1181, 1195 (Fed. Cir. 2006)(dissenting opinion).

lii *Taltech Ltd. v. Esquel Apparel, Inc.*, 604 F.3d 1324, 1335 (Fed. Cir. 2010)(dissenting opinion).

liii http://www.patentlyo.com/patent/2010/06/measuring-the-plague-of-inequitable-conduct.html.

Regarding materiality, the court required a "but- for materiality" standard. In other words, the standard for materiality now requires that "but for" the alleged deception, the USPTO would not have allowed the claim. Further, "[i]n making this patentability determination, the court should apply the preponderance of the evidence standard and give claims their broadest reasonable construction." The court also recognized an exception to the requirement for but-for materiality, finding that "[w]hen the patentee has engaged in affirmative acts of egregious misconduct, such as the filing of an unmistakably false affidavit, the misconduct is material."

The number of successful inequitable conduct defenses asserted has plummeted due to the strict new requirements for pleading and proving inequitable conduct imposed by the *Therasense* decision. District courts are dispensing with many allegations of inequitable conduct now at the pleading stage, eliminating the need for separate hearings on inequitable conduct issues.

Misuse of a patent is sometimes treated as a form of inequitable conduct, but it is more commonly treated as a separate affirmative defense. The elements of misuse are either a violation of antitrust laws or an effort to expand the scope or term of a patent beyond appropriate limits. For example, it is patent misuse for a patentee to file suit against products of a defendant that are far beyond the proper scope of any claims of the patentee's patent, or to seek damages or an injunction beyond the expiration of the patent. Often such unreasonable demands are accompanied by threats to the defendant's customers. If the misuse is proved, the patentee could be barred from recovering any damages until it has "purged" the misuse by abandoning its unreasonable assertions and dissipating any negative effects they caused.

### Willfulness

If the jury (or judge, in a bench trial) finds that the asserted patent has been infringed, it is often asked to determine whether such infringement was "**willful**."A finding of willful infringement allows the judge to award enhanced damages under 35 U.S.C. § 284, which provides in relevant part that the court may increase the damages award by up to three times the amount found. This is a potent consequence of a showing that a defendant's infringement was willful.

The standard for showing willfulness has evolved over the years, but in 2007, the Federal Circuit significantly altered the standard governing willful infringement by requiring the patentee to prove that (1) the accused infringer "acted despite an objectively high likelihood that its actions constituted infringement of a valid patent," and (2) the "objectively defined risk . . . was either known or so obvious that it should have been known to the accused infringer."[lv] The first prong of this test is objective, whereas the second prong is subjective and involves the accused infringer's actual state of mind. Each prong requires that the infringer knew the patent existed at the time it infringed.

liv *Therasense, Inc. v. Becton, Dickinson & Co., 649 F.3d 1276, passim (Fed. Cir. 2011).*

lv *In re Seagate, 497 F.3d 1360, 1371 (en banc).*

Because an infringer cannot be shown to have willfully infringed if it did not know the patent existed, some companies have adopted a "head in the sand" approach to others' patents. This practice is thought to make sense when the field is very crowded (i.e., there are many patents owned by different patentees covering many different aspects of a product or service) because trying to uncover all the potentially relevant patents that could be asserted against a new product or service is extremely costly, if not impossible. This practice is used most frequently by large companies that can afford to deal with a patent infringement lawsuit should one be filed. Small companies and entrepreneurs, especially in emerging fields, often take great care to search for and work around any existing patents that might be close to their new product or service because they can ill afford patent litigation. Of course, searching for potentially troublesome patents and trying to avoid them is no guarantee of not getting sued. Not only are there more than two million patents in force,[lvi] but creative patentees are not above taking a patent that was thought to cover one product and arguing it is broad enough to cover what a new market entrant has introduced.

In 2012, the Federal Circuit again addressed the willfulness standard, and adjusted it again.[lvii] With regard to the objective prong of the willful infringement test, the Federal Circuit concluded:

> "We believe that the court is in the best position for making the determination of reasonableness. This court therefore holds that the objective determination of recklessness, even though predicated on underlying mixed questions of law and fact, is best decided by the judge as a question of law subject to de novo review."

This further restricts the opportunity for a patentee to prove that a defendant's infringement was willful. The patentee must first convince the district court that the defendant acted despite an objectively high likelihood that its actions constituted infringement of a valid patent. Only after that will the patentee be able to present evidence of the defendant's alleged subjective intent to the jury in an effort to convince the jury that the infringement was willful.

Patentees preferred the pre-*Bard* opportunity to present all of their willfulness evidence to the jury during the liability trial. They wanted this ability because they believed, probably correctly, that it helped the jury conclude not only that the defendant was a "bad actor" who willfully ignored the patentee's rights, but also bolstered the underlying issue of infringement itself. Post-*Bard*, the patentee can only present willfulness evidence if it is able to convince a more dispassionate judge that the defendant acted objectively recklessly, which is a higher hurdle to overcome.

If the patentee convinces the judge on the objective prong, and the jury on the subjective prong, resulting in a jury verdict of willful infringement, the issue of enhanced damages passes back to the court for determination after the trial.

Because the *Bard* case was decided in mid-2012, little empirical evidence exists on its effect on the frequency with which significant enhanced damages are awarded by the courts. However, even before *Bard*, the evidence suggests that such awards were falling. Before the Seagate restrictions were imposed in 2007, 81.4 percent of cases finding willful infringement resulted in an award of enhanced damages, but after Seagate, that number fell to 54.9 percent.[lviii]

---

lvi See Dennis Crouch, *How Many US Patents are In Force?*, http://www.patentlyo.com/patent/2012/05/how-many-us-patents-are-in-force.html.

lvii *Bard Peripheral Vascular Inc. v. W.L. Gore & Assoc's. Inc.*, 682 F.3d 1003, 1006-07 (Fed. Cir. 2012).

lviii Christopher B. Seaman, *Willful Patent Infringement and Enhanced Damages After In Re Seagate: An Empirical Study*, 97 Iowa Law Review 417, 466; http://www.uiowa.edu/~ilr/issues/ILR_97-2_Seaman.pdf.

## Exceptional Case

Courts have discretion to award reasonable attorneys' fees in patent infringement cases that are deemed "exceptional."[lix] The Federal Circuit has referred to this provision as a deterrent to bringing of clearly unwarranted suits on invalid or unenforceable patents.[lx]

Normally, the losing party is not liable to pay the winner's attorneys' fees—a practice referred to as the "American Rule." The rationale for this is that any party should be able to approach the court for relief without fear of having to pay an adversary's attorney's fees. Thus, the provision of the Patent Act that permits an award of attorneys' fees is an exception to the rule that each party bears its own costs in litigation.

Congress said that it intended the rule allowing an award of attorneys' fees to be applied sparingly and "that recovery of attorneys' fees will not become an ordinary thing in patent suits.[lxi] The Federal Circuit repeatedly limited district court discretion to award attorneys' fees to only those cases in which the district court found clear and convincing evidence of bad faith or at least gross negligence by the losing party in bringing or maintaining the suit, and any such determination was reviewable *de novo* on appeal.[lxii] But in April 2014, the Supreme Court struck down these restrictive Federal Circuit interpretations and held:

> "[A]n 'exceptional' case is simply one that stands out from the others with respect to the substantive strength of a party's litigating position (considering both the governing law and the facts of the case) or the unreasonable manner in which the case was litigated. District courts may determine whether a case is 'exceptional' in the case-by-case exercise of their discretion, considering the totality of the circumstances [and without any] precise rule or formula for making these determinations."

In a companion case, the Supreme Court also rejected the rule that exceptional case determinations should be reviewed **de novo** on appeal.[lxiii]

There are increasing calls for a change to the American Rule, to require losing parties to pay the winner's attorneys' fee. The principal purpose of such a change would be to deter so-called "patent trolls," entities that acquire patents for the sole purpose of making money by filing lawsuits, threatening crippling litigation expenses, and demanding settlements at or slightly more than the cost of litigation.[lxiv] It is questionable whether such a change would in fact deter the so-called trolls or instead preclude small entities and entrepreneurs from pursuing legitimate claims due to the uncertainty of the outcome of any lawsuit. Even the most "bulletproof" patent can be subject to unexpected challenges from previously undiscovered prior art or the vagaries of a jury decision favoring the defendant for reasons other than the merits. Enforcing a patent requires resources, or the availability of a contingency fee lawyer willing to take the outsized costs, and risks that patent litigation can entail. Thus, shifting the responsibility for the winner's attorneys' fees to the losing party could effectively preclude small entities and individuals from even filing a lawsuit. The 2014 Supreme Court's *Octane Fitness* and *Highmark* cases, and how district courts exercise their newly expanded discretion in finding a patent case exception under 35 U.S.C. § 285, may dissuade Congress from enacting a "loser pays" exception for patent cases.

---

lix 35 U.S.C. § 285

lx *Mathis v. Spears*, 857 F.2d 749, 754 (Fed. Cir. 1988).

lxi S. Rep. No. 1503, 79th Cong., 2d Sess. (1946) (discussing the predecessor statute to 35 U.S.C. § 285)

lxii *Mathis v. Spears*, 857 F.2d 749, 754 (Fed. Cir. 1988) and *Brooks Furniture Mfg., Inc. v. Dutailier Int'l, Inc.*, 393 F. 3d 1378, 1381-2 (Fed. Cir. 2005).

lxiii *Highmark Inc. v. Allcare Health Management System, Inc.* (572 U.S._)(No. 12-1163. Argues February 26, 2014-Decided April 29, 2014).

lxiv See Section 2.10, *infra.*

## Entry of Judgment

The winning party seeks entry of a judgment that grants it the relief to which it is entitled, based on the jury's verdict and the rulings of the court. First, the judgment will declare who the winning party is. Then, it will set forth the relief or remedies to which the winning party is entitled. The relief may include damages, as awarded by the jury and supplemented by the court if there was a timing difference in the calculation of the damages by the jury and the date on which they are finally awarded. A winning patentee is also entitled to prejudgment interest on the damage award, calculated at the rate specified by law, to compensate for the time value of money lost due to the delay in obtaining damages. The judgment may also set forth the post judgment interest due, for any delay between the entry of the judgment and the payment of the award to the patentee by the losing parties.

A successful patentee may also be entitled to injunctive relief, barring further sales of the infringing product or service. This is the most potent relief available to patentees. Prior to 2006, it was presumed that a patentee who proved patent infringement was irreparably injured and entitled to an automatic injunction. But in 2006, the Supreme Court rejected the presumption and ruled that, in all other kinds of cases, a successful patentee is required to prove each of the following requirements for injunctive relief: (1) that it has suffered an irreparable injury; (2) that remedies available at law are inadequate to compensate for that injury; (3) that considering the balance of hardships between the plaintiff and defendant, a remedy in equity is warranted; (4) that the public interest would not be disserved by a permanent injunction.[lxv]

Usually, patentees who are competitors of the infringer can meet these requirements. However, patentees who are not competitors of the infringer are usually unsuccessful in convincing courts that they are entitled to injunctive relief, and are left with only money damages(usually an on going reasonable royalty) to compensate for future infringement. This removes the most serious risk an alleged infringer faces—being barred from the market—making fighting cases through trial more palatable than before. This new rule from the Supreme Court has driven many plaintiffs out of federal court and into the International Trade Commission (ITC), when the allegedly infringing products are imported, because the ITC issues exclusion orders and cease and desist orders (roughly equivalent to federal court injunctions barring further sales) without regard to the requirements the Supreme Court laid down in the *eBay* decision.[lxvi]

## Motion for Judgment as a Matter of Law

Called a "JMOL" motion, the premise of a motion for judgment as a matter of law is that the jury did not have a legally sufficient evidentiary basis for deciding the case as it did, and the court should intervene and decide the case in favor of the party moving for the JMOL. The moving party must explain in detail what legally required evidence is missing from the trial record. The opposing party (i.e., the party that won the jury verdict) then has the opportunity to identify in the trial record where the allegedly missing evidence is found, and the judge decides who is correct. The court must consider the evidence in the light most favorable to the nonmoving party. Thus, most JMOL motions fail. But the losing party always files such a motion because it is a chance to challenge the jury's verdict and avoid the remedies the winning party is demanding.

## Motion for a New Trial

JMOL motions are usually accompanied by a motion for a new trial, arguing that the jury's verdict was against the manifest weight of the evidence or the jury's verdict was grossly inadequate or excessive.[lxvii] Other grounds also exist, such as newly discovered evidence that could not have reasonably been discovered earlier.

The decision to grant or deny a new trial rests with the sound discretion of the judge, who typically presided during the trial and has a keen understanding of the evidence that was introduced and whether the jury's

lxv *eBay Inc. v. MercExchange, L.L.C*, 547 U.S.388 (2006).

lxvi See footnote 7, *supra*.

lxvii See Rules 50 and 59, Fed. R. Civ. P.

verdict was against the weight of that evidence. The court's decision is not whether the court would have decided the case the same way, but whether there is sufficient evidence in the record to support the jury's verdict. The court must view the evidence in the light most favorable to the nonmoving party. Thus, most new trial motions, like most JMOLs, are unsuccessful.

## 2.8 Appeals

**Figure 2.11** (credit: Photograph by North Charleston via flickr / CC BY 2.0)

### Learning Objectives

After completing this section, you will be able to

- Understand what happens after a jury verdict is entered.
- Appreciate the chances of success of appeals based on fact versus legal issues.

Once the post-trial motions are decided and the judgment entered, the losing party may appeal to the Federal Circuit Court of Appeals. This is the one federal appellate court in the United States that hears all appealed cases involving patent disputes. Almost all patent cases that conclude with a trial, or after a decision on summary judgment, are appealed. This is partly because the cost of an appeal is orders of magnitude less than the case up to that point (e.g., tens or hundreds of thousands of dollars vs. hundreds of thousands or millions of dollars). In addition, overall the Federal Circuit affirms in full less than 60 percent of the patent cases it decides on the merits.[lxviii] Thus, it is well worth it for the losing party to pursue an appeal, because overall it has a 40+ percent chance of partial or full relief from the judgment below. Of course, the reversal rate varies by the nature of the issues before the Federal Circuit and the standard of review the court applies. Legal issues (such as claim construction, summary judgment, and jury instructions) are reviewed **de novo**, without deference to the district court's or jury's decision. This makes it much more likely that the Federal Circuit will reverse a decision because it need not give any deference to the decision of the district court. Fact issues (like infringement, many aspects of validity, and damages) are reviewed on a less flexible standard (i.e., does substantial evidence support the decision), such that the Federal Circuit (like the district court) is not free to substitute its own judgment for that of the jury. Evidentiary rulings, and other issues associated with how the trial was conducted are reviewed under the least flexible standard of review—abuse of discretion. It is rare that the Federal Circuit finds that a district court abused its discretion.[lxix]

For example, the Federal Circuit reverses claim construction decisions at a rate nearly twice as high as decisions without claim construction issues (32 percent vs. 18 percent).[lxx] It is not surprising, then, that most appeals to the Federal Circuit focus at least in part on claim construction as a basis for the appeal.

Appeals at the Federal Circuit are usually resolved within 18–24 months. Oral argument is usually scheduled within a year, depending on how much time the parties take to file their appeal briefs. Oral argument is requested and granted in almost all patent appeals. The argument occurs in the Federal Circuit courthouse in Washington, D.C., before a panel of three judges, although yearly the Federal Circuit travels to other cities to hear arguments at local law schools, which allows students, local practitioners, and the public to attend more easily. The parties are typically given 15 minutes per side to make their arguments, and after the argument, the court renders a written decision within 3–6 months.

## 2.9 Litigation Alternatives

### Learning Objectives

After completing this section, you will be able to

- Understand the various alternative methods of dispute resolution.
- Distinguish the pros and cons of arbitration versus mediation.

The high cost, delay, and disruption of litigation motivate many adversaries to seek alternatives to litigation to resolve their disputes. Mediation and arbitration are two popular alternative dispute resolution (ADR) methodologies. A thriving business exists in the United States providing adversaries the resources to conduct mediations or arbitrations. Retired or former judges or lawyers are available to serve as mediators or arbitrators.

ADR is an increasingly popular way to resolve disputes because it is often faster, less expensive, and private, as compared with the public lawsuit procedures outlined above. The interactions among the parties and the

lxviii http://www.patentlyo.com/files/caseload_patent_infringement_affirmance_and_reversal_rates_2001-2010.pdf.

lxix For a deeper understanding of appellate standards of review in patent cases, see Michel, Paul R., Circuit Judge, CAFC, "Appellate Advocacy—One Judge's Point of View, The Federal Circuit Bar Journal, Vol. 1, No. 2, Summer 1991 (makes analogy to baseball and is readable).

lxx Ted Sichelman, Myths of (Un)Certainty at the Federal Circuit, 43 Loy. L.A. L. Rev. 1161 (2010). Available at: http://digitalcommons.lmu.edu/llr/vol43/iss3/27.

mediators/arbitrators can be kept confidential, as can any settlements reached. Confidentiality is a driving force behind ADR.

## Mediation

Mediation is simply an exchange between adversaries overseen (i.e., "mediated") by an individual with expertise and/ or training in helping parties reach agreement. Often, the mediator will require the parties to submit their positions and relevant documents in a pre-mediation brief. Usually, each pre-mediation brief is confidential and only seen by the mediator and the party submitting it (i.e., the opposing party does not see the other side's mediation brief). The mediator will review the materials submitted and then set a date for the parties to meet with the mediator, usually in the mediator's offices or a neutral location (such as a hotel conference room). Each party commits to bring to the mediation one or more people with the authority to settle, so that the people at the mediation can discuss the dispute and reach an agreement settling it without having to seek approval from others.

At the mediation, the mediator typically starts by meeting with all the parties together, and reviews the dispute and the issues that require settlement. The mediator will then meet with each party separately, engaging in "shuttle diplomacy," in an attempt to bring the parties to a common middle ground. Occasionally, when it may appear that the parties' respective positions leave a gap between them, the mediator may make a "mediator's proposal" that tries to bridge that gap. If the parties agree, typically a written agreement will be signed before they end the mediation—which may be a list of terms for later fleshing out in a full agreement or an actual final settlement agreement. Because anything left to later discussion can give rise to further disputes, most mediators try to get the parties to a full, signed agreement before they depart the mediation.

Perhaps surprisingly to some, mediation often succeeds, if not the first time, then weeks or months later, after the parties have a chance to think things through. Mediations can be conducted while litigation is pending, or before litigation is filed. In the latter case, often the parties will sign a "standstill agreement" that promises that neither will file a lawsuit against the other on the subject matter of the mediation until they agree the mediation has failed.

District courts and the Federal Circuit often have mediation programs that attempt to help the parties resolve their disputes voluntarily. Increased attention is given to these programs as the resources of the courts have dwindled and the caseloads increased because each successful mediation is one less case that requires the resources of the court.

## Arbitration

The principal difference between mediation and arbitration is decisiveness. Mediations result in settlements only if all parties agree to a resolution. In most arbitrations (so-called "binding arbitrations"), the parties agree to be bound by the decision of the arbitrator(s). There is a nonbinding version of arbitration, where the parties ask the arbitrator(s) to render a decision, but do not agree to be bound by it. In practice, these are actually mediations because they result in a settlement only if all parties agree to the result. Such nonbinding arbitrations are most often used when the parties have attempted to reach a mediated settlement but reach an impasse on one or more critical issues. They may then agree to submit those impasses to nonbinding arbitration, where one or more arbitrators (usually experts on the subject matter of the impasse issues) evaluate the facts, as presented by the parties, and render a decision that the parties can review to understand how an impartial third party looks at the issues. This often helps the parties craft a mediated settlement on their own.

Most arbitrations are binding, and resemble lawsuits and trials more than mediations. The parties may agree to submit their dispute to a single arbitrator (like a retired judge), but most often a panel of three arbitrators is appointed to hear the case. The parties may agree on all three arbitrators, drawn from a list of suitable candidates provided by the American Arbitration Association[lxxi] or some other entity in the arbitration business, or each party selects one arbitrator and those two arbitrators pick the third.

The parties agree on the rules that govern the arbitration, which can limit discovery, evidence, witnesses, and trial time, in whatever manner the parties agree. Once the parties agree on the rules, the arbitration is controlled by the arbitration panel, which enforces the rules and renders a binding decision. Usually, arbitration decisions are not appealable (except for gross malfeasance by the arbitrators), but the parties can provide for appeal rights if they choose. But prolonging the resolution of the dispute by allowing an appeal is contrary to the cost and time-savings objectives of most arbitrations.

Arbitrations have become particularly popular for resolving patent disputes that cross international borders and involve multiple patents issued by different countries. No one court can resolve such disputes, so international arbitration, with arbitrators expert in different countries' laws can fill the gap.

## 2.10 Patent Trolls and Efforts to Thwart Them

**Figure 2.12** (credit: Photograph by Alexandre Dulaunoy via flickr / )

### Learning Objectives

After completing this section, you will be able to

- Appreciate the threat posed by patent trolls to innocent businesses.
- Understand the difference between legitimate patent holders enforcing their rights and extortionist patent trolls who try to game the legal system.

lxxi http://www.adr.org/aaa.

Starting in the 1990s, but increasing in the new millennium, a type of plaintiff with a particular litigation and settlement strategy gained notoriety in the United States—the so- called "patent troll." By 2012, the majority of patent suits were brought not by businesses making products covered by patents they owned and seeking to halt competitors believed to be infringing their patents, or even by small entities and entrepreneurs pursuing legitimate claims, but instead by what some detractors call "patent trolls" (after the mythical creatures that demanded payment for safe passage over a bridge).[lxxii] Although some have more recently attempted to discern a difference between what they consider "good" and "bad" trolls by labeling the former "non-practicing entities" (NPEs) or "patent monetization entities" (PMEs), for the purposes of this section, we will refer to such entities as trolls.

As plaintiffs, trolls seek to take advantage of the fact that U.S. patent litigation costs have become so high that many defendants are willing to pay to make such cases go away. Trolls file lawsuits not to protect a business from an infringing competitor, but to derive settlement revenue from defendants willing to settle for less than litigation costs. Trolls often acquire patents of ambiguous scope and questionable value, file suit against multiple defendants, and rely on the presumption of validity accorded all issued patents to extract settlements for less than it would cost any one defendant to defend against the infringement claim. Because trolls have few documents other than the patents and their file histories, and even fewer employees, they are not subject to the outsized expense of discovery that a commercial business with warehouses of documents and scores of employees faces in patent litigation. Because discovery costs for such defendants are so much greater than for troll plaintiffs, defendants feel pressure to settle for less than the cost of litigation, lining the pockets of trolls. Such activities in the aggregate have proven very profitable for trolls, and expensive for defendants.

Spurred by target companies, the America Invents Act legislation in 2011 (see infra, Section X.3.3) included a change in rules governing the joinder of parties, stating:

> "...accused infringers may not be joined in one action as defendants or counterclaim defendants, or have their actions consolidated for trial, based solely on allegations that they each have infringed the patent or patents in suit."

This eliminated a tool of trolls—namely, filing a single case against scores or even hundreds of alleged infringers.[lxxiii] However, trolls simply adapted by filing multiple lawsuits and seeking consolidation for discovery, which increases their costs somewhat but avoids the purpose of the change.

More recently, politicians have scrambled to propose a myriad of different legislative fixes, from shifting the cost of unsuccessful litigation to plaintiffs, to staying litigation against customers of another's product until a suit against the manufacturer is concluded.[lxxiv] Even President Obama was involved, asserting his administration's own views for a solution.[lxxv]

---

lxxii In 2012, one article suggests 56 percent of patent infringement cases filed in the United States were Filed by trolls: https://lexmachina.com/2013/04/09/lex-machina-releases-the-aia-500-expanded/. Another put the number at 62 percent: http://www.lexology.com/library/detail.aspx?g=1e1a0e7bd9a6-4366-818f-a6935ab0fabe&utm_source=Lexology+Daily+Newsfeed&utm_medium=HTML+email+-+Body+-+Federal+section&utm_campaign=Calibar+IP+section+subscriber+daily+feed&utm_content=Lexology+Daily+Newsfeed+2013-04-29&utm_term.

lxxiii See, http://www.americanbar.org/publications/landslide/2012_13/march_april/joinder_over_year_after_america_invents_act.html.

lxxiv "See http://www.ipo.org/wp-content/uploads/2013/06/Patent-Litigation-Bills-Summary-Comparison-Chart-EXPANDED.pdf, http://patentlyo.com/patent/2013/03/guesteDitorial-throwing-trolls-off-the-bridge.html, http://www.ipwatchdog.com/2013/08/13/congress-sirens-song-patent-litigation/id=44573/, https://truthonthemarket.com/2013/03/15/the-shield-act-when-bad-studiesmake-bad-laws/."

lxxv http://www.nytimes.com/2013/06/05/business/president-moves-to-curb-patent-suits.html?_r=0.

Not everyone thinks legislation is appropriate, or even necessary. A panel at Yale Law School in April 2013 yielded decidedly mixed views.[lxxvi] And then Chief Judge Rader of the Federal Circuit Court of Appeals coauthored an op-ed piece in the *New York Times*, recommending that judges should use 35 U.S.C. §285 to foil patent trolls by imposing costs and sanctions at the judicial level.[lxxvii] But again, not everyone thinks that is realistic.[lxxviii] The Supreme Court embraced Judge Rader's recommendation in its 2014 decisions in *Octane Fitness* and *Highmark*, significantly broadening the district court's discretion in finding a case exceptional and awarding attorneys' fees. (See *supra*, Section 2.7, "Exceptional Case.") But even with such expanded discretion and power, trial judges cannot rule on the merits of a case without some basis for it, and that requires money spent by defendants. Thus, it is not easy for a district court judge to stop what trolls rely upon, namely the use of litigation expense and leverage to extract settlements. Getting to the merits of the claims takes time and significant expense—often more than the cost to settle, with no assurance as to outcome.

As of early 2015, the problem of trolls remains a subject of widespread discussion and debate. Legislation that was proposed in 2014 to address the problem is stalled, and although new legislation is still being discussed, many experts believe that the state and federal actions already taken to rein in abusive patent litigation—including important U.S. Supreme Court decisions in 2015 regarding software patentability and fee-shifting in exceptional cases—make it less likely that new legislation will be introduced any time soon.

District courts, for example, have already begun applying the standards recently announced by the Supreme Court in *Octane Fitness* and *Highmark*, and may be more willing to make abusive patent litigants pay attorneys' fees. Time will tell if the new fee-award judicial regime will lessen the pressure to implement legislation against abusive litigants. The Eastern District of Texas, one of the most popular venues for patent litigation in the United States, has added a new Track B docket, which specifically addresses a number of proposals considered by Congress, including early disclosure of certain information, such as licensing information, as well as very early disclosure of both the damages sought and the method of calculating those damage.[lxxix]

Meanwhile, a growing number of state legislatures and state attorneys general have also begun using consumer protection laws to clamp down on patent trolls.[lxxx] And the White House in 2014 issued a series of Executive Orders intended to further curb patent litigation abuse and strengthen the patent system.[lxxxi]

Finally, a movement is taking hold within the patent licensing industry itself to develop a voluntary code of conduct or standards of ethical behavior. Companies like Conversant and Dominion Harbor Group have committed themselves publicly to a set of ethical guidelines for patent licensing, and other companies are also considering doing so.[lxxxii] The Licensing Executives Society of the U.S. and Canada (LES), the industry's principal professional organization, is also developing a set of "best practice" guidelines for ethical patent licensing activity.

The importance of patents to America's economic prosperity and competitiveness ensures that competing interests will continue to strive for an advantage commercially, legislatively, and judicially. Change will continue after the publication of this chapter. The status quo does not last long in our field.

---

lxxvi http://www.patentlyo.com/patent/2013/05/patent-troll-panel-at-yale-law-school.html.

lxxvii http://www.nytimes.com/2013/06/05/opinion/make-patent-trolls-pay-in-court.html.

lxxviii http://www.techdirt.com/articles/20130605/09065423327/chief-patent-judge-speaks-outagainst-patent-trolls.shtml.

lxxix http://mcsmith.blogs.com/eastern_district_of_texas/2014/02/eastern-district-of-texas-resumescase-tracking-with-track-b-for-patent-cases.html.

lxxx http://www.conversantip.com/blog/states-stepup-fight-against-patent-trolls/.

lxxxi http://www.conversantip.com/blog/usadministration-takes-smart-steps-to-strengthenthe-patent-system/.

lxxxii http://www.conversantip.com/news-article/iam-guidelines-for-ethical-patent-licensingprovide-basis-for-new-approach-to-thetroll-debate/ and http://finance.yahoo.com/news/finjan-holdings-commits-licensingbest-130000509.html

## Assessment Questions

1. Responsibility for legally enforcing patents rests with which of the following bodies?
   A. The U.S. Patent and Trademark Office (USPTO)
   B. The U.S. Department of Justice.
   C. The owner of the patent, suing in a federal civil lawsuit.

2. Patent owners have which of the following rights under the law?
   A. The exclusive right to "practice" the patent—meaning the exclusive right to make or sell products based on the patent.
   B. The right to exclude others from making, using, offering for sale, selling, or importing the invention covered by the patent throughout the United States.
   C. Both of these.

3. Which of the following is required in order to infringe a patent?
   A. Intending to infringe the patent.
   B. Making, using, or selling the patented invention without authorization.
   C. Knowing that the patent exists.

4. Which of the following is the legal definition of patent infringement?
   A. One or more of a patent's claims match (or "read on") the features and functions of a device or process.
   B. A device or process that performs a "substantially similar" functions to those described in a patent's claims.
   C. Both of the above are correct.

5. Which of the following illustrates the "doctrine of equivalents"?
   A. If a device performs substantially the same function in substantially the same way as your patent claim, infringement exists if any differences are insignificant.
   B. A patent calling for an "adhesive" connection (describing glue as the preferred adhesive) may be infringed by a device using a Velcro® fastener.
   C. Both of the above are correct.

6. If you believe your patent is being infringed, you have how many options for recourse?
   A. Two. You can sue the infringer in federal court, or ignore the infringement.
   B. Three. Besides the two above, you can simply demand he stop infringing.
   C. Four. You can sue the infringer, demand he stop infringing and pay monetary damages, offer the infringer a license in return for royalties, or ignore it.

7. Patent infringement suits can take years and cost millions of dollars. Which of the following is another option patent owners have in seeking redress for infringement?
   A. Litigation financing in exchange for a share of any damages.
   B. Out-of-court license and royalty settlements.
   C. Contingency lawyers take the case for a share of any damages.
   D. All of the above.

8. If you think multiple parties are infringing, what is your best strategy?
   A. Sue them one at a time, so they don't gang up on you.
   B. Pick the one with the biggest pockets, as the settlement will likely be larger.
   C. Sue them all simultaneously, and let them sort out their differences.

9. Should you alert an infringer beforehand that you intend to file suit?
   A. Always. This gives them the opportunity to settle prior to you filing a costly suit.
   B. Never. They can then sue you preemptively, giving them the vital initiative in seeking a venue of their choice and a declaratory judgement of noninfringement.
   C. Yes, but only if you file suit simultaneously or shortly afterwards.

10. How often do plaintiffs win at trial?
   A. 60 to 75 percent of the time.
   B. 80 to 90 percent of the time.
   C. 40 to 50 percent of the time.

11. Which of the following is NOT a valid reason for filing a motion to dismiss once a suit is filed in a federal court?
   A. Improper jurisdiction.
   B. Improper venue.
   C. Improper (or invalid) patent.
   D. Failure to state a proper claim.

12. Which of the following is NOT a possible defense in a defendant's answer to a claim?
   A. The patent is invalid.
   B. The patent is not infringed.
   C. The plaintiff waited too long to file suit.
   D. The patent covers a nonessential part of the allegedly infringing product.

13. Why have defendants increasingly turned to post-grant review proceedings at the PTO, such as *inter partes review*, since the America Invents Act was passed in 2011?
   A. The PTO is less likely to judge that a patent has been infringed.
   B. It's quicker than waiting for a trial.
   C. The PTO has shown a strong likelihood of finding challenged patents invalid.

14. What role does discovery play in an infringement case?
   A. Through production of documents and interrogatories, either side may discover information that may be decisive in confirming or rebutting infringement claims.
   B. Discovery is often an endless fishing expedition that escalates the costs to both parties exponentially.
   C. Both of these describe the role of discovery in an infringement case.

15. What is the most critical pretrial phase of every patent infringement case?
   A. Discovery.
   B. Summary Judgment.
   C. Claims construction (or Markman) hearings.
   D. The Verdict.

16. Why do courts usually seat seven to nine jurors rather than six or twelve in most patent cases?
   A. You need an odd number of jurors to break a tie vote on the verdict.
   B. Six jurors won't be enough for a legal verdict if one is excused during trial, and twelve jurors will likely take too long to decide the case.

**17.** Why are patent trials often thought of as morality plays?

A. The facts of the case, not each party's moral views, are all that matters to a jury.
B. It is immoral to spend $3 million to $10 million on a patent suit.
C. Each party casts itself as in the right and its opponent as doing them wrong.

**18.** Which of the following is the definition of inequitable conduct?

A. Deceiving or misleading the patent office to grant a patent.
B. Deceiving or misleading a jury during opening arguments.
C. Deceiving or misleading the opposing party during the discovery phase.

**19.** What's the standard for proving willful infringement, leading to enhanced damages?

A. Selling a product despite knowing that a patent exists that the product might be infringing.
B. Selling a product despite an objectively high likelihood that it infringed a valid patent and that this risk was known or should have been known to the infringer.
C. Deliberately not conducting a prior art search to determine if a patent exists that your product might be infringing.

**20.** What is the standard for imposing attorneys' fees on the losing party to a patent suit?

A. Convincing evidence of bad faith or gross negligence by the losing party.
B. A case that "stands out from others" in the weakness of the plaintiff's case or the unreasonable or abusive manner in which it was litigated.

**21.** What is often the most serious damage that a court can impose upon an infringer?

A. A very large award for monetary damages.
B. Pre- and post judgment interest payments on the damage award.
C. Injunctive relief barring further sales of the infringer's products.

**22.** Which of the following explain why patent infringement verdicts are almost always appealed?

A. The cost of an appeal is orders of magnitude less than the cost of the trial itself.
B. Legal issues such as claim construction are reviewed **de novo** - meaning, without regard to the previous trial's rulings.
C. The U.S. Court for the Federal Circuit, the appeals court, affirms in full less than 60 percent of the patent cases it decides on the merits.
D. All of the above.

**23.** As an alternative to litigation, mediation is different from arbitration in what way?

A. Mediations result in settlements only if both parties agree.
B. In arbitrations, the parties are bound by the decision of the arbitrator.
C. Both of these are accurate.

**24.** Which of the following is the definition of a "patent troll"?

A. A patent owner who licenses their patents rather than makes or sells products.
B. A patent owner whose main source of revenue is patent litigation.
C. A patent owner whose main source of revenue is "nuisance settlements" for less than the cost of litigation.

3

# Copyright Basics

**Figure 3.1** (credit: modification of work "Copyright symbol under magnifying glass" by Marco Verch/flikr.com, CC BY 2.0)

## Chapter Outline



## Introduction

## 3.1 The Basics of Copyright

**Figure 3.2** (credit: Wikimedia Commons / CC BY-SA 3.0)

### Learning Objectives

After completing this section, you will be able to

- Understand the theoretical and legal underpinnings of copyright.
- Appreciate the important differences between copyrights and patents.

A copyright is an intellectual property right granted by a government to the author of an original literary, dramatic, musical, artistic, or other eligible creative work that gives them the exclusive right to control how the work is published, reproduced, performed, or displayed—as well as whether or not derivative works (e.g., a movie version of a novel) may be produced.

In the United States, the legal foundation for copyright is set forth, along with that for patents, in Article 1, Section 8, Clause 8 of the U.S. Constitution. This clause gives Congress the authority to "promote the progress of Science and useful Arts, by securing for limited times to authors and inventors the exclusive right to their respective writings and discoveries."[i]

Congress and the courts have interpreted the terms "authors" and "writings" very broadly so as to include the creators of a wide variety of artistic and intellectual works. Title 17 of the United States Code authorizes the grant of a copyright to the authors of "original works of authorship"—including literary works, dramatic works, choreographic works, graphic works, audiovisual works, sound recordings, and architectural works. In most cases, a copyright lasts for the life of the author plus 70 years.

### How to Obtain a Copyright

In America, the copyright system is administered by the U.S. Copyright Office, which is part of the Library of

i U.S. Constitution Arr. 1, § 8

Congress and maintains a registry of copyrighted works. Interestingly, registration is not required to obtain a copyright. It is automatically granted to an author at the moment of creation—i.e., as soon as the work is expressed in a tangible form that allows it to be seen or copied, such as being written on paper or on a computer, or recorded as video or audio. Registration is only required if a copyright holder wants to initiate a copyright infringement suit in federal court.

## Copyrights vs. Patents

Unlike the case with patents, the United States never developed an examination system for determining whether or not a creative work merits copyright protection. That's because while the validity of an invention can be evaluated fairly objectively based on its utility, novelty, and non- obviousness, the merit of any cultural work is a far more subjective affair, as demonstrated by the frequency with which publishers reject novels that later go on to become literary classics.

What the patent and copyright systems share, however, is the recognition that unless the inherent property rights of inventors and authors to their creations are protected, the wellsprings of creation and productivity would be negatively affected by the reduced incentive. Both systems also share the public policy goal of marshaling the benefits of individual creativity—whether technological, as in the case of inventions, or cultural, as in literary works—to the public good so that these promote the progress of the nation and the "general welfare" of its citizens.

How to promote that general welfare, however, was approached very differently by the Founders in the case of patents than it was with copyright.

**Figure 3.3** A portrait of Supreme Court Justice Henry Baldwin. (credit: modification of work by Wikimedia Commons / Public Domain)

The explicit intention of patent law, explained Supreme Court Justice Henry Baldwin in *Whitney v. Emmett* (https://openstax.org/l/Whitney_v_Emmett) (1831), was "to benefit the inventor, in the belief that maximizing individual welfare leads to maximum social welfare." Inventors, after all, created tools that enabled the new nation to free itself from dependency on foreign imports and develop industries of its own. Whatever incentives were needed to prod these technologically creative people to take on the challenge and succeed were well worth the bargain (see Chapter 1).

### The Rights of Authors and the Public Interest

When it came to copyright, however, the rights of authors were thought to conflict with those of the public to a far greater extent. "Democratic values emphasized equal and widespread access to learning and the importance of information flows for maintaining political freedom, whereas strong copyrights impinged on the fullest attainment of these objectives," notes Bowdoin College historian Zorina Khan, author of *The Democratization of Invention: Patents and Copyright in American Economic Development*, which won the Alice Hanson Jones prize for outstanding work in economic history in 2005.[ii]

As an example, a copyright owner's right to prevent unauthorized use of their work may at times be constrained by the public's First Amendment right of free speech—hence the doctrine of "fair use" (more on this later).

It was believed that a strategy of strong patent rights but weaker copyrights also better reflected the differing incentives that motivated inventors and authors. Inventors, many felt, were driven primarily by economic gain, whereas authors were often interested as much in the prospect of celebrity and reputation as they were in monetary reward.

Supreme Court Justice John McLean emphasized that this distinction between patents and copyrights exists in the structure of U.S. intellectual property law itself. In *Wheaton v. Peters* (1834) (https://openstax.org/l/Wheaton_v_Peters) , the first high court ruling on copyright, he wrote:

> "It has been argued at the bar that as the promotion of the progress of science and the useful arts is here united in the same clause in the Constitution, the rights of authors and inventors were considered as standing on the same footing. But this, I think, is a non-sequitur ... for when Congress came to execute this power by legislation, the subjects are kept distinct and very different provisions are made respecting them."[iii]

To understand why the Founders gave greater weight to the public domain in copyright law than they did in patent law, it's important to examine the origin and development of early copyright systems and their political and economic impact on society.

## 3.2 Early Copyright Systems

### Learning Objectives

After completing this section, you will be able to

- Understand the role early copyright systems played in enforcing monopolies.
- Appreciate the degree to which authors' rights were ignored at that time.

As was the case with patents, the granting of book privileges (now called copyrights) began in the Republic of Venice in the fifteenth century. Prior to that, printed books were considered part of the public domain and anyone could copy or reproduce them. But in 1492—the same year Columbus sailed the Santa Maria to the New World—a Milanese author named Donatus Bossius petitioned the sixth duke of Milan, Gian Galeazzo Sforza, for an exclusive privilege for his book, arguing that without such a privilege he would be unjustly deprived of the fruit of his effort. He was granted a ten-year privilege, and the practice soon spread throughout Europe.

The French copyright system was introduced in 1498. Exclusive rights to not only books but also translations, maps, type designs, engravings, and artwork were granted by the monarch for periods initially ranging from

ii B. Zorina Khan, *The Democratization of Invention: Patents and Copyrights in American Economic Development, 1790O1920*, Cambridge University Press, 2005.

iii *Wheaton v. Peters*, 33 U.S. (8 Pet.) 591 (1834)Retrieved from http://supreme.justia.com/cases/federal/us/33/591/case.html *courtesy of B. Zorina Khan.*

two to ten years. There were stipulations attached to such grants, sometimes including even price controls on the published works.

It is important to realize, however, that authorship was not required for the granting of early copyrights. In fact, the early copyright systems of Europe more often than not enabled printers and publishers to establish quite effective monopolies over the commerce in books, the arts, and other cultural works that limited the diffusion of culture in society. The owners of such privileges may have waxed poetic about "droit d'auteur" (authors' rights), but this was often just a way of deflecting public criticism of their monopolistic power and superprofits.

Indeed, this was most glaringly revealed in the grant of exclusive privileges to French opera. According to a 1929 book by Henry Prunières,[iv] Louis XIV in 1669 granted a perpetual monopoly over all operatic performances in France to Jean-Baptiste Lully, the director of the Paris Opera. Lully also gained sole publication rights to opera librettos, and sold shares in the rights to printers. He then used his copyright privilege to limit the number of musicians who could perform outside the Paris Opera and to suppress competitors like the Comédie Francaise. In the end, Lully became fabulously rich and bequeathed his monopoly rights to his heirs.

Not exactly your starving artist asking merely to enjoy the fruits of his work.

Early copyright systems also quickly evolved into means of censorship and surveillance of the population's reading habits. The 1566 Edict of Moulins in France, for example, required that any new book had to be approved and licensed by the Crown. Manuscripts first had to be read and approved by a censor before a permit was granted to print a book. The permit could be revoked if officials or influential citizens later complained about the book's content.

**Figure 3.4** The Marble Court. Versailles Palace, France. (credit: photograph by Kimberly Vardeman via flikr / CC BY 2.0)

Interestingly, a decree in 1777 enabled authors who did not sell off their rights to gain a copyright in

iv Henry Prunières, *"La vie illustre et libertine de Jean-Baptiste Lully,"* Librairie Plon, Paris, 1929, courtesy of B. Zorina Khan.

perpetuity. But like the A.J. Liebling quote about freedom of the press belonging only to those with enough wealth to own one,.so, too, were authors' inalienable rights often just a lofty theory trumped by harsh economic reality. Because few authors had the capital required to print a book, they usually sold off their "exclusive rights" to commercial publishers.

Much the same situation prevailed in the English copyright system, where copyright law began as a monopoly grant to benefit favored guilds and as a means to censor public opinion on behalf of the Crown.

## The Statute of Anne

In 1557, the Worshipful Company of Stationers was granted a royal privilege that enabled it to control the book trade for the next 150 years. Only in 1709 did a new copyright statute, the **Statute of Anne**, begin to erode the monopolistic power of the Stationers Company. It stipulated that a copyright could be obtained by anyone, and instead of a perpetual right, the term was limited to 14 years with the right to renew for one additional 14-year term. According to Professor John Feather of Loughborough University in Britain, the statute "wholly ignored the authors of books, and certainly was not intended to confer any additional rights on them."[v]

Assessing early European copyright systems as a whole, Zorina Khan observes that they "resulted in 'odious monopolies,' higher prices and greater scarcity, large transfers [of money] to officials of the Crown and their allies, and pervasive censorship [while it also] disadvantaged smaller book producers, provincial publishers, and the academic and broader community."[vi]

It wasn't until 1774 in England, in the landmark case *Donaldson v. Beckett*, that a court ruled that authors have a fundamental right to their writings—at least until publication, after which the Statute of Anne still gave the rights to the publishers. The immediate claim in the case was whether Scottish bookseller Alexander Donaldson had acted as a pirate when he published an edition of James Thomson's *The Seasons*, a work for which Thomas Beckett and other London booksellers claimed the copyright. But the larger principle at issue was whether copyright was a limited right granted by government under the Statute of Anne, or a common law right of publishers that existed in perpetuity despite the limitations of the statute.

The case would prove pivotal in deciding not only the future of publishing, but also of authors, in whose name the London publishers claimed to be acting. The court took the claim of authors' rights further than the publishers ever intended, however. It reaffirmed the limited statutory nature of copyright and also recognized that authors—with the decline of patronage, authors were only then emerging as independent professionals writing for a mass market of book buyers—were the true originators and proprietors of the product of their own creative labors.

v John Feather, *"Publishing, Piracy, and Politics: An Historical Study of Copyright in Britain,"* Mansell, New York, 1994, courtesy of Khan.

vi Op. cit., Khan.

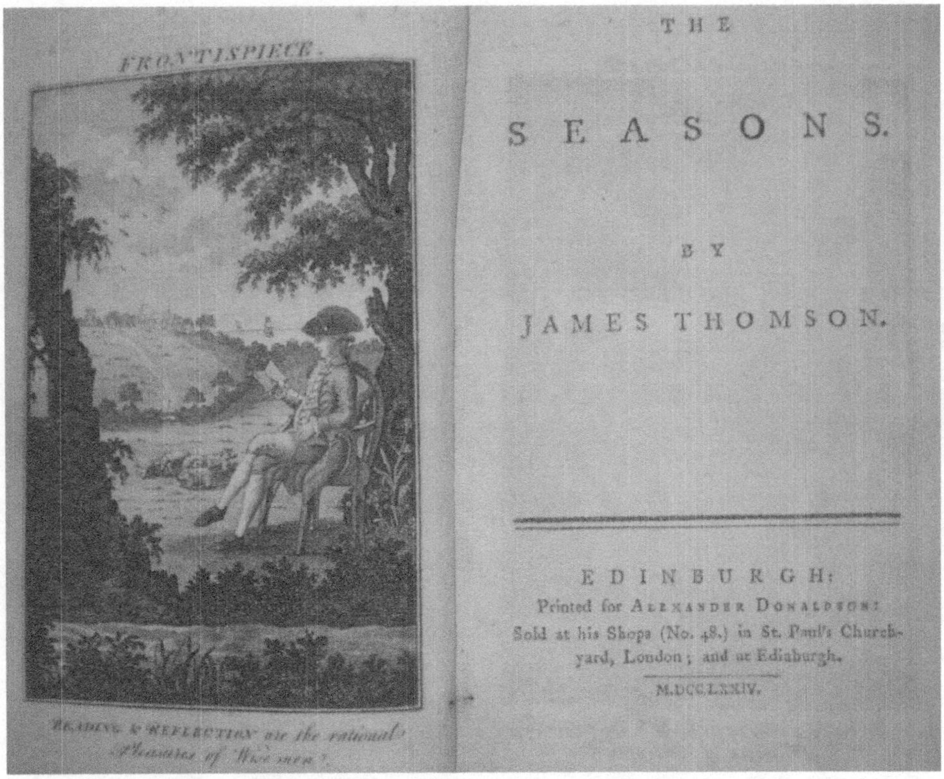


**Figure 3.5** Photograph of Frontispiece – The Seasons by James Thomson Published by Alexander Donaldson. This work is published from the United States. (credit: Wikimedia Commons / Public Domain)

As Michel Foucault would put it nearly two centuries later,

> "The coming into being of the notion of 'author' constitutes the privileged moment of individualization in the history of ideas, knowledge, literature, philosophy, and science."

In the century after *Donaldson v. Beckett*, European copyright systems expanded to include sheet music, maps, design, sculpture, and even lectures. The doctrines of "work for hire" and "fair use" would emerge (more on these later), but the law would still remain largely arbitrary, confused, and frequently injurious to the public until late in the nineteenth century.

However, the process of transforming copyright from a scheme of monopoly privileges for publishers into a property right for the actual creators of cultural works had begun.

## 3.3 Copyright in America

**Figure 3.6** (credit: photograph by Kenneth C. Zirkel via Wikimeda Commons / CC BY-SA 3.0)

### Learning Objectives

After completing this section, you will be able to

- See the origins of copyright law in the United States.
- Appreciate the importance the Founding Fathers attached to the public need for widespread access to learning and information.

Ever practical, the Founding Fathers sought to construct an intellectual property regime that above all else would encourage the growth of commerce and industry in order to ensure the survival of the young American nation during its precarious beginnings.

For patent law, this meant creating the maximum possible incentives to those whose ingenuity would spur the development of agriculture and domestic industry. As economist Jonathan Hughes once noted, entrepreneur-inventors like Eli Whitney, who developed a cotton gin in 1793 that increased agricultural production a hundredfold, were"the vital few" upon whom the nation depended for progress. That's why early Supreme Court Justice Joseph Story argued that patent rights were "sacred," and the just reward for their contributions to society.

But in copyright law, a different approach was taken—one that acknowledged authors' rights but placed far greater emphasis on the public's need for widespread access to learning and on the growth of markets. James Gilreath, the Library of Congress historian who in the late nineteenth century painstakingly reconstructed Thomas Jefferson's massive library catalog burned by the British in 1814, explained the Founders' view this way:

> "The constitutional copyright provisions' emphasis on the useful arts sought not to bolster a professional literary establishment of novelists, poets, and critics such as the one that existed in

> England, but rather to ensure that books with demonstrably practical benefits to society would be available to readers of the new Republic."

This emphasis was certainly in tune with the realities of American book trade. Domestic publishers mainly produced newspapers, almanacs, and practical guides—reading material of useful value to a nation that needed to build an entire economy from scratch. Most important literary works, on the other hand, were imported from Britain and France.

As a result, even in colonial times, states that passed copyright laws did so only with explicit rules that ensured widespread public access to knowledge and information.

Take colonial Connecticut's 1783 copyright law, for example. It certainly contained all the right rhetoric about authors' natural rights:

> "Whereas it is perfectly agreeable to the principles of natural equity and justice, that every author should be secured in receiving the profits that may arise from the sale of his works, and such security may encourage men of learning and genius to publish their writings; which may do honor to their country, and service to mankind."[vii]

But it also made it quite clear that copyrighted books had to be offered at reasonable prices or the state would issue a compulsory license enabling anyone to copy these at will. No one failed to get the point.

After the Constitutional Convention and the establishment of Congress, the first federal copyright statute was signed into law by President George Washington on May 31, 1790, less than two months after the first patent law was approved.

The law stipulated that "the author and authors of any map, chart, book or books already printed within these United States, being a citizen or citizens thereof, shall have the sole right and liberty of printing, reprinting, publishing and vending such map, chart, book or books" for a period of 14 years, with the right of renewal for another 14 years. The Founders' belief that 28 years was the proper maximum copyright term stands in sharp contrast to today's controversial maximum copyright term of life-plus-70 years, an issue we will discuss later in this chapter.

Anyone violating a copyright "shall forfeit all and every copy and all and every sheet to the author or proprietor who shall forthwith destroy the same." What's more, "offenders shall also forfeit and pay the sum of fifty cents for every sheet which shall be found in his or her possession." As a final disincentive to infringers, the law allowed copyright owners to file suit "in any court of record in the United States within one year after the cause of action."

---

vii State of Connecticut. (1906). Copyright Laws Passed by the Original States: 1783-1786. In T. Solberg (Ed.), *Copyright Enactments of the United States, 1783-1906* (2 ed., pg. 11). Retrieved from http://books.google.com/books?id=xNA9AAAAIAAJ&oe=UTF-8

Columbian Centinel.

By Authority

**Figure 3.7** The US Copyright Act of 1790 reprinted in the Colombian Centinel, published 17 July 1790. (credit: Wikimedia Commons / Public Domain)

Still, the law's focus on the public interest was clear in the first five words of the text: *"An Act for the Encouragement of Learning*, by securing the Copies of Maps, Charts and Books, to the Authors and Proprietors of such Copies, during the Times therein mentioned."

The failure in the text to distinguish between "authors" and "proprietors" (i.e., publishers, printers, and booksellers), of course, also suggested that Congress did not view copyright as an innate or moral right of authors. In fact, copyright was conditional upon the author or proprietor depositing a copy of the work in the district court and paying a fee of 60 cents.

Another sign that the emphasis of U.S. copyright law was to facilitate the diffusion of knowledge over the protection of authors' inherent property rights was provided by this sentence:

> "Nothing in this act shall be construed to extend to prohibit the importation or vending, reprinting or publishing within the United States, of any map, chart, book or books by any person not a citizen of the United States."

In other words, America's first copyright law explicitly authorized the piracy of foreign cultural works in order to promote widespread citizen access to the benefits of learning.

And that's exactly what Americans did, unabashedly pirating European culture and resisting for a century all attempts to alter what Europeans called its "obnoxious laws."

The first American to receive a U.S. copyright, one month after the Copyright Act was signed into law, was John Barry for his spelling book. The first woman granted a copyright was Mrs. Mercy Warren of Massachusetts for her *Poems, Dramatic and Miscellaneous.*

**Figure 3.8** Portrait of Mercy Otis Warren (1728-1814), American writer and first woman in the United States to be granted a copyright. (credit: portrait by John Singleton Copley via Wikimedia Commons / Public domain)

Over the next decade, half of all copyrights went to proprietors, proving yet again that the law's concern was not chiefly with the rights of authors. Most of these were for practical books such as atlases, dictionaries, and textbooks, as one would expect in a society hungering for practical knowledge and lacking in homegrown literary works equal in sophistication to those of the Europeans.

## The Pirates of Copyright

As late as 1835, 65 percent of science books, 92 percent of business texts, and 75 percent of law books published in the United States were written by Americans. But even then, a half century after independence, only a third of poetry and drama books published in America were written by Americans.[viii]

"A nation of artificers and innovators, both as consumers and producers, American citizens were confident of their global competitiveness in technology, and took an active role in international patent conventions," explains Khan. "Although they excelled at pragmatic contrivances, Americans were advisedly less sanguine about their efforts in the realm of music, art, literature and drama."

According to Ainsworth Spofford, the Librarian of Congress from 1864 to 1897, "a group of publishing houses in the [U.S.], which made a specialty of cheap books, vied with each other in the business of appropriating English and continental trash, and printed this under villainous covers, in type ugly enough to risk a serious increase of opthalmia among American readers."[ix]

And not just "trash," either. America gained a notorious reputation internationally for its piracy of English and European literary classics—a practice greatly encouraged by the protectionist levying of tariffs as high as 25 percent on imported books.

viii Op. cit., Khan.

ix "*The Question of Copyright*," compiled by George Haven Putnam, G.P. Putnam's Sons, New York, 1896, courtesy of Zorina Khan.

**Figure 3.9** (credit: Original artist: Joseph Ferdinand Keppler (1838-1894)Restoration: Adam Cuerden via Wikimedia Commons / Public domain)

Put another way, America in those days was seen as a nation of technological innovators and cultural pirates.

Between 1790 and 1875, more than a hundred petitions were submitted to Congress to bring the United States in line with international copyright laws. All were defeated by publishers' and printers' lobbies. It wasn't until 1891 that the Chace Act granted copyright protection to select foreign authors—but only if their work was published in the United States on or before the publication date in their own countries, and only if the actual printing was done here. The United States failed to qualify for admission to the Berne Convention on copyright until 1988, an astonishing 102 years after the convention.

Such piracy had its costs, however—and not just to foreign authors and publishers. According to Arthur Schlesinger, "So long as publishers ... could reprint, or pirate, popular English authors without payment of royalty, and so long as readers could buy such volumes far cheaper than books written by Americans, native authorship was at a marked disadvantage."[x]

Some believe this helps to explain why no great American novels were written in the early nineteenth century. Only in the mid-1800s, with the emergence of novelists like James Fenimore Cooper, Nathaniel Hawthorne, and Henry Wadsworth Longfellow did a change in the relative balance of authorship between Americans and foreigners begin to take place. More and more authors took up the pen and influenced American culture, including Harriet Beecher Stowe, who copyrighted Uncle Tom's Cabin in 1851. Nonetheless, it wasn't until the early twentieth century, after the United States began to comply with international copyright standards, that Americans became the majority of best-selling authors in the United States.[xi]

---

x Arthur M. Schlesinger, *The Rise of the City, 1878-1898*, McMillan, New York, 1933.

xi Alice Hackett and James Burke, *Eighty Years of Best Sellers, 1895-1975*, Bowker, New York, 1971.

**Figure 3.10** An engraving of Nathaniel Hawthorne made by H. W. Smith circa 1880. (credit: Wikimedia Commons / Public Domain)

It would be far too simplistic, of course, to ascribe the late- blooming of American literature simply to weak copyright laws and the prevalence of cheap pirated foreign literature. There are organic reasons why a young nation, and a new culture, needs time to develop its own literary voices. But it is also true, as research worldwide has repeatedly demonstrated, that where weak intellectual property protections exist in developing nations (like today's China or early nineteenth-century America), citizens have an excessive incentive to copy and insufficient incentive to invent and create for themselves.

## 3.4 Eligible Works

**Figure 3.11** Parthenon Marbles, East Pediment. Photograph taken at the British Museum by Justin Norris via flikr / CC BY 2.0

### Learning Objectives

After completing this section, you will be able to

- Know what kinds of creative work are eligible for
- Grasp the broad definition of "authors" and "literary works."

### Can I Copyright That?

Before reading this section, please watch this overview video (https://openstax.org/l/CanICopyright) covering the basics of copyright law—eligible works, the distinction between ideas and their expression, the rights granted to copyright owners, and is copyright term—life plus 70 years.

Title 17 of the United States Code Section 102 explicitly delineates eight categories of original works that are eligible for copyright.

This list, while broad, actually includes a far more extensive range of work than the average citizen might imagine. For example, copyrightable works also include software.

### Copyrighting Software

Why is software copyrightable? It's because an appellate ruling in the 1983 case of *Apple v. Franklin* (https://openstax.org/l/Apple_v_Franklin) held that software was a kind of "literary work" and therefore eligible for copyright.

The court noted that the Copyright Act defined the term "literary work" as follows:

> "Literary works are works, other than audiovisual works, [that are] expressed in words, numbers, or other verbal or numerical symbols or indicia, regardless of the nature of the material objects, such as books, periodicals, manuscripts, phonorecords, film, tapes, disks, or cards, in which they are embodied."[xii]

Based on this definition, the court determined that a computer software program "is an appropriate subject of copyright."

Note, however, that copyright does not extend to the elements of works of authorship that are potentially

xii *Apple Computer, Inc. v. Franklin Computer Corp.*, 714 F.2d 1240 (3d Cir. 1983) Retrieved from http://bulk.resource.org/courts.gov/c/F2/714/714.F2d.1240.82-1582.html.

patentable processes. And indeed, beginning in the 1990s, software companies began increasingly to patent those elements of their new software that could be described as patentable processes, precisely in order to secure the stronger protections of patent law.

In any event, software is but one example of how the courts have tended to interpret broadly the eight categories of eligible subject matter. Just as technology drove the expansion of eligible subject matter into ever new realms—e.g., first photographs and then motion pictures—the courts have also expanded the definitions of all eight categories of eligible subject matter to include maps, games, puzzles, toys, fabric design, and many other creations.

## Ideas to Copyrightable Works

However, not everything is copyrightable—far from it. Just as patent law makes a sharp distinction between ideas and their application—i.e., you cannot patent an idea for a better mousetrap but you most certainly can patent a new, non-obvious, and useful apparatus that catches mice—so, too, does copyright law differentiate between ideas and their expression. You cannot copyright, for example, the idea of an epic space opera in which a mystical cadre of Jedi knights wielding laser swords battle galactic evil, but you can copyright the particular expression of that idea in the screenplay and motion picture *Star Wars*.

Because it is an abstract concept or idea, Einstein's formula $E = MC^2$ is also not copyrightable. It is true that Einstein was the first to derive the famous formula involving mass and energy, which at first blush seems to fit the requirement for creative authorship in a copyrightable work. But the formula was derived from observation of natural physical laws, and must remain in the public domain lest private intellectual property rights create a blockade that prevents scientists and mathematicians from continuing their research and teaching.

Also noncopyrightable are names, addresses, and other known facts that are not creatively compiled. That's why a phone book cannot be copyrighted, whereas the *creative* compilation of facts in a Chinese-American phone directory listing "Bean Curd & Bean Sprout Shops" may be under certain conditions, as a judge ruled in the 1991 case *Key v. Chinatown* (https://www.openstax.org/l/KeyVChinatown) .

To be copyrightable, a creative work must not only be *expressed* in a tangible form that allows it to be seen or copied (i.e., put to paper or some other medium), but it must also be *original*. The requirement for originality in copyright has its parallel in the necessity for novelty in patents. But this parallel works only to a point, for a copyrighted work need not be novel in the strictest sense to be original.

As Arthur R. Miller and Michael H. Davis explain in their textbook on intellectual property for law students:

> "The author's ideas and themes may have appeared in earlier works, Indeed, much of the expression may have been produced before. But copyright will be available to [this] second author if his is a work of independent creation."[xiii]

To reiterate, a copyrightable work must not only fit under one of the eight broad categories of eligible subject matter, but it must also be:

- Independently created.
- Expressed or fixed on a tangible medium that can be seen or copied.
- Creatively authored or compiled.
- Not a fact or abstract idea.

---

xiii Arthur R. Miller and Michael H. Davis, *Intellectual Property: Patents, Trademarks, and Copyright in a Nutshell.* (5th ed., p. 25). St. Paul MN: West Publishing Co., 2007.

## 3.5 Rights and Term

### Learning Objectives

After completing this section, you will be able to

- Discern the specific rights granted to copyright owners.
- Understand the term of those rights as well as in some cases their limitations.

Just as common law property rights grant owners' exclusive powers of possession, use, and distribution, so, too, does copyright law provide for six roughly analogous exclusive rights:[xiv]

1. The right to reproduce the copyrighted work
2. The right to prepare derivative works
3. The right to distribute copies or phonorecords of the copyrighted work to the public by sale or other transfer of ownership, or by rental, lease, or lending
4. The right to perform the copyrighted work publicly
5. The right to display the copyrighted work publicly
6. The right to perform sound recordings publicly through a digital audio transmission.

These rights are exclusive to copyright owners—only they or those to whom they have legally assigned their rights can act upon them. Only the author of a copyrighted book, for example, can decide to make copies of (i.e., publish) the work and prepare derivatives of the book, such as a movie version of it. If any person other than the author and copyright owner were to make a movie based on the book, that person would infringe the copyright.

The term or time period of a copyright varies. For an individual, the term of a copyright is the life of the author plus 70 years after the author is deceased. For a work with two or more authors, the term expires 70 years after the last author's death. Finally, for works that are "made for hire," or anonymous or pseudonymous works, the copyright term lasts 95 years from the first publication or 120 years from the year of the work's creation, whichever comes first.[xv] As examples, assume a musical artist writes a song that is published and performed under their name. The copyright will last 70 years beyond their death, and could conceivably be quite valuable to their heirs.

On the other hand, imagine that an anonymous Korean War soldier's diary, dated "December 1951" is discovered in an antique shop in the year 2013 and published that same year. Ordinarily, the copyright for an anonymous work would last for 95 years from the date of first publication, expiring in the year 2108. But because the date of creation is known to be 1951, the copyright would expire in 2071, or 120 years after it was written.

As noted earlier and discussed later in Section 3.9 of this chapter, these lengthy terms for copyright are controversial and opposed even by many supporters of copyright.

### Work for Hire

According to U.S. law, a **work for hire** is:

> "a work prepared by an employee within the scope of their employment, or a work specially ordered or commissioned for use as a contribution to a collective work, as a part of a motion picture or other audiovisual work, as a translation, as a supplementary work, as a compilation, as an instructional text, as a test, as answer material for a test, or as an atlas, if the parties expressly agree in a written instrument signed by them that the work shall be considered a work made for hire."[xvi]

---

xiv Derived from 17 U.S.C., § 106 Retrieved from http://www.law.cornell.edu/uscode/text/17/106

xv Derived from 17 U.S.C., § 302 (c) Retrieved from http://www.law.cornell.edu/uscode/text/17/302

xvi 17 U.S.C., § 101 Retrieved from http://www.law.cornell.edu/uscode/text/17/101

Imagine that you are an employee of a company, and you are asked to write one section of a white paper on a subject of interest to the industry. Or let's say you're a contractor hired to perform that same task under a "work for hire" arrangement. You will not own the copyright to that section of the white paper when it is completed, nor can you publish or use it if you leave the company and go to work for someone else. Although it is your creation, it is owned by the employer, who often uses your work product as part of an integrated project involving other contributors. The copyright for this particular white paper will last for 95 years from the year of first publication, or for 120 years from the year of its creation, whichever expires first.

### First-Sale Doctrine

It is important to note, however, that an author's distribution rights (No. 3 above) are strictly limited by what is known as the first-sale doctrine, which terminates those distribution rights once he sells or distributes the work to someone else. For example, once the author of a copyrighted novel lets a publisher distribute copies of that novel to a bookstore, the author's distribution rights to those copies are ended and the bookstore can do whatever it wants with them—sell them, rent them, give them away, or throw them in the dumpster. The bookstore owner cannot, however, make additional copies of the book because the first-sale doctrine does not limit a copyright owner's *reproduction* right (the first right listed above).

The first-sale doctrine was first delineated in the 1908 Supreme Court case *Bobbs-Merrill Co. v. Straus* (https://www.openstax.org/l/BobbsMerrillCoVStraus) . The Bobbs-Merrill Co. distributed copies of a novel titled *The Castaway* to retailers with the proviso that these be sold for exactly one dollar. Printed right in the book itself, in fact, right after the title page, was the following notice:

> "The price of this book at retail is $1 net. No dealer is licensed to sell it at a less price, and a sale at a less price will be treated as an infringement of the copyright."

Retailers, however, sold the book for less than a dollar and the Bobbs-Merrill Co. sued one of them. The high court found that once copies of the book were sold, the distribution rights of the author terminated as to those copies.[xvii] The ruling came to be known as the first-sale doctrine and was codified into law as 17 U.S.C., § 109. The statute distinctly draws the line at distribution rights, leaving all other rights to the copyright owner.

It's the first-sale doctrine that explains why Amazon.com and eBay allow users to resell secondhand copies of printed books, music, and movies at prices of their own choosing—but only if those copies were legally obtained. It is still illegal to sell pirated works.

In 2011, however, a new case in the United States Court of Appeals for the Second Circuit—*John Wiley & Sons, Inc. v. Supap Kirtsaeng* (https://www.openstax.org/l/SecondCircuit2011) —waived the first-sale doctrine in cases where the copies of the copyrighted work were manufactured abroad.[xviii] But in March of 2013, the U.S. Supreme Court overturned that ruling in a 6-to-3 decision that affirmed that Mr. Kirtsaeng's rights after first sale trumped the publisher's right to ban imports. He couldn't make unauthorized copies of the book. But just as with secondhand books or Gucci bags bought at a flea market, if the books had been bought legally (regardless of whether they had been imported or sold originally in the United States), Mr. Kirtsaeng had a right to sell them.

The first-sale doctrine was also limited by *Vernor v. Autodesk* (https://www.openstax.org/l/VernorVAutodesk) , when an appeals court in 2010 ruled that software was not subject to the first-sale doctrine because purchasers of software were actually only licensees and therefore could not resell the software to others.

Does the first-sale doctrine apply to digital music, such as your iTunes library? In a case involving the start-up company ReDigi, U.S. District Court Judge Richard J. Sullivan ruled on March 30, 2013, that a resale of digital

---

xvii Derived from *Bobbs-Merrill Co. v. Straus*, 210 U.S. 339, 350 (1908) Retrieved from http://caselaw.lp.findlaw.com/scripts/getcase.pl?court=us&vol=210&invol=339.

xviii *John Wiley & Sons, Inc. v. Kirtsaeng*, 654 F.3d 210, 99 U.S.P.Q.2d 1641, 2011 ILRC 2481 (2d Cir. 2011) [2011 BL 211086] Retrieved from http://bit.ly/HOTFlb.

music that involved creating a new copy on someone else's computer while erasing the copy on your computer actually concerned the reproduction right, not the distribution right, and the first-sale doctrine therefore did not apply. (You could sell your hard drive that has your music files on it, but most people would not want to do that!) But this decision is likely only the first round in what many feel will ultimately be a successful effort to create legal markets for secondhand digital goods.

### First-Sale vs. Moral Rights

The first-sale doctrine does not affect an author's moral rights, which under U.S. copyright law are limited only to certain works of visual art but under European copyright statutes are more broadly applied to other kinds of copyrightable work. Derived from the French concept of droit d'auteur, these give authors the power to protect the integrity of their work as well as the right of attribution. [xix] Preserving the integrity of a work means that the author has the right to prevent its intentional distortion, mutilation, or modification by others. Authors also have the right to control the use of their name in relation to the work.

Both of these rights, however, have limitations. Under U.S. law, because moral rights are *personal*, they exist only for the life of the author. Only the author can enforce those rights; they cannot be transferred by the author to heirs or anyone else.

As noted at the beginning of this chapter, registration is not required in order to enjoy copyright protection. Once an author puts words to paper, paint to canvas, or software code into a digital file, it is immediately protected by copyright and nothing more is required.

Although the requirement of registration as a condition of federal copyright protection was discarded over a century ago, when Congress passed the Copyright Act of 1909, the requirement that proper copyright notice be affixed to copies of published works survived much longer. It was only dropped in 1989, when the United States joined the Berne Convention and had to amend its copyright law to comply with the terms of that convention. Notice and registration of copyright are now discretionary, but recommended. Registration of a copyright provides a legal record of copyright ownership in cases where infringement is alleged, and in fact is required before the author can even file suit for infringement.[xx] To register a published work, an author will usually need to submit two copies of the work to the U.S. Copyright Office.

## 3.6 Infringement and Remedies

### Learning Objectives

After completing this section, you will be able to

- Discuss the specific requirements for proving copyright infringement.
- Understand how copyright is affecting a changing music industry.

### What If Someone Infringes Your Copyright?

Before reading this section, please watch this overview video (https://openstax.org/l/WhatIfInfringeCopyright) covering what you can do if your novel, blog post, photograph, or song is used by another without permission, and what the famous "Blurred Lines" copyright trial means to you.

xix Zemer, L. (2011). Moral Rights: Limited Edition. Boston University Law Review, 91(4), 1524. Retrieved from http://www.bu.edu/law/central/jd/organizations/journals/bulr/volume91.

xx 17 U.S.C., § 411

Derived from the common law of trespass, **infringement** of a copyright or any other intellectual property right occurs when a person violates the exclusive rights of its owner. The term gets its meaning from the word "fringe"—implying a boundary that cannot be crossed. As laid out in Sections 106 through 122 of Title 17 of the U.S. Code and subject to certain exclusions, infringement occurs when a person copies, distributes, performs, or displays all or part of a copyrighted work (or in the world of television, conducts a secondary transmission of a cable system without the express consent of the cable system owner). Copyright infringement requires proof of two things. First, it requires proof that the defendant actually copied from the plaintiff's work. That makes it different than patent infringement, which can take place even if the defendant independently came up with the invention that was patented by the plaintiff. Proof of copying can be obtained either directly, by the defendant admitting the act, or, indirectly, by showing that he had access to the plaintiff's work, and that there are similarities between the works that make independent creation unlikely. Second, infringement requires proof that the allegedly infringing work is substantially similar to the plaintiff's work.[xxi] The second requirement is there to make clear that not all copying amounts to infringement. For example, copying of a general theme, such as a detective solving a murder mystery, would not be considered infringement.

There are two ways to demonstrate the similarity of an allegedly infringing work and the original copyrighted work. "Fragmented literal similarity" may be shown by demonstrating that the infringing work contains specific copied elements of the original work. For example, suppose that one travel writer wrote a guide to Florida that contained a chapter on Key West, and a second writer copied that chapter and included it in their otherwise independently researched and written guide to Florida. In that case, we could point to specific sentences and paragraphs in the two works that were identical, even if other sentences and paragraphs were not.

Or, to take another example, in today's music scene, certain genres of music use pieces or "samples" of previous sound recordings that are then mixed into a new sound recording. Unless the artist doing the sampling licenses the sound recording (and maybe the underlying musical work as well), the sampling could be considered infringing.

## Copyright Infringement in the Music Industry

Take Kanye West, for example. He was recently sued for sampling Sly Johnson's song "Different Strokes" and using it in a new song called "The Joy" on Kanye's and Jay-Z's *Watch the Throne Album*. The case was settled out of court for an undisclosed amount.

The second type of similarity—called comprehensive nonliteral similarity—involves the borrowing of patterns without necessarily borrowing specific elements. In the case of a novel, for example, one author might infringe by copying the plot of another novel, even though he used different words to describe the action taking place. Similarly, a composer of a song might write lyrics and music that closely borrowed patterns from another song, even though he did not use the exact same words and notes.

Again, take Kanye West. He was also recently sued by Vincent Peters, a local Chicago artist, not for sampling his music but rather for employing substantially similar concepts and wording in Kanye's megahit "Stronger." The judge did not agree, finding that Kanye's song had actually used concepts and phrasing that were "common ideas" and in the public domain—specifically, Friedrich Nietzsche's phrase, "That which does not kill us makes us stronger."[xxii]

But by far, the most significant copyright infringement case in recent years concerning music was the March 10, 2015, verdict against Robin Thicke and Pharrell Williams, the performer and primary songwriter-producer

xxi Derived from *Computer Assoc. Int'l v. Altai, Inc.*, 982 F.2d 693, 701 (2nd Cir. 1992) Retrieved from homepages.law.asu.edu/~dkarjala/cyberlaw/ComputerAssocsVAltai.

xxii Mitchell, D. (2011, November 28). *Kanye West Invokes Nietzsche in Copyright Battle.* Retrieved from http://tech.fortune.cnn.com/2011/11/28/kanye-west-invokes-nietzsche-in-copyrightbattle/.

of the 2013 pop hit "Blurred Lines." A federal jury ruled that Thicke and Williams committed copyright infringement by using elements of the 1977 Marvin Gaye classic R&B hit "Got to Give It Up." The jury awarded Gaye's family $7.3 million—a very significant penalty—but the Gaye family announced that they will also seek an injunction against further radio and concert performances of the song, which will certainly give them leverage in negotiating future royalties and songwriting credit.

The case is significant, even beyond the outsize monetary award, because it challenges the growing practice in contemporary music production of incorporating elements, features, themes, and even the "feel" and "mood" of the work of other artists and genres.

Larry Iser, an intellectual property lawyer who has represented artists like Jackson Browne and David Byrne, criticized the verdict. "Although [Marvin] Gaye was the Prince of Soul," Iser told the *New York Times*, "he didn't own a copyright to the genre, and Thicke and Williams' homage to the feel of Marvin Gaye is not infringing."

Despite the critics, musicians and producers will likely be more cautious in the future. In addition to the "Blurred Lines" case, singers Sam Smith and Tom Petty reached a settlement in 2015 granting songwriting credit and royalties to Petty on Smith's song "Stay With Me," which bore some resemblance to Petty's hit "I Won't Back Down."

## Actual and Statutory Damages

As we see in the above case, infringing a copyrighted work can carry very significant penalties. The copyright owner has the right to recoup damages and lost profits from infringement. There are two kinds of damages—actual and statutory. The copyright owner may only receive one or the other form of damages.[xxiii]

The Recording Industry Association of America (RIAA), for example, was awarded major damages from Jammie Thomas in 2009 for her willful statutory infringement of 24 copyrighted songs that she had uploaded to the music sharing site Kazaa. Because the infringement was found to be willful, the court in its discretion raised the damages maximum from its usual $30,000 per act of infringement to $80,000 per infringement. That $80,000, times 24 songs that were infringed, resulted in a damage award of $1,920,000[xxiv] After several trials and appeals, however, the damages assessed against Thomas were reduced to $222,000.

Take note, infringers—the risks can be very great, indeed.

Only the owners of registered copyrights may file for statutory damages. That's another reason why it's a good idea to register your copyright.

Sometimes, though, the copyright owner's most important remedy for infringement will be an injunction that forces the infringer to stop illegal actions that cause continuing damage to their rights. The grounds for getting that injunction, however, have tightened in recent years and now require the plaintiff, or copyright owner, to provide substantial evidence of infringement that cannot be repaired without an injunction.

As the court of appeals for the ninth circuit put it in 2011:

> "Our long-standing precedent finding a plaintiff entitled to a presumption of irreparable harm on a showing of likelihood of success on the merits in a copyright infringement case, as stated in *Elvis Presley v. Passport Video* and relied on by the district court, has been effectively overruled. In other words, 'Elvis has left the building.' Accordingly, we hold that even in a copyright infringement case, the plaintiff must demonstrate a likelihood of irreparable harm as a prerequisite for injunctive relief, whether preliminary or permanent."[xxv]

---

xxiii Derived from 17 U.S.C., § 504 Retrieved from http://www.law.cornell.edu/uscode/text/17/504.

xxiv Kravets, D. (2009, June 18). *Jury in RIAA Trial Slaps 2 Million Fine on Jammie Thomas.* Retrieved from http://www.wired.com/threatlevel/2009/06/riaajury-slaps-2-million-fine-on-jammie-thomas/

xxv http://scholar.google.com/scholar_case?case=7153487234107458840&hl=en&as_sdt=2&as_vis=1&oi=scholarr

Individuals who infringe copyrighted material face not only restitution for damages and lost profits and impoundment and destruction of materials, but strict criminal penalties as well. To be subject to criminal penalties, the infringer must have willfully infringed the copyright. For those doing so for commercial advantage or private financial gain, the sentence may be up to five years for a first offense, and ten years for a second offense.[xxvi]

We have focused solely on the federal penalties for infringement. That's because, with the passage of the 1976 Copyright Act, federal copyright law now preempts state laws. State laws governing breach of contract, violations of trust, trespassing, conversion, invasion of privacy, defamation, and deceptive trade practices still exist, however, and these may also be employed by a copyright owner seeking redress for other harms caused by infringing activity.

## 3.7 The Fair Use Defense

### Learning Objectives

After completing this section, you will be able to

- Understand the nature of fair use and how it serves the public interest.
- Appreciate the continuing debate over just vagaries in what is considered fair use.

### Is It Fair Use or Infringement?

Before reading this section, please watch this overview video (https://openstax.org/l/FairUseOrInfringement) covering Fair Use is an enigma—indeed, no one even knows how many words of a copyrighted work one can legally copy as "fair use." Here, at last, is everything you need to know about Fair Use.

Title 17 of the United States Code allows the copying and use of copyrighted material for specific **purposes**—including criticism, comment, news reporting, teaching (involving multiple copies for classroom use), scholarship, or research. The statute also describes four **factors** that draw on the precepts first discussed by Supreme Court Justice Story 150 years earlier to determine if the use of a copyrighted work is infringement or "fair use."[xxvii]

Based on these factors, which are not meant to be all inclusive, a judge must determine if the use of copyrighted material is within the bounds of fair use. What makes that determination sometimes difficult is the challenge of weighing a variety of purposes—was the work used for criticism, comment, news reporting, teaching, scholarship, or research?—in concert with various factors (such as how much was used, and whether it was for commercial gain or not).

In the crucial 1973 Supreme Court case of *Williams & Wilkins v. United States* (https://www.openstax.org/l/WilliamsWilkinsVUS) , for example, the divided justices affirmed a lower U.S. Court of Claims decision that the benefits of freely distributing photocopies of medical journal articles to nonprofit government research libraries outweighed the reduction of potential revenue to the publisher of those journals.[xxviii]

### Parody

One of the purposes for which copyrighted work may at times be freely used is parody. As a federal court ruled in one 1993 case:

---

xxvi Derived from 18 U.S.C., § 2319 Retrieved from http://www.law.cornell.edu/uscode/text/18/2319

xxvii 17 U.S.C., § 107 Retrieved from http://www.law.cornell.edu/uscode/text/17/107.

xxviii *Williams & Wilkins v. United States*, 487 F.2d 1345 (1973) Retrieved from http://fairuse.stanford.edu/primary_materials/cases/c487F2d1345.html.

> "The heart of any parodist's claim to quote from existing material is the use of some elements of a prior author's composition to create a new one that, at least in part, comments on that author's work."[xxix]

And the greater the "transformative" nature of the new work, the less likely it infringes the original work.

A case involving the Fox TV show *Family Guy* illustrates the point. In Bourne Co. v. Fox (https://www.openstax.org/l/BourneCoVFox) , the court found that a Family Guy episode in which the character Peter Griffin sang a revised version of the song "When You Wish Upon a Star" called "I Need a Jew" was a parody and thereby a fair use of the original material. The outrageous if not offensive visuals and words employed in the *Family Guy* parody were so substantially different in character and form from the original use of the song in the Walt Disney movie *Pinocchio* that no one could ever confuse the two or fail to realize that Fox's use was a parody.

## Transformative or Theft?

A very interesting case involving fair use was decided by the U.S. Court of Appeals for the Second Circuit on April 25, 2013. It overturned a 2011 district court ruling that artist Richard Prince had acted illegally by using another artist's photographs to create a series of collages and paintings. Such borrowing of another's work is considered fair use only if it is "transformative" in some substantial way, and the district judge held that it was not because the collages did not comment on the original work explicitly. The federal circuit disagreed, holding that explicit references to the original work are not required so long as the required "transformation" is manifested by "an entirely different aesthetic" in the secondary work.

According to the appeals court:

> "Where [the original artist's] serene and deliberately composed portrait and landscape photographs depict the natural beauty of the Rastafarians and their surrounding environs, Prince's crude and jarring works are hectic and provocative."

## Fair Use for Public Good

The fair use clause also allows libraries and archives that are open to the public, or researchers in a specialized field, to use copyrighted materials for the purpose of preservation and security of the material or as a deposit for research. These libraries and archives can keep up to three copies of a copyrighted work, but a copyright notice must be included on each copy. Libraries and archives will not be held liable for "unsupervised use of reproducing equipment located on its premises" if there is a notice on the equipment that a copy may be subject to copyright law.[xxx] Any use of photocopied copyrighted materials must be specifically for private study, scholarship, or research, and any other use constitutes infringement. Photocopying copyrighted materials in a business setting is also infringing if used outside of research.

Academic institutions also are protected by specific rules regarding fair use, pursuant to an agreement between representatives of the publishing industry and of academic institutions negotiated in the 1970s. The photocopying of a copyrighted work for the classroom is permitted if it is limited to:

- A chapter from a book
- An article from a periodical or newspaper
- A short story, short essay, or short poem, whether or not from a collective work
- A chart, graph, diagram, drawing, cartoon, or picture from a book, periodical, or newspaper.

[xxxi]

---

xxix *Campbell v. Acuff-Rose Music*, 510 U.S. 569 (1994) Retrieved from http://www.law.cornell.edu/supct/html/92-1292.ZS.html.

xxx 17 U.S.C. § 108 Retrieved from http://www.law.cornell.edu/uscode/text/17/108.

xxxi Library of Congress. (2009, November). Reproduction of Copyrighted Works By Educators And Librarians. Retrieved from

But even in the above academic uses, limitations apply regarding the size of both the audience and the content to be copied. For example, teachers may photocopy works only for students enrolled in the class. The photocopied material must also pass brevity, spontaneity, and other tests. "Brevity" means no more than 250 words of a poem, 2,500 words of a prose work, or 10 percent or 1,000 words of an excerpt of a prose work may be used. In addition, the decision to photocopy the material must be spontaneous; the photocopied material must be used only for one course and one class term; no more than one poem, article, story, or essay—and no more than two excerpts—may be copied from the same author; and such bulk photocopying must be limited to nine instances per class during one term.[xxxii]

**Figure 3.12** Verbatim from source: "The President greets the cast and crew of 'Hamilton' after seeing the play with his daughters at the Richard Rodgers Theatre in New York City." (Official White House Photo by Pete Souza) (credit: Pete Souza via Wikimedia Commons / Public Domain)

Finally, copyrighted works may not be photocopied and used in educational settings as a substitute for required texts, photocopies may not be mandatory, and you cannot charge for the photocopied work (although you may recoup the costs of photocopying).[xxxiii]

## 3.8 Changes in Copyright Law

### Learning Objectives

After completing this section, you will be able to

- See how copyright law has continually adapted to technological change.
- Note how digital entertainment industries in particular have been affected by changes in copyright law.

---

http://www.copyright.gov/circs/circ21.pdf.

xxxii Derived from The President and Fellows of Harvard College. (2008). *Copyright Law Guidelines* Retrieved from http://hfs.fas.harvard.edu/copyright.html.

xxxiii Copyright Law Revision (House Report No. 94-1476) Retrieved from http://uscode.house.gov/download/pls/17C1.txt.

Throughout the more than 226-year history of copyright in the United States, technological innovation and changes in consumer behavior have continuously forced Congress and the courts to embrace new forms of copyrighted media and new ways of distributing and consuming it.

## The Copyright Act of 1976

As noted earlier, the nineteenth century saw copyright expand to include a variety of new technologies, such as mechanical reproductions of musical compositions (player pianos and phonographs), photography, and eventually motion pictures. But those changes were small compared with the enormous advances of the twentieth century. The invention of radio, broadcast television, cable television, the video cassette recorder (VCR), personal computers, computer software and video games, digital audio recorders, compact discs, the digital video recorder (DVR), the Internet, iTunes media players, and now the streaming of music and movies all offered consumers new forms of creative content—and offered creators a new means of reproducing and distributing it. Each of these required an adjustment in U.S. copyright law.

Take the advent of cable television in the 1960s and 1970s. Early court cases like *Fortnightly Corp. v. United Artists* (https://www.openstax.org/l/FortnightlyVUnited) in 1968 and *Teleprompter v. CBS* (https://www.openstax.org/l/TeleprompterVCBS) in 1974 held that the rebroadcast of broadcast television shows over cable television systems did not constitute a "performance" and therefore did not infringe the copyright in those shows. The **Copyright Act of 1976**—the most significant revision of copyright law since 1909—remedied this failure to see cable broadcasts as performances and extended copyright protection to works performed over cable TV.

**Figure 3.13** A television studio with a greenscreen setup. (credit: photograph by Jorge Franganillo via flikr / CC BY 2.0)

The Copyright Act of 1976 made several other major changes to the law. It also codified "fair use" into the statutes rather than simply the common law, granted statutory copyright protection as soon as a work was reduced to a concrete form rather than only when registered, and began to bring the United States into compliance with international copyright law rather than continue to stand apart from it.[xxxiv]

## The Computer Software Rental Act of 1990

The next major copyright issue arose with the emergence of personal computer software in the 1980s. Software companies and independent developers lobbied Congress to curtail the illegal copying of copyrighted software. As a result, the Computer Software Rental Act of 1990 was passed, prohibiting the unauthorized rental, lease, or lending of a computer program for commercial gain. Individuals, however, could still make personal copies for their own use, and libraries were permitted to lend software.[xxxv]

The hope was that this would curb the rampant software piracy then costing U.S. firms roughly $1 billion per year in lost sales and rentals. The law probably did slow piracy inside the United States. But by 2010, software piracy worldwide had grown into a $10 billion a year business.

## The Audio Home Recording Act of 1992

Hoping to prevent similar piracy in the emerging digital audio field, the Audio Home Recording Act of 1992 amended copyright law to require manufacturers and importers of digital audio recording devices to install technology to prevent the illegal copying of copyrighted music. It also mandated that royalties be paid to copyright owners for every device sold.

**Figure 3.14** Pirate Bay is one site known for dir ecting users to unauthorized pirated copies of songs, movies, and other works. Despite many attempts to take down and/or block the site, pr oxies still spring up. (credit: The Pirate Bay via Wikimedia Commons / Copyrighted free use)

When it came to performance rights—one of the six exclusive rights of copyright owners—the last 150 years have witnessed major changes in the way musical performances are distributed and consumed. The American

---

xxxiv Arthur R. Millerand Michael H. Davis, *Intellectual Property: Patents, Trademarks, and Copyright In a Nutshell.* (5th ed., p. 25). St. Paul MN: West Publishing Co., 2007.

xxxv Library of Congress. (2003). *The Computer Software Rental Amendments Act of 1990: The Nonprofit Library Lending Exemption to the "Rental Right".* Retrieved from http://www.copyright.gov/reports/software_ren.html

Society of Composers, Authors and Publishers (ASCAP) was formed in 1914 to develop a system whereby royalties could be obtained for composers whose songs were performed live—and later on, over the newly invented technology of radio. Today, 435,000 U.S. composers, songwriters, lyricists, and music publishers rely upon ASCAP to secure royalties for their work performed over TV, CD, and every new media that has come after radio.

The other three performing rights organizations are SESAC, formed in 1930; Broadcast Music, Inc. (BMI), formed in 1939; and SoundExchange, which in 2007 was granted the sole right by the Copyright Royalty Board to represent performers whose music airs on satellite radio (such as SIRIUS XM), Internet radio (like Pandora), cable TV music channels, and similar platforms for streaming sound recordings. The Recording Industry of America Association (RIAA), formed in 1952, represents record labels and music distributors and has played an important role in ensuring that their rights are respected even as new technologies for distributing recorded music have emerged.

The RIAA lobbied Congress to enact the **No Electronic Theft Act of 1997**, for example, which made it a criminal offense to reproduce or distribute music by electronic means (i.e., over the Internet). Nonetheless, by 2002, some 3.6 billion songs a month were still being downloaded illegally, thanks to music sharing sites like Napster, which had been launched in 1999 and at its peak facilitated the downloading (much of it illegal) of 80 million songs. Indeed, many college dormitory networks became overloaded with MP3 musical file transfers.

At the time, many Internet pundits, enthralled with the misquoted notion that "information wants to be free" online, insisted that downloading technology made it impossible for musicians and their labels to enforce their copyrights on the Internet. For its part, Napster claimed that they should not be held responsible for any illegal downloading committed by users.

But the RIAA and musicians brought suits for contributory infringement. In court cases like *A & M Records, v. Napster* (https://www.openstax.org/l/AMVNapster) and *Metallica v. Napster* (https://www.openstax.org/l/MetallicaVNapster) , judges and juries repeatedly found Napster guilty of infringement and it was forced into bankruptcy in 2002.

Music piracy still exists, of course. But in place of Napster, music consumers now have legal music download sites such as Apple's iTunes music store that sell digital music with permission from, and appropriate royalties to, their copyright owners. Surveys show that most consumers don't really want to steal music. They just want convenient, low-cost online access to it. Most consumers also appear to recognize that if music creators cannot make a living from their work, they won't be able to keep making music.

Meanwhile, digital rights management (DRM) technologies had been developed that have the potential to limit the piracy of copyrighted content. Companies in various content industries lobbied Congress to pass the **Digital Millennium Copyright Act of 1998 (DMCA)**. This law made it a crime to disseminate technology or services that could circumvent DRM measures used to control access to copyrighted movies, music, and books. It also increased penalties for copyright infringement on the Internet.

But in an appropriate concession to online services that merely hosted user content, the DMCA limited the liability of online services for copyright infringement committed by their users, so long as they acted to remove the offending content once informed of it.

### Viacom vs. YouTube

In 2007, however, Viacom filed suit against YouTube and its corporate parent Google for copyright infringement, claiming that the popular video-sharing site was committing "massive intentional copyright infringement" for not taking sufficient steps to prevent or remove some 160,000 unauthorized clips of Viacom's entertainment programming posted by users. Google argued that the DMCA's "safe harbor" provisions shielded them from liability for the actions of its users, and a district court judge ruled in favor of Google in 2010. But in April of 2012, a court of appeals vacated that decision and ruled that Viacom had presented enough evidence to warrant a trial. Viacom was seeking more than $1 *billion* in damages from YouTube, but in March of 2014, the parties quietly settled the seven-year-old case.

A key factor in spurring the settlement is that Google has in the interim addressed the concerns of content owners like Viacom by creating a system that allows them to track their content when posted on YouTube and then request it be taken down or run with ads.

## Extending Copyrights

The same year that saw passage of the DMCA also witnessed the passage of the **Sonny Bono Copyright Term Extension Act**, which added an additional 20 years to the term of copyright—extending it for most works to the life of the author plus 70 years after the author is deceased. Critics called it the "Mickey Mouse Protection Act" because it effectively extended the copyrights of many of the characters and content of the Walt Disney Company, which lobbied strongly for the bill. They argued that copyright law was historically designed to serve a public purpose and ought to defer to the public interest, as it has throughout U.S. history. As the *New York Times* put it:

> "When Senator Hatch laments that George Gershwin's 'Rhapsody in Blue' will soon 'fall into the public domain,' he makes the public domain sound like a dark abyss where songs go, never to be heard again. In fact, when a work enters the public domain it means the public can afford to use it freely, to give it new currency."

Even a staunch defender of intellectual property rights like Professor Richard Epstein of the NYU School of Law—he was rated one of the top legal thinkers of modern times by the journal *Legal Affairs*—believes that the copyright term of life- plus-70s years is too long.

"My own view is that no commercial property right should ever be tied to life, and the extra 70 years is far too long," he argues. "It has the potential to create an anti-commons that deprives the public of its rights to freely access cultural works. Copyrighted works should pass into the public domain after 28 years, which was the approach of the Founders."

The debate over the Copyright Term Extension Act, not surprisingly, continues.

In the international sphere, meanwhile, the late twentieth century also saw the United States finally agree to the **Berne Convention** in 1988, joining the following year. The purpose of the convention is to ensure fair and reciprocal copyright protection for member nations. Although it did not create an international copyright per se, it did require the United States to amend its copyright law to comply with certain Berne provisions, such as a ban on registration as a condition of copyright. But overall, the convention facilitated the reciprocal cross-border protection of creative works while leaving most details of each nation's copyright laws to member states.

One proposed bill that didn't make it into law was the *Consumer Broadband and Digital Television Promotion Act of 2002.* It attempted to deal with continuing piracy of copyrighted works by requiring every medium and every device for the consumption of copyrighted works to implement digital rights management (DRM) technology. But the bill was considered too draconian—too *1984*, if you will—and failed to pass.

To be sure, many companies have voluntarily implemented elements of DRM technology, to the chagrin of many consumers. Some electronic book readers (e-books) limit the ability of users to read books only on those devices, preventing interoperability between Kindle and iPad e-book readers, for example. Some music labels install software on their CDs to prevent copying of the music. And some Blu-ray and DVD movie players do not allow for the creation of transformative copies. In fact, iTunes, a very popular way to manage music and other media, used to employ a DRM system that limited the transfer of songs to five authorized computers.

Groups like the Free Software Foundation argue that "The motive for DRM schemes is to increase profits for those who impose them, but their profit is a side issue when millions of people's freedom is at stake." But their argument is undercut by the simple reality that if content creators can't make a living from it, most will stop creating and take day jobs to pay the rent. This has always been the copyright bargain in America—protection for the rights of creators but only so long as it serves the public interest.

And enabling creators to keep creating is clearly in the public interest.

## E-Books

A more legitimate concern regarding DRM is that, whatever its perceived benefits for publishers and distributors, it is holding back innovation and consumer rights in digital content industries. This is especially evident in the burgeoning e-book market, which exploded from barely 10 percent of U.S. book sales in 2011 to 30 percent of all book sales by 2013. But a growing number of e-book publishers have now concluded that unless they meet consumer demands to ease these DRM anti-piracy provisions, further growth could be constrained.

According to Microsoft's Chief Intellectual Property Strategy Counsel Tom Rubin, a leading voice on this issue, that's because DRM makes the e-book reader experience much less enjoyable and useful than that for printed books. According to Rubin:

> "When I buy a printed book, I can choose where to buy it—whether from a small neighborhood bookstore, a large chain bookstore, a grocery store, drug store, other retail establishment, or an online retailer. I can even buy books at a steep discount by going to second-hand stores, garage sales, and flea markets. "You can't do that with an ebook. "Then after I buy a print book and bring it home, I can write notes in the margin, share those passages or even the whole book with friends and colleagues, and even photocopy a few pages for my book club. "You can't do that with an ebook."

Rubin says the fault here lies not in the technology, which already exists to enable these capabilities in e-books and also augment them with rich audio, video, and social media. Rather, it lies in the business arrangements underlying the publication and distribution of e-books.

The e-book you buy, for example, is often available from only one source—and usually only readable on one proprietary device. You can't access it from any device you want, nor can you use the e-reader app of your choice. This balkanization of the market diverts resources from enhancing the user experience into defending the turf of incumbent players.

But it's not just the balkanization of the market that hinders competition and innovation. Some publishers now believe that the digital rights management (DRM) controls they employ to prevent piracy are actually preventing many consumers from fully embracing e-books. After all, as many book buyers have angrily noted, you can't even download the digital version of a print book that you've already purchased unless you pay a second time.

## Publishing DRM Free

> "The consumer ebook market is an emerging and changing one, and we want to offer customers as many choices as possible."
>
> -Elsevier spokeswoman Suzanne BeDell

In response to consumer complaints, some publishers have dispensed with DRM controls. *Harry Potter* author J. K. Rowling has launched her own website, *Pottermore.com*, to sell her e-books DRM free, enabling readers to enjoy them on any device they choose. Interestingly, the piracy of *Harry Potter* books has declined by 25 percent since DRM was dropped in 2012.

Also in 2012, Tor Books, a major science fiction publisher owned by MacMillan, went DRM free as well, with no apparent harm to its sales—and to the delight of its customers.

Then there's the big U.S. tech publisher O'Reilly, which has been DRM free since its inception. O'Reilly, which has one of the most loyal customer bases in publishing, signed a deal on April 16 of 2013 with Elsevier, the world's largest publisher of scientific and health information, to distribute more than 1,200 titles DRM free. (It also distributes all Microsoft e-books DRM free.)

"The consumer ebook market is an emerging and changing one, and we want to offer customers as many choices as possible," explained Elsevier spokeswoman Suzanne BeDell.

And finally, although the prestigious Harvard Business Press still sells its books on Amazon with DRM restrictions, it recently started selling books on its own site DRM free.

These early publisher moves to dispense with DRM restrictions parallel what happened in the digital music industry a decade ago. For the first few years after the launch of the iTunes music store in 2003, piracy-wary music publishers required Apple to sell its songs with DRM controls that limited the kind and number of devices consumers could play them on.

But on February 6, 2007, Apple CEO Steve Jobs wrote an open letter to the industry urging music publishers to let iTunes sell music DRM free:

> "DRMs haven't worked, and may never work, to halt music piracy. If such requirements were removed, the music industry might experience an influx of new companies willing to invest in new [music distribution systems]."

This, said Jobs, would obviously be "positive for the music companies."

And sure enough, once publishers agreed to license digital music DRM free later that same year, the market exploded. In 2013, iTunes announced the sale of its twenty-fifth billionth song!

Ultimately, argues Rubin:

> "Success [for ebook publishers] can only come with the satisfaction of legitimate consumer needs—most especially the need for an ebook experience that is every bit as good or better than that of their beloved printed books."

### Recent Copyright Laws

The debate over DRM in e-books is likely to be center stage in the copyright debate in coming years. In the meantime, it's worth mentioning three other copyright-related laws that were passed during the last decade or so.

One, the Technology, Education, and Copyright Harmonization (TEACH) Act of 2002 enabled educators to use certain copyrighted performances and displays for educational purposes.[xxxvi] The bill was focused on the fast-growing arena of distance education, whose students number 12 million and are growing rapidly.

Also that year, the Small Webcaster Settlement Act of 2002 eased royalty burdens for small webcasters who don't have the resources of the major content distributors.[xxxvii]

Finally, the Family Entertainment and Copyright Act of 2005 mandated fines and possible imprisonment for the unauthorized recording of motion pictures in theaters. It also enabled consumers to use new technologies to screen out or skip over some 14 different categories of objectionable content in movies played on DVD players and other devices.[xxxviii]

---

xxxvi Technology, Education, and Copyright Harmonization (TEACH) Act of 2002, Div. C, Tit. III, Subtitle C of the 21st Century Department of Justice Appropriations Authorization Act, Pub. L. No. 107-273, 116 Stat. 1758, 1910 (Nov. 2, 2002) Retrieved from http://thomas.loc.gov/cgi-bin/query/z?c107:S.487.ES.

xxxvii Derived from Small Webcaster Settlement Act of 2002 (SWSA), Pub. L. No. 107-321, 116 Stat. 2780 (Dec. 4, 2002) Retrieved from http://thomas.loc.gov/cgi-bin/query/z?c107:H.R.5469.ENR.

xxxviii Family Entertainment and Copyright Act of 2005, Pub. L. No. 109-9, 119 Stat. 218 (Apr. 27, 2005), codified at various sections of Titles 17 and 18 U.S. Code. Retrieved from http://www.copyright.gov/legislation/pl109-9.html.

## 3.9 New Technology Challenges to Copyright

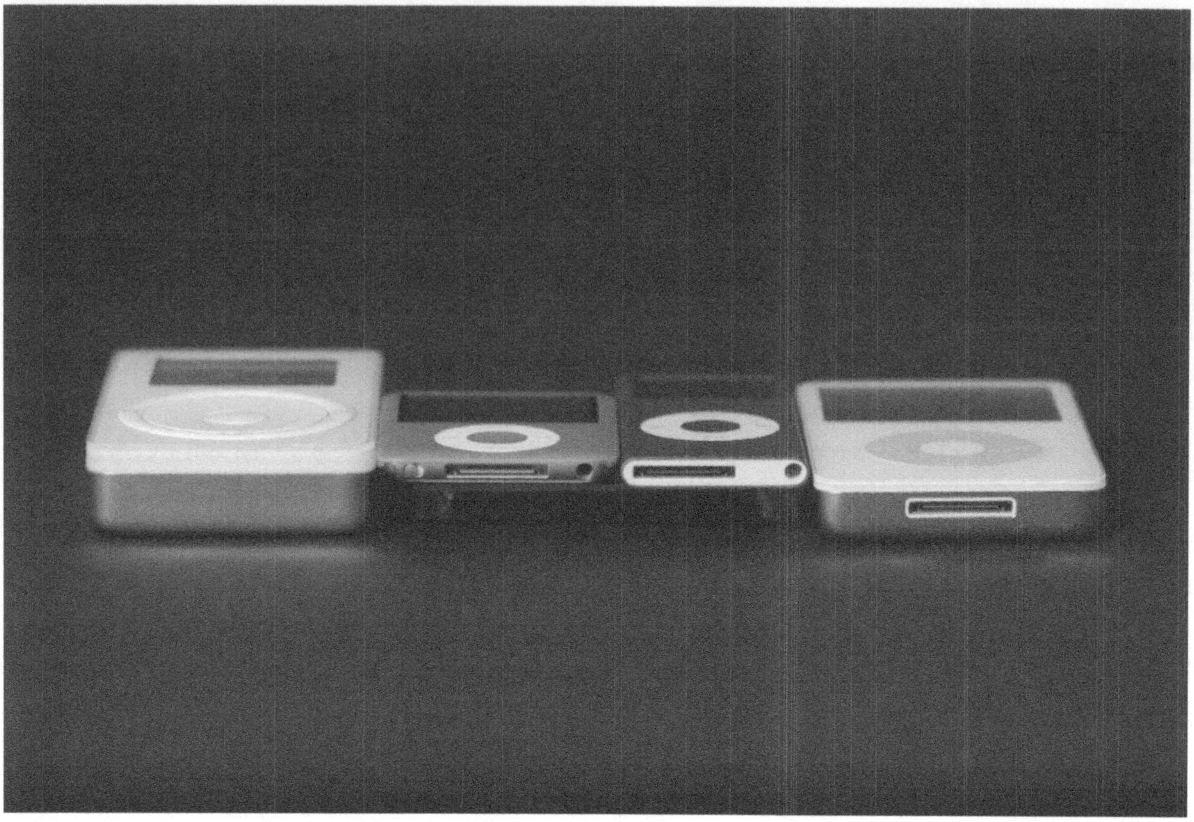

**Figure 3.15** (credit: photograph by Ivailo Djilianov via flikr / CC BY 2.0)

### Learning Objectives

After completing this section, you will be able to

- See how a changing music industry has been affected by copyright.
- Appreciate the challenges that continued technology advances may pose for copyright in the future.

One of the newest technology challenges facing copyright law concerns royalty rates for streaming music online. As it stands, royalty rates are much lower for music played over satellite and cable radio outlets like Sirius XM than they are for music streaming services like Pandora.

### Music Streaming

Rates are set by the federal Copyright Royalty Board (CRB), a three-judge panel, but currently they apply a different rate for streaming music than they do for satellite and cable music. Sirius pays about 8 percent of its revenue to record companies and artists. Pandora, however, claims it must pay a rate per song streamed that amounts to 44 percent of revenue. So it pushed for the introduction in September 2012 of the Internet Radio Fairness Act, which would make the rates for Internet radio companies the same as those for satellite and cable radio.

This bill was opposed not only by many musical artists and their organizations, but by many copyright experts as well. In November of 2012, a who's who of musicians and singers—including stars from Motown, rock and roll, country, rap, and jazz—published an open letter in *Billboard* magazine opposing Pandora's plan to cut artists' pay and make more money, as they put it in the letter, "on the backs of hard working musicians and singers."

In November of 2013, Pandora quietly abandoned efforts to seek legislation that would help reduce the royalties paid to rights holders. Instead of pursuing legislation, Pandora said it will focus its efforts on lobbying the CRB.

In early December 2015, the music industry waited breathlessly for the CRB's decision on royalty rates. Pandora had petitioned the CRB to reduce the current statutory rate of 14 cents per 100 songs to 11 cents per 100 songs starting in 2016. But music labels and artists represented by a royalty collection organization called SoundExchange wanted the statutory royalty rate raised to 25 cents per 100 songs—an 80 percent increase—and then by 1 cent every year after that until 2020. Collectively, music streaming services have a combined listenership of 100 million people and are the fastest-growing revenue source for artists and music labels.

On December 16, 2015, in a victory for record labels and artists, the CRB ruled that online radio firms will have to pay 17 cents per 100 plays of songs through 2020.

### TV Streaming

Another new technology challenge to copyright involved television broadcasters and an upstart television service called Aereo that at one point rented dime-sized antennas for $8 per month that act like long-range rabbit ears to people with digital video recorders, enabling them to watch and record over-the-air network channels like NBC or Fox without paying the much-larger fees for cable or satellite service.

TV broadcasters argued that Aereo violated their copyrights by rebroadcasting their TV signals. Aereo, however, claimed that it was the subscribers who were doing the transmitting, and that Aereo merely rented a tool that enabled people to watch a private performance—much like they do when they tape a TV show and watch it in their living room.

The case, which had the TV and technology industries on edge, was decided in their favor on June 25, 2014, by the U.S. Supreme Court, which ruled that Aereo had infringed the rights of copyright holders. Five months later, Aereo declared bankruptcy.

## 3.10 Alternative Forms of Copyright

**Figure 3.16** (credit: Kristina Alexanderson via flikr / CC BY 2.0)

### Learning Objectives

After completing this section, you will be able to

- Understand how alternative forms of copyright are emerging in today's increasingly digital ecosystem.

Up to now, we have focused on traditional copyright situations in which an author usually pursues some sort of monetary gain in exchange for the use of their creative work as well as situations in which the author also wants to prevent any alteration of their work. But what if an author simply wants to get their work out before the broadest possible readership and monetary gain is not an issue? What if an author would welcome others adding to the original work? In these cases, there are new kinds of copyright licenses that may be employed by authors.

### Creative Commons

The development of the **Creative Commons** represents a voluntary private sector alternative to traditional copyright that coordinates the creation and consumption of content among a wide variety of individuals and institutions—all without a hint of government intervention. In doing so, Creative Commons captures a whole section of the market for which broad dissemination of content and not financial gain is key, which is something that could not be done as effectively by either traditional copyright or the public domain.

The Creative Commons License is currently available in six flavors:

All of these licenses require the work to be copyrighted because the Creative Commons license is based on copyright. Although Creative Commons licenses can provide authors with added opportunities to have their work distributed and used, these licenses do not allow authors to limit any of the rights otherwise available under copyright law, such as fair use.

Creative Commons licenses also cannot be revoked, which means that if copies of your work are distributed under a Creative Commons license, they will always be distributed that way. If, for example, you distribute your amazing new video under a Creative Commons license and it generates five million page views on YouTube—and then 20th Century Fox offers you a seven-figure deal for exclusive rights to distribute your video—you will not be able to prevent everyone on the planet from continuing to distribute your video for free on the Internet.

### Open Access

Another alternative copyright approach is called open access, founded by the Budapest Open Access Initiative in 2002. Open access encourages scholars to provide the fruits of their research online without expectation of payment.[xxxix] The aim here is to open up scholarly research far more widely than is currently the case, but open access adherents face a key challenge in the fact that many scholarly articles are published in expensive journals as "works made for hire." This means that the rights belong to the journals, not the authors. But open access supporters are working with publishers to try to overcome this limitation and create more opportunities for scholarly research to be made more widely accessible at lower cost.

**Figure 3.17** (credit: art designer at PLoS, modified by Wikipedia users Nina, Beao, and JakobVoss via Wikimedia Commons / CC0)

Finally, open source software licensing also offers an alternative to traditional copyright. An open source license for computer software allows the source code to be used, modified, and/or shared under certain defined terms and conditions set by the Open Source Initiative, an educational, advocacy, and stewardship organization formed in 1998. An open source license allows end users to modify the source code for their own purposes. Open source licensed software is mostly available free of charge, though this does not always have to be the case.

## 3.11 Copyright in a Changing World

### Learning Objectives

After completing this section, you will be able to

- Understand how copyright law is showing signs of strain today.
- Realize that it may very well need to adapt to an increasingly mobile world.

---

xxxix Chan, L., Cuplinskas, D., Eisen, M., Friend, F., Genova, Y., Guedon, J., Hagemann, M., Harnad, S., Johnson R., Kupryte, R., Manna, M., Rev I., Segbert, M., Souza, S., Suber, P., & Velterop J. (2002, February 24). *Budapest Open Access Initiative*. Retrieved from http://www.soros.org/openaccess/read.

Comprehensive copyright reform may soon be on the horizon. On March 20, 2013, Register of Copyrights at the United States Copyright Office Maria A. Pallante testified before the House Judiciary Committee that the time had come for a comprehensive review and updating of the Copyright Act.

According to Pallante:

> "The law is showing the strain of age and requires your attention. [People] increasingly are accessing content on mobile devices and fewer and fewer of them will need or desire the physical copies that were so central to the $19^{th}$ and $20^{th}$ century copyright laws."

The list of issues requiring attention is long, involving everything from copyright term and digital rights management restrictions on digital content to the legality of developing secondary resale markets for digital content as exist with traditional printed content.

The debates may be contentious, as they always are when intellectual property rights are involved. But U.S. copyright law has throughout our history demonstrated a remarkable ability to adapt to new economic, social, and technological realities, and there is no reason to doubt that it will continue to do so.

## Assessment Questions

1. A copyright gives authors, artists, dramatists, architects, and other artistic creators the exclusive right to control what?
   A. How their work is published, reproduced, performed, or displayed.
   B. The price at which their work is sold, performed, or displayed.
   C. Whether or not the work becomes a classic on art, theater, or literature.

2. Copyright is made possible by Article 1, Section 8, Clause 8 of the U.S. Constitution, which also gives Congress the authority to do what?
   A. Declare war.
   B. Grant patents.
   C. Make all laws necessary and proper to enforce copyrights.

3. Congress and the courts have interpreted the terms "authors" and "writings" very broadly to include which of the following as eligible for copyright? (Choose all that apply)
   A. Graphic works.
   B. Novel, non-obvious and useful inventions.
   C. Architectural works.

4. When is a work considered copyrighted?
   A. Once it is officially registered with the U.S. Copyright Office.
   B. Once the U.S. Copyright Office grants an official copyright.
   C. Once it is expressed in a tangible form that allows it to be seen or copied.

5. There is an extensive examination system for getting a patent approved. Why is there not a similar system in place for copyrights?
   A. The merit of an artistic or literary work is a wholly subjective determination.
   B. Merit has nothing to do with whether or not a creative work is copyrightable.
   C. Patent examiners can all agree that an invention is novel, non-obvious and useful, but art critics may never all agree that any one painting is beautiful.
   D. All of the above.

6. Which <u>two</u> public policy goals are served by granting copyrights? (Choose all that apply)
   A. By protecting the property rights of artists to their creations, the wellsprings of creation do not dry up for lack of incentive.
   B. Copyrights ensure that artists and writers won't be taken advantage of.
   C. Cultural creativity serves the public good and promotes literacy and learning.

7. How were copyrights viewed very differently from patent rights in terms of the interests of the general public?
   A. Copyrights were thought to be in less conflict with the public interest.
   B. Copyrights were enforced with the same diligence as patent rights.
   C. Patent rights were seen as more beneficial to the public than copyrights.

8. The policy of strong patent rights and weaker copyrights also reflected what differences in the motivations of inventors compared with authors?
   A. Authors were not generally interested in economic gain.
   B. Authors were motivated only by the prospect of economic gain.
   C. Both artists and inventors sought economic gain, but authors also tended to be rewarded by celebrity and reputational gain as well.

9. Copyrights began to be formally issued in what part of Europe?
   A. France in the sixteenth century.
   B. England under Queen Anne.
   C. The Republic of Venice in the fifteenth century.

10. Initially, to whom were copyrights given?
   A. Authors.
   B. Artists.
   C. Printers and publishers.

11. The copyright granted in 1669 to Jean-Baptiste Lully, director of the Paris Opera, gave him exclusive rights to? (Choose all that apply)
   A. All operatic performances.
   B. The publication of operatic librettos.
   C. The number of musicians who could perform outside the Paris Opera.
   D. Bequeath his copyright monopoly to his heirs.
   E. All of the above.

12. How did early copyrights evolve from business monopolies into instruments of censorship and surveillance?
   A. Bookstores sent the authorities records of who purchased what books.
   B. Books had to be read and approved by a censor before a permit was granted to print the book.

13. What did the 1709 Statute of Anne do to copyright practices?
   A. It required that copyrights be given to multiple printers, not just one monopoly.
   B. It enabled copyrights to last as long as 150 years.
   C. It enabled anyone to get a copyright lasting 14 years with the right to renew.

14. In general, early European copyright systems achieved what results?
   A. Created monopolies, high prices, censorship, and wealth for the Crown.
   B. Guaranteed authors' rights.
   C. Prevented publishers and printers from exploiting authors and artists.

15. What was the significance of the landmark *Donaldson v. Beckett* case in England?
   A. It established that copyright was the common law right of publishers.
   B. It treated copyright as a limited right of authors for the first time anywhere.
   C. It gave Thomas Beckett the right to his own work in perpetuity.

16. After Donaldson v. Beckett, copyrights were expanded to include which of the following? (Choose all that apply)
   A. Sheet music, maps, design, and sculpture.
   B. Lectures.
   C. Inventions.

17. At the time of America's first copyright laws, publications in America were mostly focused on which of the following?
    A. Literary works.
    B. Practical guides, newspapers, and almanacs.
    C. Poetry.

18. Given America's more utilitarian focus in publishing, what was the emphasis placed in the drafting of our first copyright laws?
    A. To guarantee the rights of authors.
    B. To guarantee the rights of publishers and printers.
    C. To ensure widespread public access to knowledge and information.

19. Copyrights for U.S. citizens last for what term?
    A. 28 years.
    B. 14 years, with the right of renewal.
    C. Life-plus 70 years.

20. The first U.S. copyright law was signed by George Washington when?
    A. 1776.
    B. 1783.
    C. 1790.

21. How did America's first copyright law treat the infringement of foreign cultural works?
    A. It strongly prohibited copyright infringement whether domestic and foreign.
    B. It explicitly allowed, even encouraged the piracy of foreign works.

22. America would resist all efforts to outlaw the piracy of foreign works for how long?
    A. Until 1810.
    B. Until the end of the Civil War in 1865.
    C. Until 1891.

23. John Barry was the first American to receive a copyright. For which type of work did he receive the copyright?
    A. A novel.
    B. An almanac.
    C. A spelling book.
    D. A book of poems.

24. A half century after independence, what proportion of literary works published in America were written by Americans?
    A. 33%
    B. 65%
    C. 92%

25. What were some of the costs of America's rampant piracy of foreign books?
    A. The U.S. was regarded as an publishing outlaw by other countries.
    B. American works cost a lot more than pirated foreign works.
    C. Domestic American authorship was stunted and delayed as a result.
    D. All of the above.

**26**. When was Harriet Beacher Stowe's *Uncle Tom's Cabin* copyrighted?
A. 1837.
B. 1851.
C. 1861.

**27**. Research and historical experience demonstrate that, in the absence of intellectual property rights, nations are bound to face which of the following?
A. An excessive incentive to copy others.
B. An excessive incentive to invent or create for themselves.
C. An incentive to trade ideas and work freely.

**28**. When did U.S. authors finally become the majority of best-selling authors in the U.S.?
A. The mid-19th Century.
B. The early 20th century.

**29**. Which of the following is NOT one of the eight broad categories of copyrightable work?
A. Literary works.
B. Musical works, including any accompanying words.
C. Dramatic works, including any accompanying music.
D. Pantomimes and choreographic works.
E. Creative Ideas.
F. Pictorial, graphic, and sculptural works.
G. Motion pictures and other audiovisual works.
H. Sound recordings.
I. Architectural works.

**30**. Why is computer software eligible for copyright?
A. It cannot be patented.
B. It is considered to be a literary work, which the Copyright Act defines as a work expressed in words, numbers, or other symbols that is creatively compiled.
C. It is able to display artistic or literary work on a TV or in an e-book.

**31**. What is the difference between ideas and their expression under copyright law.
A. You can't copyright an idea for a movie, but you can patent it.
B. Ideas are just thoughts, not matter how creative. You can't copyright thoughts.
C. You cannot copyright an idea for a space opera, but you can copyright *Star Wars*—the original expression of a space opera idea put to paper or film.

**32**. Which of the following may be copyrightable?
A. A mathematical formula.
B. Facts that you have discovered through research.
C. A compiled Chinese-American phone book that uses facts.

**33**. Other than being one of the eight broad categories of creative content, which is NOT one of the other four things a copyrighted work must be.
A. Original.
B. Expressed or fixed on a tangible medium that can be seen or copied.
C. Authored or creatively compiled.
D. Not a fact or abstract idea.
E. Culturally worthwhile.

**34.** How many exclusive rights does a copyright owner have?
- A. 5.
- B. 6.
- C. 8.

**35.** If the copyright in a work lasts for 95 years from first publication, it is copyright for:
- A. An individual.
- B. A work of two or more authors.
- C. A work for hire.

**36.** How long will Michael Jackson's copyrights last? (Note: He died in 2009)
- A. Until 2025.
- B. Until 2079.
- C. Until 2110.

**37.** What is the "first-sale" doctrine?
- A. It states that copyright begins with the first sale of your manuscript to a publisher.
- B. It gives you the right to protect the integrity of your work after publication.
- C. It terminates your distribution rights after you (or your publisher) sell your work to a bookstore, art gallery, etc.

**38.** Registration used to be required for a copyright. When did that requirement end?
- A. 1976, with the passage of the Copyright Act.
- B. 1909, when Congress passed the Copyright Act of 1909.
- C. 1989, after the United States joined the international Berne Convention.

**39.** If attorneys could demonstrate in court that Kanye West "sampled" or used pieces of Sly Johnson's song "Different Strokes" in a song called "The Joy," this would be evidence of what kind of copyright infringement?
- A. Comprehensive nonliteral similarity.
- B. Fragmented literal similarity.

**40.** In 2015, a federal jury found Robin Thicke and Pharrell Williams guilty of copyright infringement of soul singer Marvin Gaye's "Got to Give It Up." They found that their song "Blurred Lines" demonstrated what form of copyright infringement?
- A. Comprehensive nonliteral similarity.
- B. Fragmented literal similarity.

**41.** In addition to the $5.3 million jury award, why was the Thicke and Williams copyright infringement case considered to be so significant within the music industry?
- A. It shows that you can't get away with stealing other people's work.
- B. The verdict seemed ironic in light of Williams's smash hit "Happy."
- C. It challenged the growing practice in music of incorporating elements, features, themes, and even the "feel" and "mood" of the work of other artists and genres.

**42.** The jury's decision also drew criticism from many copyright and music experts. Why?
- A. The $5.3 million award was thought to be outrageously large.
- B. Critics said that although Marvin Gaye may have been the Prince of Soul, he didn't own a copyright to the whole genre.
- C. Not a single word, melody, or beat from Gaye's song was actually copied.

**43.** In what way has the Marvin Gaye case already made musicians and producers more cautious?

A. Singers are more willing to license the work of previous artists from whom they gain "look and feel" ideas and inspiration.

B. Sam Smith granted Tom Petty songwriting credit and royalties to Smith's song "Stay With Me," which bore a resemblance to Petty's hit "I Won't Back Down."

C. Both of these are accurate.

**44.** Which of the following are NOT one of the types of damages that copyright owners may receive if their work is infringed?

A. Actual.

B. Punitive.

C. Statutory.

**45.** If someone willfully infringes your copyrighted work for commercial advantage or private financial gain, what may he or she also face?

A. Treble damages.

B. Criminal penalties of up to five years in prison for a first offense, and ten years for a second offense.

C. An order to publicly apologize for the infringement.

**46.** Sometimes the copyright owner's most important remedy for infringement will be an injunction. Why?

A. It immediately stops the infringer from continuing to make money from work that infringes your copyright.

B. It puts the infringer in jail where he cannot commit more infringement.

**47.** Fair use allows for the copying and use of copyrighted material for all EXCEPT which specific purpose?

A. Criticism and comment.

B. News reporting.

C. Teaching or research.

D. Political organizing.

**48.** One of the four factors considered in whether the copying or use of a copyrighted work is considered to be fair use is "the purpose and character of the use, including whether such use is of a commercial nature or is for nonprofit educational purposes." Which of the following would likely be considered fair use?

A. A profit-making magazine like *Vanity Fair* publishes a book review that quotes several thousand words of the copyrighted book being reviewed.

B. A nonprofit university distributes copies of two chapters of a copyrighted textbook to its students so they don't have to buy the textbook itself.

**49.** What major change in copyright law was NOT made in the Copyright Act of 1976?

A. It extended copyright to performances via cable television.

B. It prohibited the unauthorized rental or lease of computer software programs.

C. It codified fair use into the statutes.

**50.** The Digital Millennium Copyright Act of 1998 made it a crime to circumvent digital rights management (DRM) measures that control access to digital music and ebooks as a means of preventing piracy. So why are so many listeners, readers, and book and music publishers voluntarily abandoning DRM measures?

A. It prevents people from sharing their digital music and e-books with friends and family, like they can with regular music CDs and printed books.

B. DRM measures alienate consumers and limit their choices.

C. The elimination of DRM measures will grow the market for digital books and music much more rapidly.

D. All of the above.

**51.** Why was the Sonny Bono Copyright Term Extension Act of 1998 so controversial?

A. It put all of Sonny and Cher's formerly copyrighted music into the public domain.

B. It reduced the copyright term to that favored by the Founding Fathers—28 years.

C. It extended copyright an additional 20 years to the life of the author plus 70 years.

**52.** On December 16, 2015, the Copyright Royalty Board changed the royalty rates paid by music services like Pandora. What change was made?

A. The board reduced the rate from 14 cents per 100 songs played to 11 cents.

B. The board raised the rate to 17 cents per 100 songs played.

C. The board raised the rate to 20 cents per 100 songs played.

**53.** Which of the following alternative channels for licensing copyright never allows users to change, modify, or reuse original content?

A. Open source software licensing.

B. Open access publishing.

C. Creative Commons licenses.

**54.** Changes to copyright law in the future are likely to focus on which issues?

A. Reducing or eliminating DRM.

B. Adjusting to new advances in digital technology.

C. Enabling and regulating a secondary market for digital content.

D. Shortening copyright term.

E. All of the above.

4

# Trademark Basics

**Figure 4.1** (credit: modification of work "Close-up of TESLA trademark sign on a car" by Ivan Radic/flikr.com, CC BY 2.0)

## Chapter Outline



# Introduction

## 4.1 Core Concepts

### Learning Objectives

After completing this section, you will be able to

- Understand trademarks and their properties.
- Identify differences between trademarks and other intellectual property rights.

A **trademark** is an intellectual property right granted by a government to an individual, business, or legal entity that creates and uses a distinctive word, name, symbol, or device to distinguish its products or services from those from any other entity in the marketplace.

The original purpose of a trademark was to indicate the origin of goods and services. Trademarks thus protected the public by preventing mistakes, confusion, or deception by those who would "palm off" their goods as those of another. But it also served to protect the market and reputation (or goodwill) of the producers of goods. As modern markets evolved, trademarks also developed into guarantees of quality as well as potent marketing and advertising devices.

### Trademarks as Branding

Consider, for example, the role that Nike's "Swoosh" logo plays in its $106 billion shoe, equipment, and apparel business. In 1971, Nike founder Phil Knight paid graphic design student Carolyn Davidson a mere $35 to design the "Swoosh" logo for the fledgling new company. According to the Portland *Oregonian* newspaper, when Knight saw her design, he reportedly told her, "I don't love it, but maybe it will grow on me." Nike attorneys nonetheless registered the logo with the U.S. Patent and Trademark Office (USPTO) on June 18, 1971.[i]

Today, this one logo is estimated to be worth as much as $20 billion, and is recognized around the world as a symbol of Nike's quality workmanship and design. Indeed, its vital role in protecting Nike's market share and reputation explains why the company so strenuously protects its trademark rights from being infringed by counterfeiters. As for design student Carolyn Davidson, Phil Knight gave her Nike stock in 1983 that is today worth more than $850,000.

### Trademarks vs. Other Intellectual Property Rights

Trademarks share with other intellectual property rights the power to encourage and reward creative enterprise. Trademarks also share with patent rights and copyrights the public policy goal of marshaling the benefits of creative endeavor—in this case, the distinctive branding of one's products and services from those of others—to the public good. They do this by protecting the consumer from deception and encouraging sellers to provide quality products.

But trademarks are different from other intellectual property rights in three key respects. In the first place, the legal foundation for U.S. trademark law comes not from rights expressly enumerated in the Constitution, as is the case with patent rights and copyrights. Rather, it lies in the Commerce Clause of the Constitution, which gives Congress the authority to regulate interstate commerce and enact whatever necessary and proper legislation is required to do that.

Trademarks are also different from other intellectual property rights in that they are not limited in duration. Patents and copyright are granted only for limited periods of time because society benefits by putting an invention or literary work into the public domain once the inventor or artistic creator has recouped the costs of innovation and been rewarded for the pioneering endeavor. Trademarks, however, never hinder the sales of other products or services, so they are granted in perpetuity so long as they are not abandoned by the trademark owner.

### Trademarks Mean Business

Finally, trademarks exist only in conjunction with commercial activity. An inventor may receive a patent for a new invention and never employ or "practice" that invention in a business or research endeavor. Similarly, an author can receive a copyright for an original literary or artistic work and yet never publish, display, or sell it. A trademark, however, cannot exist by itself, apart from commercial activity.

Thus a trademark cannot be obtained by mere adoption. It can only be acquired through commercial use or in anticipation thereof—i.e., through the sale of goods and services.

---

i Allen Brettman, "*Creator of Nike's Famed Swoosh Remembers Its Conception 40 Years Later,*" the Oregonian, June 15, 2011.

# 4.2 Early Trademark Systems

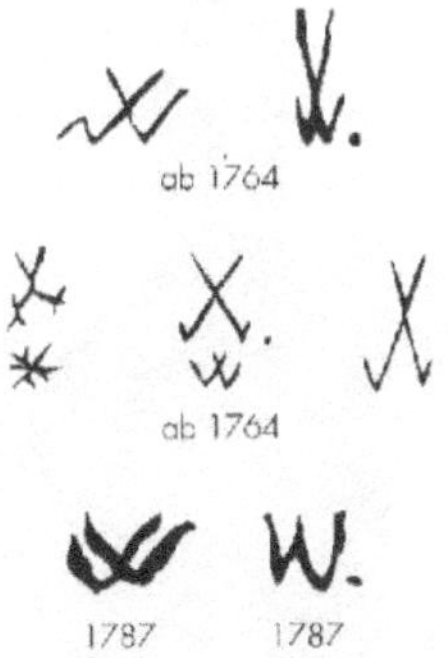


**Figure 4.2** (credit: Wikimedia Commons / Public Domain)

## Learning Objectives

After completing this section, you will be able to

- Discuss the origins of trademarks.
- Analyze examples of early forms of trademarks.

## Bronze Age Origins

Scholars of antiquity give Early Bronze Age potters the credit for creating the world's first trademarks by imprinting their works with distinctive markings. We assume that these marks were meant to indicate the origin of a particular work or the identity of its craftsman, but the historical record is not conclusive on this point. But an examination of the potters' seals found on Corinthian artifacts dating to 2000 BC suggests this is a reasonable supposition. Trade and commerce between the tribes and early civilizations of that era were expanding rapidly, and in order to be mutually beneficial, trade requires a certain amount of trust in the provenance and quality of goods. These early potters' trademarks seemed to have served that purpose by distinguishing the goods of quality craftsmen from those of unknown or uncertain sources.

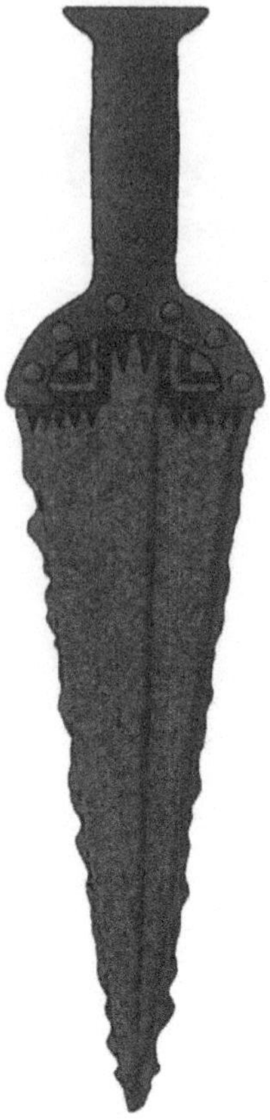

**Figure 4.3** Triangular dagger with solid handle from the Early Bronze Age, a period with some of the earliest examples of trademarks. (credit: Wikimedia Commons / Public Domain)

Trademarks have always been inextricably bound up with commerce. And as commerce grew and developed over the centuries, so did the use of trademarks. Marks have been found, for example, on works ranging from Egyptian pots to the swords of Roman blacksmiths. But it was in the medieval period, with the emergence of powerful craft guilds, that trademark usage really expanded. Their marks identified a work as being made by a particular guild or member of that guild, and therefore continued the long tradition of identifying the origin of goods. But medieval trademarks also served other functions. They became a means by which guilds could control the quality of work of fellow guild members and, because of a trademark's association with quality, ultimately, a source of competitive advantage in the market.[ii] Trademarks thus began to acquire something akin to the existential "moral rights" found in later copyright statutes—i.e., the right of a creator to defend the quality, originality, and "personality" of their work.

Trademark use in medieval times also acquired a public interest function. As Arthur R. Miller and Michael H. Davis note in *Intellectual Property: Patents, Trademarks, and Copyright in a Nutshell*, "Statutes dating back as early as the thirteenth century show that [trademark] was eventually recognized as having social consequence. These statutes were meant to protect the public by preventing the sale of unidentified goods whose quality could not be ascertained."

One notable trademark from the time was that of Löwenbräu Brewery, which claims to have used its lion mark since its founding in 1383.[iii]

ii Arthur R. Miller and Michael H. Davis, *Intellectual Property: Patents, Trademarks, and Copyright in a Nutshell.* (5th ed., p. 25). St. Paul MN: West Publishing Co., 2007.

iii Gary Richardson, *Brand Names Before the Industrial Revolution*, National Bureau of Economic Research, NBER Working Paper No. 13930, April,2008.

## Early Trademark Cases

Scholars had until only recently attributed the first reported trademark case in Anglo-American law to be *Southern v. How*, which was decided in 1618. This despite the fact that the case involved not a trademark but the sale of counterfeit jewels.[iv] Its connection to trademark came from a reference by the presiding judge to an earlier, unnamed, and unreported case in 1584 involving a suit brought by a cloth maker against another cloth maker who had used his mark. That earlier clothier case, only recently discovered and now known as *Sanforth's Case*, is now held to be the earliest reported trademark case in Anglo- American law. It establishes beyond a doubt that even 250 years before the Industrial Revolution, trademark infringement was viewed as a tort of deceit and a violation of the laws against unfair competition.[v]

To quote from a contemporary 1656 legal report:

> "The action upon the case was brought in the [Court of] Common Pleas by a clothier, that whereupon he had gained great reputation for his making of his cloth ... to his benefit and profit, and that he used to set his mark on his cloth whereby it should be known to be his cloth; and another clothier, observing it, used the same mark to his ill-made cloth [in order] to deceive him."

In the more than four centuries since then, as commerce and industry have evolved into an $80 *trillion* a year global marketplace unimaginable to the people of *Sanforth's Case* time, its verdict that trademark infringement is competition most unfair and demands redress still serves as the foundation and wellspring of worldwide trademark policies and statutes today.

# 4.3 U.S. Trademark Law

### Learning Objectives

After completing this section, you will be able to

- Grasp the basics of trademark law.
- Analyze notable trademark cases.

As the young United States rapidly developed its commerce and industry in the late eighteenth and early nineteenth centuries, propelled in no small part by the nation's unusually democratic and effective patent laws (see Chapter 1, "Section 1.5: What the U.S. Patent System Wrought"), the states developed increasingly sophisticated and complex trademark laws. Eventually, however, the transformation of America's many local and regional markets into a single, unified, national economy propelled Congress to try to federalize trademark law despite the lack of any express constitutional authority to do so. So Congress passed the first national trademark laws in 1870 and 1876. But in a set of three court challenges consolidated into a single appeal before the U.S. Supreme Court in 1879, Justice Samuel Freeman Miller ruled for the majority that the Patent and Copyright Clause (https://www.openstax.org/l/PCClause) of the Constitution gave Congress no explicit authority to regulate trademarks, and declared the 1870 and 1876 trademark laws unconstitutional.[vi]

## The Commerce Clause and the Lanham Act of 1946

Two years later, Congress instead acted under the **Commerce Clause** (https://www.openstax.org/l/CommerceClause) of the Constitution to pass the Trade Mark Act of 1881. This first national trademark law, however, only regulated trademarks used in commerce with other nations and with Indian tribes. It wasn't until 1905 that Congress passed another trademark statute regulating the use of marks within the United

iv McKenna, M. *The Normative Foundations of Trademark Law* (December 30, 2010). Notre Dame Law Review, Vol. 82, No. 5, p. 1839, 2007. Retrieved from SSRN: http://ssrn.com/abstract=889162.

v Keith M. Stolte, *How Early Did Anglo-American Trademark Law Begin? An Answer to Schechter's Conundrum*, Fordham Intellectual Property, Media and Entertainment Law Journal, Volume 8, Issue 2, 1997.

vi See *United States v. Steffens* 100 U.S. 82 (1879); *United States v. Wittemann* 100 U.S. 82 (1879); *United States v. Johnson* 100 U.S. 82 (1879) Retrieved From http://caselaw.lp.findlaw.com/cgibin/getcase.pl?court=us&vol=100&invol=82.

States.

Those two trademark laws were subsequently overhauled by the Lanham Act of 1946 (https://www.openstax.org/l/LanhamAct) , which remains the principal law of the land on trademarks in the United States to this day.[vii] It broadened national registration of trademarks, and also gave owners of unregistered marks access for the first time to the federal courts. The act also established remedies such as bars on the sale or importation of infringing products, and required the renewal of trademarks every ten years to weed out the registry trademarks that are no longer in commercial use (known as the "deadwood" prevision).[viii]

After 119 years in business, for example, the world-famous retailer Woolworth's went bankrupt in 1997 and its trademark was no longer protected. The 83-year-old Hostess Twinkies brand, however, was acquired by two private equity firms for $410 million because they see future profit in the iconic brand—and the customers who love it.

## Requirements for a U.S. Trademark

The requirement that a trademark must be actively used or intended to be used in commercial activity in order to be protected by law has been a fundamental feature of U.S. trademark law since its inception. The Lanham Act specifically requires applicants to submit "a verified statement that the mark is in use in commerce, specifying the date of the applicant's first use of the mark in commerce and those goods or services specified in the notice of allowance on or in connection with which the mark is used in commerce."[ix] A trademark is presumed to have been abandoned when its owner ceases to use it for three or more years, after which anyone else can register and use the mark.

---

vii Harvard University. (2012). *Overview of Trademark Law.* Retrieved from http://cyber.law.harvard.edu/metaschool/fisher/domain/tm.htm.

viii Op. cit., Miller and Davis.

ix 15 U.S.C. §1051 Retrieved from http://www.law.cornell.edu/uscode/text/15/1051.

## 4.4 The Four Types of Trademarks

**Figure 4.4** (credit: photograph by Mike Mozart via flikr / CC BY 2.0)

### Learning Objectives

After completing this section, you will be able to

- Identify the four types of trademarks.
- Compare differences between types of trademarks.

### Can I Trademark That?

Before reading this section, please watch this overview video (https://openstax.org/l/CanITrademark) covering the four types of trademarks and what they are used for, the subject matter of trademarks, and why trademarks are important—not just to their owners, but even more so, to the general public.

The term "trademark" is usually used to describe any of the four types of marks that can be registered with the U.S. Patent and Trademark Office. The two primary types of marks are **trademarks** and **service marks**. The two other marks—**certification marks** and **collective marks**—occur much less frequently and must meet different requirements for registration.[x]

### Trademarks

Trademarks identify *products*—i.e., physical goods and commodities—that are either manufactured, produced, grown, or that exist naturally. A trademark is a word, name, symbol, or device—or combination of these—used to identify and distinguish the source of that product. Examples of trademarks include the Nike "Swoosh" symbol, the arched "M" for McDonalds, and the apple symbol with a small curved bite taken out of it for Apple Computer.

### Service Marks

Service marks are exactly the same in principle as trademarks except that these words, names, symbols, or devices identify and distinguish the source of a *service*. Examples of service marks include the sleek silver

x United States Patent and Trademark Office. (2012, May 24). Trademarks. Retrieved from http://www.uspto.gov/inventors/trademarks.jsp

greyhound dog on Greyhound buses, and United Parcel Service's brown shield emblazoned with the bold yellow letters "UPS."

### Certification Marks

A certification mark is any word, phrase, symbol, or design—or a combination of any of these—owned by one party that certifies the goods and services of others when they meet certain standards or requirements.[xi] A certification mark identifies either the nature of a product or service—for example, that it meets the quality standards needed to receive the "Good Housekeeping Seal of Approval"—or the **origin** of products or services, as in the certification mark "Washington State" given to apples grown in that state.

### Collective Marks

Collective marks come in one of two varieties: collective trademarks and service marks, and collective membership marks. A collective trade or service mark is any word, phrase, symbol, or design that is owned by a cooperative, association, collective group, or organization and is used by its members to indicate the source of goods or services.[xii] An example of a collective trademark is the "Girl Scouts" mark seen on cookies every February, or the designation "CPA" to identify the services provided by a Certified Public Accountant.

**Figure 4.5** (credit: Wikimedia Commons / Public Domain)

A collective membership mark, by contrast, is used to indicate that a person is a member of some organization, such as a trade union or an association like the Rotary Club, but is not used to identify the source of goods and services.

## 4.5 The Subject Matter of Trademarks

### Learning Objectives

After completing this section, you will be able to

- Learn the subject matter of trademarks.
- Analyze characteristics of various forms of trademarks.

As discussed, there are four types of trademarks: trademarks, service marks, certification marks, and collective marks. But what does it mean to say that a trademark may be a "word [or phrase], name, symbol [or design], or device." The answers may in some cases surprise you.

xi United States Patent and Trademark Office. (2012, March 09). *What Is a Collective Membership Mark?*. Retrieved from http://www.uspto.gov/faq/trademarks.jsp#_Toc275426676

xii United States Patent and Trademark Office. (2012, March 09). Frequently Asked Questions About Trademarks. Retrieved from http://www.uspto.gov/faq/trademarks.jsp

## Words, Phrases, and Names

There is little confusion about what is meant by a trademarkable *word*, *phrase*, or *name*. The only point to remember here is that words, names, and phrases that are simply descriptive of the goods or services with which they are associated do not necessarily qualify for registration as a trademark.[xiii] They must be distinctive and indicate the origin of a product or service. What is meant by distinctive—and how distinctive they must be—will be discussed in the next section.

## Symbols and Devices

**Symbols** and **devices** are where things start to get interesting in trademark law. The language of the Lanham Act does not specify what is meant by a "symbol" or a "device" that can be trademarked. The U.S. Supreme Court took careful note of that fact, ruling in 1995 that, "Since human beings might use as a 'symbol' or 'device' almost anything at all that is capable of carrying meaning, this language, read literally, is not restrictive."[xiv]

In the United States, therefore, trademarks can include almost anything that carries distinctive meaning and identifies the origin of products and services. This includes slogans, letters, numbers, logos, three-dimensional designs—even colors, scents, and sounds that indicate the source of a good or service to consumers.[xv]

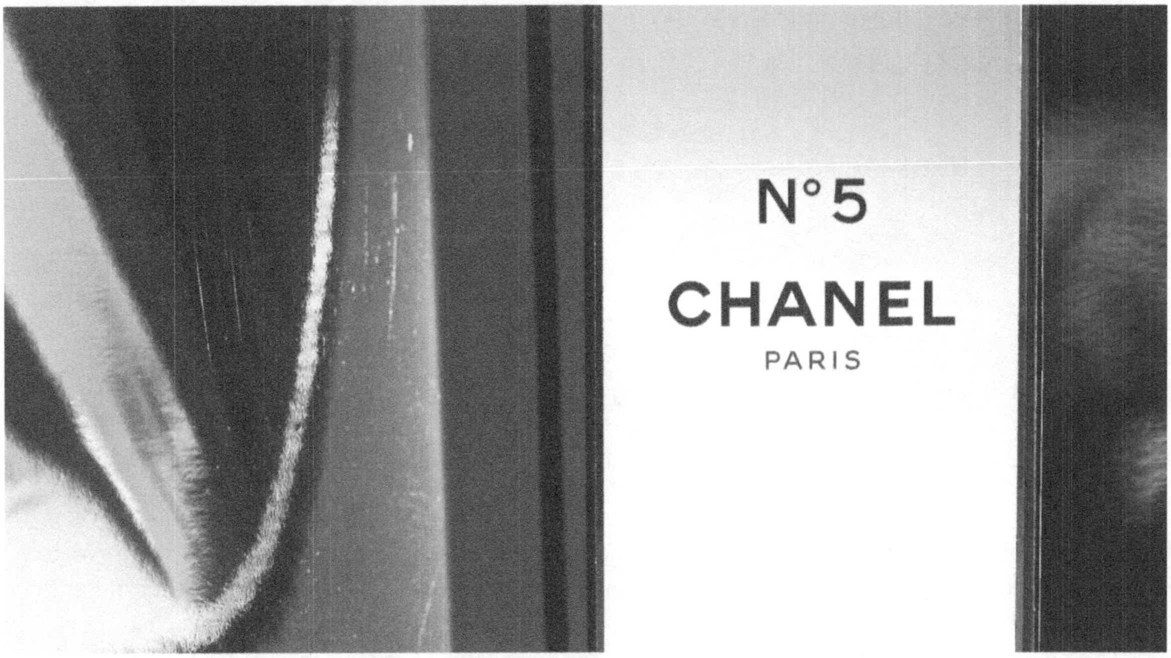


**Figure 4.6** (credit: TIGER500 via flikr / CC BY 2.0)

A trademarkable symbol can be a *number*. The number 5, for example, is a trademarked symbol of Chanel No. 5 perfume (No. 73788555). So is the number 31, which is the trademarked symbol of Baskin-Robbins 31 Flavors (No. 72172718).

---

xiii United States Patent and Trademark Office. (2012, August 09). *Trademark Manual of Examining Procedure* § 1202. Retrieved from http://tess2.uspto.gov/bin80/gate.exe?f=doc&state=nk9n3c.2.14

xiv *Qualitex Co. v. Jacobson Products Co.*, 514 U.S. 159, 7 (1995) Retrieved from: http://www.todaysengineer.org/2003/Feb/files/514U.S.159.pdf

xv Henderson, C. *International Standards for The Protection of Intellectual Property Rights: Trademarks and Geographical Indications*. Retrieved from USPTO website: www.uspto.gov/web/offices/dcom/olia/conf_gipa2007nov2/lebanont

No trademark can block the use of the numbers 5 or 31 in math. Nor have the courts allowed the trademarking of mere part numbers,[xvi] model numbers,[xvii] or grades,[xviii] because these are not distinctive enough and do not indicate the origin of the goods in question. Regular gas, also known as "87 octane," also cannot be trademarked because it doesn't tell you whether that gas comes from Exxon, Shell, or BP.

Yet despite the above, one of the most iconic trademarked numbers is 501. Originally, the number 501 was simply the lot number Levi's assigned to the famous copper-riveted waist overalls. But over time, 501 acquired meaning in the minds of consumers and came to be very strongly associated with *Levi's* brand jeans. How otherwise un-trademarkable symbols (or words and designs) can acquire secondary (trademark) meaning will be discussed in the next section.

**Figure 4.7** A label for Levi's "501" jeans, another example of a number that gained trademark protection. (credit: The original uploader was Ludovic Glucksman at French Wikipedia via Wikimedia Commons / CC BY 1.0)

As for *scents*, the fundamental case for trademarking these came about when the USPTO denied Celia Clarke's request in 1990 for a trademark for scented yarns and threads with a "fresh, floral fragrance reminiscent of Plumeria blossoms." She appealed, and the Trademark Trial and Appeal Board overruled the examiner, granting her a trademark for the scent.

"[F]ragrance is not an inherent attribute or natural characteristic of applicant's goods but is rather a feature supplied by applicant," the board noted. "Moreover, applicant has emphasized this characteristic of her goods in advertising, promoting the scented feature of her goods. Applicant has demonstrated that customers, dealers and distributors of her scented yarns and threads have come to recognize applicant as the source of these goods. . . . In her advertisements and at craft fairs, applicant has promoted her products as having a scented nature. We believe that applicant has presented a prima facie case of distinctiveness of her fragrance mark."[xix]

On the other hand, a trademark cannot be granted for any scent that serves a function other than identifying the product's source. The scent of perfumes and air fresheners, therefore, cannot be registered, nor can the sulfurous smell that serves as a warning for natural gas leaks.

xvi See *Southco, Inc. v. Kanebridge Corp.*, 258 F.3d 148, 149 n.2 (3d Cir. 2001).

xvii See *See In re Dana Corp.*, 12 USPQ2d 1748 (TTAB 1989).

xviii See *See In re Union Oil Co.*, 33 USPQ 43 (C.C.P.A.1937).

xix In re Clarke, 17 U.S.P.Q.2d 1238 (T.T.A.B. 1990) Retrieved from http://ipmall.info/hosted_resources/TTAB_Decisions/TTAB_Appeal_758429.asp

Still, there remains a good deal of uncertainty about when a scent is trademarkable and when it is not. Consider the world-famous Cinnabon smell—that sweet, sugary, cinnamon-infused scent that is absolutely unmistakable (if not also irresistible). But it is not trademarked because even though it is certainly distinctive, it cannot be easily distinguished from the smell of cinnamon buns made by any number of other bakeries.

*Sounds* can also be trademarked provided they indicate the source of the product or service with which they are associated, and indeed, there are approximately 700 trademarked sounds registered at the USPTO.[xx] These include Tarzan's Yell, the THX theme heard at the beginning of a movie, MGM's roaring lion, America Online's "You've got mail" announcement, the sequence of chimes heard with the display of the NBC logo on TV, and, naturally, the sound of a duck quacking "Aflac!" for the American Family Life Assurance Company.

## Designs and Trade Dress

A *design*, like a logo, can also be trademarked, provided it distinguishes the origin of the product or service from any other source or producer. In these trademarks, the logo must be unique and consist of more than simple stylization.

**Figure 4.8** The Pepsi logo has been tweaked a few times since 1969 but the overall design has remained recognizable and distinct. (credit: Mike Mozart via flikr / CC BY 2.0)

Bacardi for using a similar stylized "O" on its label for orange-flavored vodka. The court ruled against Geogri, however, because its design consisted merely of a stylized symbol that had not acquired a distinguishing (or secondary) meaning in the minds of consumers that enabled them to identify the producer.[xxi]

Examples of pure trademarked designs, without any associated words, include Nike's "Swoosh" and Apple's famous logo of an apple with a bite taken out of it.

This is why design trademarks often take a "design plus words" approach, as in the trademarked Lacoste logo featuring the word "Lacoste" above the famous green alligator.

---

xx See Constine, J. (2011, December 20). *Don't Let Your Company's Sound Be Stolen, Trademark it With Trademarkia.* Retrieved from http://techcrunch.com/2011/12/20/tradmark-sound-trademarkia/

xxi *Star Industries, Inc. v. Bacardi & Co., LTD.*, 412 F.3d 373 (2d Circuit, 2005) Retrieved from http://bulk.resource.org/courts.gov/c/F3/412/412.F3d.373.04-1753-.04-0831-.html

**Trade dress**, on the other hand, refers to the **overall appearance** of a product or service that indicates its source. Trade dress can include features such as size, shape, color or color combinations, texture, graphics, or even particular sales techniques. The key to claiming trade dress protection is that the attributes must be distinctive. For example, Taco Cabana has trademarked its distinctive and "festive eating atmosphere having interior dining and patio areas decorated with artifacts, bright colors, paintings and murals," and won an infringement case against a competitor restaurant called Two Pesos. By creating a theme that was similar to Taco Cabana, Two Pesos created confusion in the minds of consumers.[xxii]

A design trademark may be one part of a product's trade dress, but it is distinct from trade dress because it only covers the stylization of words, letters, numbers, or of a specific design like the Lacoste green alligator.

Imagine that an Apple competitor opened a retail store with the same colors, lighting, atmosphere, and overall look and feel as the Apple store but sold their own products. The goal would not be to stop the sale of the goods, which are not necessarily infringing any of Apple's design trademarks or patents, but to stop the competitor from infringing the look and feel of the Apple store. In this case, Apple would file a trade dress suit.

Both design trademarks and trade dress are different from design patents. Although all three cover only **nonfunctional** designs and appearances, design patents strictly protect only the new and original ornamental design of an article of manufacture, and the actual drawing of a design patent limits what is protected. A design trademark, on the other hand, protects a particular word, name, symbol, or design used in commerce to distinguish a product's source. And trade dress protects the overall appearance of the product and can include anything that gives a product or service meaning and distinguishes it from those of any other producer.

A design patent might protect the new and original ornamental design of a lamp, for example, so long as that appearance does not affect the lamp's function. A design trademark would protect the words or symbols used on the lamp that identify it as coming from a particular producer. And trade dress protects the overall "look and feel" of the lamp.

Sometimes both forms of protection can be obtained, providing an extra advantage to the owner of these rights. Examples of products with both design trademarks and design patents include the *Dustbuster* vacuum cleaner, the *Pepsi* bottle, and the *Honeywell* round thermostat.

## 4.6 The Spectrum of Distinctiveness

### Learning Objectives

After completing this section, you will be able to

- Discover the elements of distinctiveness within trademarks.
- Identify the various kinds of marks used.

The fundamental and overriding requirement for a trademark is **distinctiveness**. The requirement for distinctiveness is analogous to the requirement for **novelty** in patent rights and **originality** in copyright. Without distinctiveness, there can be no trademark.

As Miller and Davis note, "Naturally, a trademark must be distinctive if it is to serve the function of identifying the origin of goods and thereby avoid confusion, deception, or mistake. If a trademark is to protect purchasers from confusion over what they are purchasing, then the trademark somehow must be recognizable, identifiable, and different from other marks."[xxiii]

Some trade and service marks achieve distinction via their inherent nature—Nike's curved "Swoosh" check mark suggesting speed and agility, for example.

---

xxii 932 F.2d 1113, 1117 (CA5 1991), derived from: http://caselaw.lp.findlaw.com/scripts/getcase.pl?court=us&vol=505&invol=763

xxiii Op. cit., Miller and Davis.

But other marks gain distinctiveness as a result of marketing, eventually forming a powerful association over time in the minds of consumers. As an example, the term "Raisin Bran" is merely descriptive of the foods used in the cereal and would not be eligible for trademark registration had Kellogg Company not demonstrated through evidence of use (including sales, advertising expenditures, and consumer surveys) that the buying public had come to distinctively associate Raisin Bran with this particular Kellogg's cereal.

The public's distinct association of a trademark to a company is known as secondary meaning, and that is something that can only be established over time. An understanding of secondary meaning is crucial when discussing the **spectrum of distinctiveness.**

In *Abercrombie & Fitch Co. v. Hunting World, Inc.* (https://www.openstax.org/l/AFVHuntingWorld) in 1976, Judge Henry Jacob Friendly established five basic categories of marks along a spectrum of distinctiveness, ranging from "fanciful" marks that are inherently distinctive on one end and on the other end "generic" marks that are never distinctive and thus not eligible for trademark registration.[xxiv]

### Fanciful Marks

**Fanciful marks** are invented words, symbols, or devices that have no relation to the good or service being sold and have no meaning other than to distinctly identify the product or service and distinguish it in the minds of consumers from those of any other vendor. "Xerox" is a good example of a fanciful mark, as are "Google" and "Kodak." Fanciful marks are considered the strongest type of mark and are prima facie registrable with the USPTO.

### Arbitrary Marks

**Arbitrary marks** are real words in common usage that have no descriptive relationship to the product or service being sold. Examples of arbitrary marks include "Apple" (for the computer company), "Oracle" (for the software company), and "Galaxy" (for the mobile phone). Arbitrary marks are also unreservedly eligible for trademark registration.

### Suggestive Marks

**Suggestive marks** are marks that suggest or imply a quality or characteristic of the goods and services being sold. They require imagination, insight, or perception on the part of the consumer as to the nature of the article.[xxv] Examples include "iPad" for the tablet computer and "Coppertone" for the sunscreen lotion.

A suggestive mark is the minimum required for a mark to be unconditionally registrable absent a secondary meaning. Or in the words of Judge Friendly, "The validity of the mark ends where *suggestion* ends and *description* begins."[xxvi] From this point on along the spectrum of distinctiveness, things get a bit tricky.

### Descriptive Marks

A **descriptive mark** explicitly describes the purpose, nature, or an attribute of a product or service and is, therefore, not eligible for trademark registration unless a secondary meaning or association has been developed in the public's mind through usage.[xxvii] Ineligible descriptive marks include "Lightweight" and "Faster." However, if a descriptive mark takes on a secondary meaning in the public mind—"Sharp" televisions, for example, or "Windows" for windowing software—then it can be eligible for trademark registration.

---

xxiv *Abercrombie & Fitch Co. v. Hunting World, Inc.*, 537 F.2d 4, Court of Appeals. Retrieved from http://scholar.google.com/scholar_case?case=9011105700430131407&q=abercrombie+%26+fitch+v.+hunting+world&hl=en&as_sdt=2,38&as_vis=1

xxv Derived from: http://www.bitlaw.com/trademark/degrees.html

xxvi Op. cit., *Abercrombie & Fitch Co. v. Hunting World, Inc.*

xxvii United States Patent and Trademark Office. (2011, January). *Trademark Manual of Examining Procedure (TMEP) - 8th Edition*. Retrieved from http://tess2.uspto.gov/tmdb/tmep/1200.htm

The bar against descriptive marks is designed to protect for public use common concepts and language that everyone needs to use. Imagine having to pay the coiner of the term "reverse mortgage" every time you wanted to describe such a financial arrangement. It would create a nightmare of social costs, which can be prevented simply by allowing the descriptive term to remain in the public domain. The bar against descriptive marks spotlights the overall social purpose of trademarks, which is to prevent fraud and confusion in the market while not conferring a monopoly on anyone.

### Generic Marks

The last and least distinctive category of marks are **generic marks** that are simply the common name for the goods and services being sold. Examples of generic marks might be "Aspirin" for the analgesic, or the use of the word "Baskets" for a basket store without any accompanying logo or other design element to distinguish from a merely generic description of the items sold. A generic mark is never eligible for registration no matter how much evidence a mark owner offers that it has acquired a secondary meaning through advertising and marketing.

Ironically, a product or service can become so successful in the marketplace that the public begins to associate its trademark with an entire category of similar products and services. When this happens, a valid trademark can become a generic name and the trademark will be lost, as happened with both "Cellophane" and "Aspirin." To prevent this from happening, companies like "Kleenex," "Xerox," and more recently "Google" have gone to great legal and advertising expense to prevent the generic misuse of their trademarks so these remain valid.

**Figure 4.9** (credit: Microsoft via Wikimedia Commons / Public Domain)

There are many companies that sell aspirin, but aspirin itself can no longer be trademarked.

Adobe, for example, sent emails to many web authors advising them to discontinue using the term "photoshopped" and instead say that their photos were "modified by Adobe Photoshop software." Similarly, Xerox spent heavily on advertisements warning that "you cannot Xerox a document, but you can copy it on a Xerox brand copying machine."

## 4.7 Bars to Trademark

**Figure 4.10** (credit: Amazon via Wikimedia Commons / Public Domain)

### Learning Objectives

After completing this section, you will be able to

- Identify the bars to trademark.
- Dissect criteria for trademark registration.

## The Prior Use Bar

No one can register a trademark if it has been used by other parties prior to its use by the applicant. Indeed, if the applicant uses such a mark, he or she may be liable for trademark infringement.[xxviii] The only exception to the prior use bar is when the mark has been used in an entirely different market or field of business, as in the trademark "Progressive" granted to two companies, one a backpack manufacturer and the other an auto insurance company.

## The Functionality Bar

To be trademarked, no word, symbol, design, device, scent, or sound may purely or primarily serve a functional purpose. Nor can it be trademarked if its absence in or on the product inflates its cost or reduces its quality.[xxix]

Thus as noted earlier, the scent of a perfume cannot be trademarked because the core requirement of a perfume is that it have a pleasant and distinctive smell.

The design of a chair presents an interesting dilemma, however. Does the design enable a person to sit—i.e., does it have a functional purpose? Or does the design distinctively mark an otherwise perfectly functional chair as coming from an identifiable producer?

This "chicken and egg" question has confronted many applicants, trademark examiners, judges, and juries over the years. The issue is usually decided by asking whether the appearance of a product or its components is inspired more by design or by function?

The issue is most easily decided when the functionality of an item resides in a specific part of the product, and the design elements are found in other parts of the product. A great example of this is the "A Christmas Story Leg Lamp" based on the classic 1983 film comedy. The functional part of the lamp is its electronics and light fixture sitting atop the base. The base, however, is in the shape of a woman's stocking-clad leg, and is thus clearly a design feature that distinguishes the lamp from any other on the market, and it is trademarked (No. 77105065).

## Subject Matter Bars

In addition to prior use and functionality, certain kinds of subject matter are generally not eligible for trademark registration. These are surnames, geographic marks, and ornamental, immoral, or offensive marks.[xxx]

Surnames or family names such as "Smith" and "Johnson" cannot be trademarked except under certain conditions. The USPTO assesses five factors in determining whether a surname is eligible for a trademark:

- Whether the surname is rare.
- Whether the term is the surname of anyone connected with the applicant.
- Whether the term has any recognized meaning other than as a surname.
- Whether it has the "look and feel" of a surname.
- Whether the stylization of lettering is distinctive enough to create a separate commercial impression[xxxi]

---

xxviii 15 U.S.C. §1115.

xxix *Inwood Laboratories Inc. v. Ives Laboratories, Inc.*, 456 U.S. 844 (1982) Retrieved from http://supreme.justia.com/cases/federal/us/456/844/case.html

xxx United States Patent and Trademark Office.(2012, March 09). *Frequently Asked Questions About Trademarks.* Retrieved from http://www.uspto.gov/faq/trademarks.jsp

xxxi United States Patent and Trademark Office. (2011, January). *TMEP 1211.01 "Primarily Merely A Surname".* Retrieved from http://tess2.uspto.gov/tmdb/tmep/1200.htm

"If the mark's character as a surname predominates in terms of its 'primary significance to the purchasing public,' then it is prohibited," write Miller and Davis.[xxxii] But over time, if the surname becomes associated in the public mind with the distinctive origin of products or services, then it may be eligible for a trademark, as is the case with "Sears" and "Macy's."

**Figure 4.11** Macy's the brand name of the department store chain—is an example of a surname that has become eligible for trademark protection. (credit: photograph by Mike Mozart via flikr / CC BY 2.0)

Geographic marks must also be evaluated for eligibility on the basis of several factors. If a geographic mark is simply *descriptive*, the following tests apply:

- The primary significance of the mark is a generally known geographic location.
- The goods or services originate in the place identified in the mark.
- Purchasers would be likely to believe that the goods or services originate in the geographic place identified in the mark.[xxxiii]

The test above determines whether there is a literal association to the name or not. For example, if an entrepreneur launches a company called "Los Angeles Shoes" to produce shoes in Los Angeles, the name would not pass the test for trademark eligibility because the primary significance of the mark is that it is a generally known location, the product is produced in the location stated in the mark, and consumers would believe the shoes were made in Los Angeles.

The goal of the bar against geographically **descriptive** marks, then, is to protect one party from seizing ownership of a geographic term that ought to remain in the public domain.

If a geographic mark is deceptively **misdescriptive**, however, the test is as follows:

- The primary significance of the mark is a generally known geographic location.
- The goods or services do not originate in the place identified in the mark.
- Purchasers would be likely to believe that the goods or services originate in the geographic place identified in the mark.
- The misrepresentation is a material factor in a significant portion of the relevant consumer's decision to buy the goods or use the services.[xxxiv]

The goal of this test for geographically **misdescriptive** marks is to prevent the confusion and deception of the

xxxii Op. cit., Miller and Davis.

xxxiii United States Patent and Trademark Office. (2011, January). *TMEP 1211.01(a) "Primarily Merely A Surname."* Retrieved from http://tess2.uspto.gov/tmdb/tmep/1200.htm

xxxiv United States Patent and Trademark Office. (2011, January). *TMEP 1211.01(b) "Primarily Merely A Surname."* Retrieved from http://tess2.uspto.gov/tmdb/tmep/1200.htm

consumer. For example, if an entrepreneur launches a fashionable shoe business called "New York Shoes" but actually manufactures the shoes in China, he will not receive a trademark for the name because it will likely confuse or deceive consumers.

Sometimes, however, a geographic name may be trademarked, as was the case with the online retailing giant's trademark "Amazon." In this case, the geographic name "Amazon" is not indicative of the source of goods, nor are consumers under the impression that the goods sold by the retailer come from the Amazonian region of South America. In addition, the geographic nature of the name "Amazon" is not a significant factor in whether or not consumers decide to purchase books, clothing, electronics, or anything else from the company.

Nor can *ornamental, immoral,* or *offensive* marks be trademarked. Ornamental marks such as a "smiley face" logo are merely decorative and are too vague to distinguish the origin of a product or service. Immoral or offensive marks—e.g., an online dating service with a logo depicting two naked people having sex—also cannot be registered.

## 4.8 Establishing Trademark Protection

### Learning Objectives

After completing this section, you will be able to

- Identify the reasons for establishing trademark registration.
- Understand the process of trademark protection.

### Establishing Your Trademark Protection

Before reading this section, please watch this overview video (https://openstax.org/l/EstablishingTrademark) covering the "spectrum of distinctiveness" and other fancy-sounding legal terms and what they really mean in the real world of commerce and consumerism.

As in the case with copyrights, trademarks do not necessarily have to be registered with the federal government, but doing so has benefits. The owners of unregistered trademarks have the exclusive right to use the mark concerning similar goods and services in the geographic area of actual use of the mark, the right to bring civil action against infringers, and protection against false advertising. Unregistered trademarks are usually identified by the "TM" symbol displayed on the product, package, or advertising used to promote them. Trademarks formally registered with the USPTO, however, receive additional benefits:

- A legal presumption of ownership of the mark and exclusive right to use the mark nationwide on or in connection with the goods/services listed in the registration.
- Public notice of claim of ownership of the mark.
- The ability to bring an action concerning the mark in federal court.
- The use of the U.S. registration as a basis to obtain registration in foreign countries.
- The ability to record the U.S. registration with the U.S. Customs and Border Protection (CBP) Service to prevent importation of infringing foreign goods.
- The right to use the federal registration symbol ®
- Listing in the United States Patent and Trademark Office's online databases.[xxxv]

Because registration costs money, many small businesses choose to rely upon the common law protections afforded trademarks, especially when just starting up. A case in point was Google, which used an unregistered trademark for its first six years in operation. Only in 2006 did the company formally apply for a registered trademark for "Google." It was registered in 2012.

But trademark protection can be vital to a small business, as one recent case amply demonstrates. Payam "Peter" Tabibian first registered the 1950s-style red, white, and yellow logo for his start-up Z-Burger chain in

xxxv Derived from: http://www.uspto.gov/faq/trademarks.jsp#_Toc275426681

2007, a few months before he opened his first restaurant the next year in a hip Washington neighborhood. As the *New York Times* reported, "his first restaurant was an immediate hit, attracting students from nearby American University. The place [later] drew public praise when it gave free food to federal workers who were furloughed from their jobs during government budget cutbacks."

But Mr. Tabibian eventually fell out with his partners, who then tried to stop him from continuing to use his Z-Burger brand with his expanding chain of restaurants; they also demanded he transfer the trademarks to them.

But because Mr. Tabibian had done his homework and taken the time to properly register his trademarks, a federal judge ruled in August of 2015 that he was the legitimate owner of the trademarks and could continue to use them.

As James Gibson, law professor at the University of Richmond School of Law, told the *New York Times*, the Z-Burger case shows why "it is very important early on to pick a trademark that's going to work, and make sure ownership is sewn on. That's particularly true if nobody knows who you are and you're operating in a limited area. The federal trademark gives you a lot of nationwide rights."

In order for your trademark to be eligible for registration with the USPTO, however, you must actually use it in conjunction with commercial activity—i.e., with the marketing and sale of products and services—or be about to use it within six months. Absent the selling of athletic shoes and other sports attire, Nike's $20 billion "Swoosh" logo would be nothing more than a worthless doodle.

When applying for trademark registration, the applicant must file an affidavit attesting to the date the mark was first used in commerce as well as a specimen showing how the mark was first used, whether in advertising or on the product in a store setting. It is imperative that the applicant identify the earliest provable date of first use in commerce, to lessen the likelihood that another party can claim prior use of that mark and invalidate the trademark.

The USPTO also offers an "intent-to-use" application, which allows an entity to apply for a trademark that is not yet used in commerce.

"If you have not yet used the mark but plan to do so in the future, you may file based on a good faith or bona fide intent to use the mark in commerce," notes a USPTO publication. "A bona fide intent to use the mark is more than an idea, [but] less than market ready. For example, having a business plan, creating sample products, or performing other initial business activities may reflect a bona fide intent to use the mark."[xxxvi]

The mark must then be put into use within six months of receiving a "notice of allowance" from the USPTO or the applicant risks having to pay extension fees or losing the mark entirely.

If the trademark is still in commercial use five years after registration, the owner is eligible to receive an additional protection known as "incontestability," which immunizes the mark from many challenges, including challenges to validity, ownership, registration, and descriptiveness. (Incontestable marks can still be challenged on some grounds, such as genericism, functionality, and abandonment.) To receive incontestability status, a § 15 Declaration must be submitted to the USPTO.

Once incontestability is achieved, no one can contest the validity, ownership, or registration of the mark, nor can anyone contest the owner's exclusive right to use the mark. An individual or a corporate entity can register a mark.

A trademark can be assigned to others in the event of purchase or acquisition by another entity.

xxxvi *Protecting Your Trademark: Basic Facts About Trademarks*, U.S. Patent and Trademark Office, derived from: http://www.uspto.gov/trademarks/basics/BasicFacts.pdf

The §15 Declaration must include:

A. The registration number and the date of registration.
B. The fee for each class of goods/services in the registration to which the Declaration pertains.
C. A statement that declares: *-The mark has been in continuous use in commerce for a period of five years and is still in use in commerce -No final decision exists adverse to the owner's claim of ownership of the mark for the goods/services, or to the owner's right to register the mark or to keep the same on the register -No pending proceeding exists involving the claimed rights in the USPTO or in the courts*
D. A signed and dated affidavit or declaration under 37 C.F.R. §2.20[xxxvii]

There are other reasons why an owner might assign trademarks to another party, including a business name change, a security agreement, a license, a lien, as collateral for a loan, or as a result of a bankruptcy procedure. Ford used its trademarks as collateral for a $23.5 billion loan. Ford was still able to use its trademarks, but if the company had defaulted on the loan, the trademarks would have been assigned to the lender.[xxxviii]

Just like tangible assets, trademarks and other intellectual property such as patents and copyrights often have enormous value. In fact, some sources estimate that in contrast to 40 years ago, when plant, equipment, and other tangible assets comprised 80 percent of the market value of most public companies, today it is intangible assets like intellectual property, business methods, and know-how that make up roughly 80 percent of the value of public companies.[xxxix]

**Figure 4.12** The official logo of the Ford Motor Company. Ford was still able to keep its trademarks, as long as it didn't default on the

xxxvii United States Patent and Trademark Office. (21 August, 2012). *Maintain/Renew a Registration: How to Keep a Registration Alive.* Retrieved from http://www.uspto.gov/trademarks/process/maintain/prfaq.jsp

xxxviii CBS News. (23 May, 2012). *Ford Regains Assets, Including Blue Logo, After Credit Upgrade.* Retrieved from http://www.cbsnews.com/8301-505164_162-57440003-10391734/ford-regainsassets-including-blue-logo-after-credit-upgrade/

xxxix "Intangible Asset Market Value," Ocean Tomo, Retrieved from: http://bit.ly/1gldnWL

loan. (credit: JD Hancock via flikr / CC BY 2.0)

Trademarks can also be licensed to others. In 2012, licensed trademarks generated $5.45 billion for North American owners, reported the Licensing Industry Merchandisers' Association. That same year, the top 150 global brand licensors earned $230 billion in sales of trademarked products, with the Walt Disney Company alone accounting for nearly $40 billion in sales.

Abandonment of a mark results in loss of ownership and the associated rights of the mark. For a mark to be considered abandoned, it must be discontinued from active use in commerce with no intent to resume the commercial use of the mark. Evidence of nonuse for three consecutive years is usually considered to be sufficient proof of abandonment. Upon abandonment, the trademark owner loses the right to prevent others from infringing the mark.

## 4.9 Trademark Infringement

### Learning Objectives

After completing this section, you will be able to

- Identify the factors involved in trademark infringement.
- Understand the basis for determining similarity.

### Trademark Infringement and Remedies

Before reading this section, please watch this overview video (https://openstax.org/l/WhatIfInfringeTrademark) covering similarity, market confusion, vicarious infringement, and getting back what's yours.

The purpose of trademarks is to enable consumers to distinguish the source of products and services as well as help businesses defend the quality and reputation of those goods. Trademarks benefit society by protecting consumers and businesses alike, and by preventing confusion in the marketplace. This principle lies at the heart of the trademark system.

It is also the basis on which the courts rule on claims of trademark infringement. The most common way that trademark infringement causes confusion is through **similarity**. In the words of the Lanham Act, no trademark may be registered "which so resembles" another name or mark that it will be likely "to cause confusion, or to cause mistake, or to deceive."[xl]

To determine similarity, the mark must be evaluated as a whole rather than through its individual components. This is important because there are only a limited number of parts—words, names, shapes, symbols, or devices—that can be used separately or together to create a unique and distinctive trademark that indicates the origin of goods.

The courts generally look at five key factors to determine if a defendant's use of your mark is likely to cause confusion among consumers.

The two most important are:

- The similarity in the overall impression created by the two marks (including the marks' look, phonetic similarities, and underlying meanings)
- The similarities of the goods and services involved.

But the court also looks at three other factors:

- The strength of your mark.
- Any evidence of actual confusion by consumers.
- The intent of the defendant in adopting its mark.

xl See 15 U.S.C. § 1052 Retrieved from http://www.law.cornell.edu/uscode/text/15/1052

The basis for determining similarity, again, is not an assessment of the similarity between each component of two trademarks but of their totality as seen and experienced by the consumer. And the key test for similarity is **resemblance**, not **sameness**. In short, two marks do not have to be exact mirror images of each other to be legally similar. According to a 2003 decision by the U.S. Court of Appeals for the Federal Circuit, "Similarity is not a binary factor but is a matter of degree."[xli] Each and every attribute of a mark need not be replicated exactly by those of another mark to be deemed similar. But the more one mark's attributes are similar to those of another, the greater the likelihood that there is legal similarity between the marks as a whole.

The social networking site LinkedIn, for example, sports a logo made up of the joined words "Linked" and "in" displayed in a white font with the "in" component surrounded by a blue colored square with rounded edges. If a new networking site for professionals was launched that featured a logo with the same words except that the "in" component was surrounded by a red colored square, there would likely be enough similarity between the two logos to justify a case for infringement. The colors of one component of the logo may be different, but when the concept, wording, font style, and design are considered as a whole, any judge or jury would probably find the similarity between the marks so substantial as to constitute infringement.

But similarity is not the only basis for assessing infringement. The question is also whether any similarity between marks is likely to cause confusion in the minds of consumers. This takes into account such factors as the similarity of the goods and services on which the two marks are being used. If a company that made metal chains called itself "LinkedIn," that would less likely cause consumers to believe that the chains came from the same source as the social networking site, because the manufacture of chains is a very different line of business than running a social networking site.

An entity can be guilty of **contributory infringement** if it intentionally encourages the infringement of a valid mark by a third party. One can also be liable for contributory infringement if one continues to produce or distribute a product with knowledge that the beneficiary is infringing a mark. As the Supreme Court held in the 1982 case *Inwood Labs., Inc. v. Ives Labs., Inc.* (https://www.openstax.org/l/InwoodVIves), "If a manufacturer or distributor intentionally induces another to infringe a trademark, or if it continues to supply its product to one whom it knows or has reason to know is engaging in trademark infringement, the manufacturer or distributor is contributorily responsible for any harm done as a result of the deceit."[xlii]

> *"If a manufacturer or distributor intentionally induces another to infringe a trademark, or if it continues to supply its product to one whom it knows or has reason to know is engaging in trademark infringement, the manufacturer or distributor is contributorily responsible for any harm done as a result of the deceit."*[xliii]
>
> *-Inwood Labs., Inc. v. Ives Labs., Inc.*

Another type of infringement is **vicarious infringement**. The definition of vicarious infringement is somewhat convoluted, but Cornell University's Legal Information Institute describes it thusly:

> "A person may be held liable for the infringing acts committed by another if he or she had the right and ability to control the infringing activities and had a direct financial interest in such activities. The existence of direct infringement is required to establish a claim of vicarious infringement; however, it is not necessary for the alleged infringer to have intent or knowledge of the infringement."[xliv]

---

xli In re Coors Brewing Co., Fed. Cir. 2003 Retrieved from: http://www.ipo.org/AM/Template.cfm?Section=Federal_Circuit_Opinions&ContentID=4174&template=/CM/ContentDisplay.cfm.

xlii *Inwood Labs., Inc. v. Ives Labs., Inc.*, 456 U.S. 844, 854 (1982) Retrieved from http://scholar.google.com/scholar_case?case=5946191720195736097&hl=en&as_sdt=2&as_vis=1&oi=scholarr.

xliii *Inwood Labs., Inc. v. Ives Labs., Inc.*, 456 U.S. 844, 854 (1982) Retrieved from http://scholar.google.com/scholar_case?case=5946191720195736097&hl=en&as_sdt=2&as_vis=1&oi=scholarr.

xliv Derived from: http://www.law.cornell.edu/wex/vicarious_infringement.

Vicarious infringement most often occurs on Internet sites that allow outside parties to post or upload files. One such example was *Sega Enters., Ltd. v. MAPHIA* (https://www.openstax.org/l/SegaVMAPHIA) ., in which third parties uploaded unauthorized games that displayed the Sega mark to the Maphia site with the knowledge and consent of—and to the profit of—Maphia owners.

Finally, there is a form of harm called **trademark dilution**, which is described by the International Trademark Association as "the weakening of a famous mark's ability to identify and distinguish goods or services, regardless of competition in the marketplace or the likelihood of confusion. Dilution typically occurs as the result of blurring or tarnishment of the famous mark. . . . The concept of dilution developed from the idea that because some marks are so well-known and famous, they deserve an extra level of protection beyond the likelihood-of-confusion analysis. Dilution theory seeks to prevent the coexistence of a mark that is sufficiently similar to a famous mark, regardless of the goods and/or services associated with the allegedly diluting mark."

The Federal Trademark Dilution Act of 1995 and the Federal Dilution Revision Act of 2006 created a federal cause of action for trademark dilution that is separate from infringement. Generally speaking, an owner of a trademark eligible for dilution protection can prevent another company from using that mark no matter how dissimilar the goods and services of the two companies are. That makes dilution protection potentially broader in scope than infringement protection. After the 2006 revision, however, only marks that are "widely recognized by the general consuming public of the United States" are eligible for dilution protection, which means that only a very small percentage of trademarks used in the United States—undoubtedly less than 1 percent—qualify for that protection. Google has protection against dilution. Your local dry cleaner does not.

## 4.10 Trademark Remedies

### Learning Objectives

After completing this section, you will be able to

- Explain remedies for trademark infringement.
- Discuss effects of infringement.

Remedies for trademark infringement are similar to those available to owners of other intellectual property, including the possibility of receiving monetary damages for lost profits and injunctive relief. But even more so than is the case with patent and copyright owners, trademark owners almost invariably insist on injunctive (e.g. prohibiting continued sales) to cure the infringement. That's because when a trademark is infringed, the biggest loss to the owner is not necessarily revenue but the potential damage to the reputation of the brand in the minds of consumers.

Imagine, for example, that a manufacturer in Bangladesh started shipping substandard athletic shoes with the Nike "Swoosh" on them into the U.S. market. The loss of revenue resulting from U.S. customers mistakenly buying the Bangladeshi manufacturer's counterfeit shoes might not amount even to a rounding error on Nike's books. But if customers began to lose trust in the "Swoosh" symbol as a reliable indicator of Nike's quality design and manufacturing, the damage to Nike's brand and future profits could be significant. The company would want to secure an immediate injunction against the importation of the offending shoes and thereby stop the ongoing damage to its trademark and brand.

Incidentally, in cases where the products being imported are not patented or copyrighted, the courts may only require the importer to stop use of the mark, but allow for the continued importation of the product.[xlv]

In addition to injunctive relief, monetary damages may also be awarded in trademark infringement cases. Monetary damages are primarily aimed at compensating trademark owners for lost profits due to the infringing activity, and may be trebled if the infringement is deemed intentional. The courts may base an

xlv See *William R. Warner & Co. v. Eli Lilly & Co.*, 265 U.S. 526 (1924) Retrieved from http://caselaw.lp.findlaw.com/scripts/getcase.pl?court=us&vol=265&invol=526.

award on any or all of the following measures:

- The defendant's profits, either as an indicator of the plaintiff's loss or under an unjust enrichment theory.
- Actual business damages and losses suffered by the mark owner as a result of the infringement, including lost profits and the cost of notifying customers.
- Punitive damages to punish the infringer (available in state courts only)
- Reasonable attorneys' fees incurred by the mark owner to prosecute the case.

## 4.11 Fair Use of Trademarks

**Figure 4.13** (credit: Kellogg's via Wikimedia Commons / Public domain)

### Learning Objectives

After completing this section, you will be able to

- Discuss fair use of trademarks.
- Identify examples of fair use cases.

Not every use of a trademark is infringement.

Individuals and entities may be permitted the fair use of another's trademark under two conditions. These are known as **nominative fair use** and **classic fair use**.

**Nominative fair use** covers many occasions on which a party other than the trademark owner is using the mark another party to refer to genuine goods or services. An example of nominative fair use is when an auto repair shop advertises that it repairs BMWs and Hondas. It is using the mark "Honda" to refer to cars genuinely produced by the Honda Motor Company, and simply asserting that it is able to conduct repairs on those cars. Another example of nominative fair use is use of a competitor's trademark in comparative advertising. When Verizon advertises that it has better coverage than AT&T, it is making nominative fair use of

AT&T's mark because it is actually referring to AT&T's services.

Under nominative fair use, the entity using the trademark is permitted to use only so much of the mark as is necessary to identify the good or service to which it is referring, and cannot imply any sponsorship or endorsement by the mark holder (unless, of course, the repair shop really is a BMW- or Honda- approved repair facility). Another example is the use of another's trademark for the purpose of a product review.

**Classic fair use** occurs when a trademark is used in good faith for its primary meaning, and no consumer confusion is likely to occur. Classic fair uses typically involve marks that are descriptive. For example, even though Kellogg's has gained secondary meaning for the mark "All Bran," another cereal manufacturer might be able to describe its cereal as "all bran," if indeed it consists entirely of the hard outer layers of cereal grains.

Although fair use of trademarks is in many ways similar to the fair use of copyrights, there are differences. Under copyright law, you can use a copyright for the purpose of parody. You can also use trademarks for the purpose of parody, but whoever does so must be very careful to avoid confusion in the marketplace and diluting or tarnishing the trademark in question.

## Assessment Questions

1. What is the purpose of the intellectual property right we call a trademark?
   A. To protect the inventions of businesses.
   B. To indicate the origin of goods or services.
   C. To reward businesses for their creative works.

2. Which of the following is NOT true of trademarks?
   A. They protect the public by preventing confusion or deception about the source of goods and services.
   B. They protect the market reputation and goodwill of the producers of goods.
   C. They are granted at the moment of creation.
   D. They are excellent marketing and advertising tools.

3. How much did Nike pay a graphic designer in 1971 to produce its swoosh logo now estimated to be worth as much as $20 billion?
   A. $850,000.
   B. $25,000.
   C. $35.

4. What value do trademarks provide society?
   A. They encourage and reward creative enterprise.
   B. They marshal the benefits of this creativity to the public good.
   C. They protect the consumer from deception.
   D. All of the above.

5. What is the legal foundation for federal trademark law?
   A. The Commerce Clause of the U.S. Constitution.
   B. Article 1, Section 8 of the U.S. Constitution.
   C. State laws.

6. How are trademarks different from patents and copyrights?
   A. They are not limited in duration.
   B. They do not hinder the sale of similar products and services by others.
   C. They cannot be obtained by mere adoption, but only through commercial use.
   D. All of the above are true statements.

7. Why did trademarks not emerge until the start of widespread trade in the Bronze Age?
   A. There was no government agency to register trademarks before that time.
   B. That was when written records of trademarks could be printed.
   C. Widespread trade requires a certain level of public trust in the provenance and quality of goods, which trademarks helped to build.

8. Besides indicating the source of a good or service, how did trademarks change with the emergence of guilds in the Middle Ages?
   A. The guilds issued trademarks only to their own members.
   B. They became a means by which guilds could ensure the quality of work done by guild members.
   C. The guilds started charging money to issue a trademark.

**9.** What is one of the oldest trademarks still in existence?
A. The Royal Dutch Tulip Company.
B. Wedgewood china.
C. Löwenbräu Brewery.

**10.** What is the significance of an old lawsuit known as *Sanforth's Case*?
A. It proves that 250 years before the Industrial Revolution, trademark infringement was viewed as deceit and a violation of laws against unfair competition.
B. It is the first trademark infringement case known to be recorded.
C. It serves as the foundation for modern trademark laws and policies.
D. All of the above.

**11.** What caused U.S. trademark laws to evolve from a patchwork of state laws into a unitary federal trademark system?
A. The Industrial Revolution transformed America's many local and regional markets into a unified national economy.
B. Producers of goods and services began to grow into national entities.
C. State laws often conflicted with each other.
D. All of the above.

**12.** Why were the first two national trademark laws ruled unconstitutional by the Supreme Court?
A. The court ruled that they infringed on non-trademark owners' first amendment rights to free speech.
B. The court ruled in 1879 that the patent and copyright clauses of the Constitution gave Congress no authority to regulate trademarks.
C. The court ruled that they were too vaguely written.

**13.** What was the chief weakness of the Trade Mark Act of 1881?
A. It only regulated the trademarks used in commerce with other nations and with Indian tribes.
B. It only allowed for the registration but not the enforcement of trademarks.
C. It derived its authority from the Commerce Clause of the U.S. Constitution.

**14.** The Lanham Act is the principal federal law on trademarks in the United States. Which of the following was NOT a feature of trademark law enacted by the act?
A. It broadened the national system of trademark registration.
B. It set the trademark renewal period.
C. It required registration of trademarks before owners could gain access to the federal courts for redress.
D. It established remedies in the case of infringement.

**15.** When does federal law create a presumption of trademark abandonment?
A. When its owner ceases to use it in commerce.
B. When its owner ceases to employ it throughout the national territory of the United States.
C. When its owner ceases to use the trademark in commerce for three or more years.

**16.** Of the four individual types of marks, what does a trademark identify?
A. Services provided to either consumers or other businesses.
B. Physical goods or commodities that are manufactured, produced, grown, or that exist naturally.
C. Both of the above.

17. A collective mark identifies a trademark owned by a member of a certain organization. True or False?
    A. True.
    B. False.

18. A certification mark indicates what?
    A. The certified or verified origin of a product or service.
    B. A product or service that meets certain standards or requirements.

19. A trademark may be a word (or phrase), name, symbol, or device. Which of these do the following trademarks represent?
    A. Chanel handbags.
    B. The MGM lion's roar.
    C. Tiffany's blue color.
    D. The power-on chime in Apple's Mac computers.

20. Why has no company been able to gain trademark protection for "87 Octane" as a brand of gasoline?
    A. It's a number.
    B. It's not trade dress.
    C. It doesn't indicate the origin of the gas—whether Exxon, Shell, or another company.

21. What's the difference between a design protected as a trademark and trade dress?
    A. A trademark-protected design consists of a discrete symbol or logo on the product or service, whereas trade dress is its overall "look and feel."
    B. A trademarked trade dress covers a product or service's overall features like its size, shape, and color combinations rather than a particular symbol or design.
    C. Both of these.

22. In what way are trademarked designs and trade dress similar to design patents?
    A. All three protect the unique look of a company's products from being infringed.
    B. All three protect only the nonfunctional elements of the product's appearance.
    C. Both of these.

23. What is the trademark world's corollary to novelty in patents?
    A. Non-obviousness.
    B. Distinctiveness.
    C. Originality.

24. Of the following five categories of marks—fanciful, arbitrary, suggestive, descriptive, and generic—which one of them can never be protected as a trademark?
    A. Descriptive.
    B. Generic.
    C. Fanciful.

25. Which kind of mark is owned by the following companies?
    A. Apple.
    B. Xerox.
    C. Coppertone.
    D. Windows.

**26.** Why was the store Toys "R" Us able to gain trademark protection for its name, even though "toys" is a generic word used by thousands of toy stores nationwide?

A. Because Toys "R" Us was the first to use the name "toys" and thus has priority.
B. Because Toys "R" Us was the first to use the name nationwide.
C. Because of the fanciful spelling of its name.

**27.** Why did "Cellophane" and "Aspirin" lose their trademarks

A. The original companies making these products went out of business.
B. The public came to associate the name with an entire category of similar products.

**28.** What are some of the bars to getting a trademark?

A. The prior use bar.
B. The functionality bar.
C. Subject matter bars.
D. All of the above.

**29.** If geographic marks that are deceptively misdescriptive are ineligible for trademark protection, then why was Amazon able to gain trademark protection for its name, which refers to a geographic area of South America?

A. The name "Amazon" is not indicative of the geographic source of the retailer's goods, nor do consumers think those goods come from the Amazonian region.
B. The name "Amazon" is not a factor in whether or not consumers decide to purchase books, clothing, electronics, or anything else from the company.
C. Amazon's brand stands for low prices and great customer service, not for anything of a geographic nature.
D. All of the above.

**30.** As with copyrights, trademarks do not have to be registered with the federal government, but doing so gives their owners all of the following additional rights EXCEPT for which one?

A. The exclusive right to use the mark in their geographic area of business.
B. The ability to seek assistance from the U.S. Customs and Border Protection Service in preventing the importation of infringing foreign goods.
C. The exclusive right to use the mark nationwide.
D. The right to use the federal registration symbol ® instead of the ™ symbol.

**31.** You can't file a trademark registration application unless you are currently engaged in business.

A. True.
B. False.

**32.** Which of the following explains why a trademark owner may assign it to another?

A. A business name change.
B. A bankruptcy proceeding.
C. As collateral for a loan.
D. All of the above.

**33.** How does trademark infringement harm consumers?

A. By confusing consumers about the source of goods or services.

B. By allowing others to "palm off" lower-quality knockoffs in place of the high-quality goods they are seeking to buy.

C. By damaging trust between consumers and providers of goods and services.

D. All of the above.

**34.** How is the "similarity" between two marks in a trademark infringement case determined?

A. By examining each individual component of a mark and seeing if another mark uses individual components that are similar.

B. By examining the totality of the two marks as seen and experienced by the consumer in the context of the goods or services on which they are used and seeing if they are similar enough to cause confusion or deception.

**35.** What is trademark dilution as opposed to trademark infringement?

A. Dilution occurs when a mark famous to the general American public is blurred or tarnished by a similar mark, regardless of whether that mark is used on similar goods or services.

B. Dilution occurs when a trademark grows weaker in the minds of consumers as a result of its owner not advertising or featuring it prominently enough on products.

**36.** Which of the following is true about trademark remedies?

A. Damages can be significantly increased if trademark infringement is deemed willful.

B. Courts frequently use injunctions based on trademark law to stop the importation of products that once carried infringing marks even after those marks have been removed.

C. Federal trademark law also provides for punitive damages for trademark infringement.

**37.** A party may be permitted the fair use of another's trademark under two conditions, known as **nominative fair use** and **classic fair use**. Which of the following is an example of nominative fair use?

A. When a business compares its products with those of a competitor, with no intent to confuse customers as to the source of the competitor's goods.

B. When a trademark of another is used to refer to that other's goods or services in legitimate connection with one's own, such as a notice on the packaging of a small company's graphic design program that it can run on the Microsoft Windows operating system.

C. Both of the above are correct.

5

# Trade Secret Basics

**Figure 5.1** (credit: modification of work "hush!" by Pixel Addict/flikr.com, CC BY 2.0)

## Chapter Outline



## Introduction

## 5.1 Trade Secret Protection

**Figure 5.2** (credit: modification of work by Michael Galpert via flickr / CC BY 2.0)

### Learning Objectives

After completing this section, you will be able to

- Define trade secrets.
- Identify the advantages and disadvantages of protecting intellectual property through trade secrets.

### What Is a Trade Secret?

**Trade secret** law is a source of protection for intellectual property that serves as an alternative to patent or trademark law. Whereas patent and trademark law require that the intellectual property to be protected be publicly "disclosed" (for example, through a patent application), trade secret law requires precisely the opposite—that is, that the intellectual property to be protected *not* be publicly disclosed. The subject matter of a trade secret may be virtually any information that is of value as a result of not being generally known.

There is enormous **economic value** in trade secrets—for companies and countries. A study released in March of 2014 estimated that trade secret misappropriation costs the world's top 40 economies between 1 percent and 3 percent of their gross domestic product each year.[i]

Unlike copyright and patent law, there is no formal requirement of "novelty" or "tangibility" under trade secret law. Rather, trade secret protection is extended to information that has independent economic value by virtue of not being generally known or readily ascertainable by others, and which has been subject to reasonable efforts to avoid public disclosure.

### Advantages and Disadvantages of Trade Secret Law

There are both advantages and disadvantages to protecting intellectual property through the use of trade secret law. The decision of whether to use trade secret law as opposed to other legal means of protecting knowledge or information is governed primarily by the nature of the intellectual property to be protected.

### Advantages

One of the main advantages of trade secret law is that it provides indefinite future protection. Unlike the 20-year time limit that underlies the protection granted to a patent holder, there is no definite time limit

i "*Economic Impact of Trade Secret Theft*," PricewaterhouseCoopers, retrieved from: http://pwc.to/1sVx3AP

placed on the protection granted to a trade secret owner. This indefinite future protection granted to trade secrets is appealing, assuming that the intellectual property to be protected is likely to remain generally unknown well into the future. For example, if the intellectual property to be protected is a method of manufacturing a product that can be determined from examining the product, then the best way to protect the new method of manufacture might be through a patent. On the other hand, if the new method of manufacturing the product cannot be determined from examination of the product, then the best way to protect the intellectual property might be to treat it as a trade secret.

### Disadvantages

Although there is no definite expiration of the protection granted to trade secrets, the protection prohibits only the disclosure or use of the trade secret by one to whom the secret was disclosed in confidence. Unlike patent law, trade secret law does not offer any affirmative protection against the use of the same intellectual property that is independently derived or reverse engineered by a competitor. Consequently, if the intellectual property to be protected is a new method of manufacturing a product, and if that method of manufacture is ascertainable from an examination of the product, then the best form of protection for the intellectual property is most likely that offered by patent law.

The same analysis applies to intellectual property that is likely to be independently derived by a competitor. For as the U.S. Supreme Court noted in *Bonito Boats v. Thunder Craft Boats* (https://www.openstax.org/l/BonitoVThunderCraft),[ii] state trade secret law has never given the holder of a trade secret protection against reverse engineering by the public or a competitor. The Supreme Court commented that in order to receive protection from reverse engineering, the holder of the intellectual property must seek the protection of federal patent law.

**Pros and Cons of Trade Secret Law**

| Pros | Cons |
|---|---|
| Trade secret law provides indefinite future protection, so long as the trade secret stays a secret. Trade secret protection has no expiration date. | If someone came up with the same idea on their own, the trade secret is no longer protected by law. |
| Trade secret protection prevents the disclosure or use of the trade secret by one to whom the secret was disclosed in confidence. | Trade secret law does not give the holder of a trade secret protection from reverse engineering by the public or a competitor. |

**Table 5.1**

Whereas patent and trademark law involve an affirmative assertion of an intellectual property right, trade secret law only actively operates after a misappropriation or threatened misappropriation of the trade secret has occurred. Due to this difference in the way trade secret law protects intellectual property, the protections given to trade secrets are largely dependent on classifications of information made by courts. Thus, the foundation and development of trade secret law in the United States is inherently tied to the statutes protecting trade secrets, and the court decisions defining and interpreting the statutory protections created for trade secrets.

ii 489 U.S. 141 (1989).

## 5.2 The Foundations of Trade Secrets Law

### Learning Objectives

After completing this section, you will be able to

- Identify the roots of trade secret law in the United States.
- Explain the purpose of the Uniform Trade Secrets Act.

Unlike patents and copyrights that are issued in accordance with federal law, trade secret protection until very recently emanated from state law. But on May 11, 2016, the federal Defend Trade Secrets Act (DTSA) was signed into law, thereby creating a federal cause of action for trade secret misappropriation that largely mirrors the current state of the law under the Uniform Trade Secrets Act (UTSA), which has been adopted by 48 states.

Trade secret law in the United States is largely rooted in the English legal tradition, and was first incorporated through the court-made common law. The general consensus is that trade secret law originated in England in the early 1800s.[iii] Early cases dealt with trade secret concepts not in modern trade secret vernacular but instead through the guise of jurisdictional or restraint of trade terms. The trade secret concept began in American jurisprudence in the case of *Vickery v. Welch* (https://www.openstax.org/l/VickeryVWelch) , 36 Mass. 523 (1837). The Massachusetts Supreme Court first expounded on trade secret law in modern terms in *Peabody v. Norfolk* (https://www.openstax.org/l/PeabodyVNorfolk) , 98 Mass. 452 (1868). In the 145 years since the Peabody decision, the courts, including numerous federal courts, have addressed trade secret issues and have contributed to the current body of trade secret law. However, because each state may regulate trade secret law independently, each state has developed its own legal regime, involving a mixture of both statutes and common law, to regulate and protect trade secrets.

### Uniform Trade Secrets Act

In an effort to harmonize and standardize trade secret law in the United States, the Uniform Law Commission[iv] published the Uniform Trade Secrets Act (UTSA) (https://www.openstax.org/l/UTSA) in 1979. The UTSA sought to create a uniform trade secret law regime from state to state. However, the UTSA itself was not binding upon states at publication. In order for the UTSA to be successful, the states themselves needed to adopt and enact the model UTSA statute created by the commission. In 1980, Minnesota became the first state to adopt the UTSA. Since 1980, most states have adopted the UTSA, many with the 1985 amendments to the act. New York and Massachusetts remain the last states that have yet to adopt the UTSA. Although the UTSA harmonized various state law approaches to trade secrets, each state enacts the UTSA with any modifications or customizations the state legislature desires to make. Thus, although most states have adopted the UTSA, each state may have a slightly different adaptation of the UTSA.

One important provision of the UTSA is section 7, which deals with the interaction of the UTSA and state law. Section 7 preempts certain state law causes of action. Section 7 "displaces conflicting tort, restitutionary, and other law...providing civil remedies for misappropriation of a trade secret."

### Trade Secret Misappropriation

Although this section seems to indicate that the UTSA broadly replaces all state laws dealing with **misappropriation** of trade secrets, there is debate as to what constitutes "conflicting tort, restitutionary, and other law." Additionally, what it means for a common law remedy to be "based on" misappropriation of a

---

iii Michael Risch, Why Do We Have Trade Secrets?, 11 Intellectual Property L. Rev. 1 (2007) (citing Restatement (Third) of Unfair Competition § 39 cmt. a (1995).

iv The Uniform Law Commission, also known as the National Conference of Commissioners on Uniform State Laws, is a nonpartisan, nonprofit organization that promotes the uniformity of law from state to state. The Commission publishes "model laws" that states are then able to adopt and enact.

trade secret is often contested. Owners seeking to recover damages for misappropriation generally argue that only common law causes of action that have elements identical to the UTSA are preempted, while defendants argue that any cause of action used to protect trade secrets is preempted because it is duplicative of the UTSA. Despite this potential conflict between the UTSA and state common law, this chapter focuses on the main body of trade secret law as governed by the UTSA.

## 5.3 Elements of a Trade Secret

### Learning Objectives

After completing this section, you will be able to

- Identify the key criteria used to qualify as a trade secret.
- Explain how ideas can be protected as trade secrets.

To qualify as a trade secret, the information in question must meet two essential criteria. First, the information must attain its value from the fact that it is not generally known.

Second, the owner of that information must take reasonable efforts to maintain its secrecy. Absent these two elements, information does not qualify as a trade secret and is not entitled to trade secret protections that prevent or remedy misappropriation under the UTSA.[v]

Trade secrets are not limited to particular subject matters, although the knowledge or information to be protected need not take any particular form. A trade secret can be information or knowledge in the form of a formula, pattern, compilation, program, device, method, technique, or process. Although the UTSA defines what may be a trade secret, various courts interpreting the UTSA have come to different conclusions on what type of material should be considered a trade secret. For example, whereas courts have found that an insurer's database is a trade secret under Wisconsin law, a similar database was found not to be a trade secret in Rhode Island.[vi]

### The Value of Secrets

For information or knowledge in any of the above forms to be considered a trade secret, it must derive independent economic value because it is not generally known to, nor readily ascertainable by, other persons who can profit from its disclosure or use. Some examples of information courts have found to be trade secrets include computer software, sales information, customer information, and manufacturing formulas. However, merely because information is not known to the public does not necessarily make the information a trade secret. For example, information that is not generally known by the public but is known by different manufacturers in the same industry likely does not qualify as a trade secret.[vii]

---

v The UTSA defines a trade secret as "information, including a formula, pattern, compilation, program, device, method, technique, or process, that (i) derives independent economic value, actual or potential, from not being generally known to, and not being readily ascertainable by proper means by, other persons who can obtain value from its disclosure or use, and (ii) is the subject of efforts that are reasonable under the circumstances to maintain its secrecy."

vi Compare *American Fam. Mut. Ins. Co. v. Roth* 485 F.3d 930, 933 (7th Cir. 2007); *APG Inc. v. MCI Telecommunications Corp.* 436 F.3d 294, 307 (1st Cir 2006).

vii See e.g. *Ruckelshaus v. Monsanto Co.*, 467 U.S. 986, 1002 (1984); *Speedry Chemical Products, Inc. v. Carter's Ink Co.*, 306 F.2d 328, 331 (2d Cir 1962).

Material that is ascertainable through public sources generally does not derive independent economic value justifying trade secret protection. If the information in question cannot be quickly or easily ascertained from examining or testing the publicly available product, then it is more likely to be a trade secret.[viii] Conversely, if the information may be discovered through public observation of the product or the company's displays, it is unlikely to be a trade secret.[ix] For example, customer lists are not considered trade secrets when the identity of the customers could potentially be discovered through public sources. However, identical information if not available through public sources could constitute a trade secret.[x] Additionally, processes or systems that are simply a compilation of known information generally do not rise to the level of trade secrets. The courts, however, are still quite divided on this issue.

**Figure 5.3** (credit: modification of work by Nial Bradshaw via flickr / CC BY 2.0)

## Protecting Ideas as Trade Secrets

In addition to information, certain ideas may constitute trade secrets. Although ideas were not protected as trade secrets under common law, the UTSA provides protection for certain novel and concrete ideas. For example, remedies for misappropriation of an idea may be permitted based on the existence of a confidential relationship. The elements that must be proven under this common theory are: (1) a novel or original idea; (2) reduced to concrete form; (3) disclosed to the defendant in a confidential relationship, i.e., one in which it would be implied that use would not be made without compensation; and, (4) used by the defendant.

Protection of an idea may also be permitted on the basis of a contractual relationship with the defendant. Parties may enter into a contract to protect an idea being submitted or disclosed to another person or company. The major benefit of a contract to the submitter of an idea is evidence of a protected disclosure that is deserving of trade secret protections. The major benefit of a contract to the recipient of an idea is the establishment of the ground rules under which compensation, if any, will be payable to the submitter.

Corporations that receive unsolicited ideas many times grapple with how to best protect use of those unsolicited ideas. To protect themselves from the uncertainties of trade secrets law, the idea must be converted from an unsolicited idea to a solicited idea. This may be accomplished by contacting the submitter and alerting them that the idea will be considered only with the understanding that the use of the idea, and decisions regarding compensation for that idea, rest solely with the corporation.

Whether the trade secret takes the form of information or an idea, the owner of that trade secret must show

viii See *Morlife, Inc. v. Perry*, 56 Cal. App. 4th 1514 (1st Dist. 1997).

ix See *MicroStrategy Inc. v. Business Objects*, S.A., 331 F. Supp. 2d 396,417 (E.D. Va. 2004).

x Compare *Inflight Newspapers, Inc. v. Magazines In-Flight, LLC*, 990 F. Supp. 119, 129-30 (E.D.N.Y. 1997) (holding that the plaintiff's customer lists were not trade secrets because the customer identity could be easily found through publicly available means, such as the Internet, trade shows, and trade directories) with *North Atl. Instruments, Inc. v. Haber*, 188 F.3d 38, 44 (2d Cir. N.Y. 1999) (finding that a customer list kept in confidence may be treated as a trade secret).

not only that the trade secret was not generally known or readily ascertainable, but also that the lack of general knowledge of the trade secret conferred some value to the owner. When the owner derives a profit from licensing the use of the protected information, the value to the owner is quite apparent. However, in cases where the owner is seeking to show he was injured in the marketplace or through the loss of profits after costly research and development, the value may only become apparent by inference. But even if information is not generally known and gives the owner some value, the information is not a trade secret unless the owner takes steps to protect the secrecy of the information.

## 5.4 The Secrecy Requirement

**Figure 5.4** (credit: Rob Pongsajapan via flickr / CC BY 2.0)

### Learning Objectives

After completing this section, you will be able to

- Explain the steps that businesses can take in order to protect trade secrets.
- Describe how trade secrets can be accessed through passive and active disclosure.

The second element necessary to gain trade secret protection is evidence that the trade secret's owner made a reasonable effort to maintain secrecy. This flexible standard set out by the UTSA is often a point of contention, which results in litigation. To determine whether a piece of information rises to the level of a trade secret, courts often engage in a highly factual inquiry into the security measures taken by the owner to protect a trade secret. For as the Supreme Court has noted, if an owner has not taken steps to protect the trade secret, their proprietary interests may be diminished.[xi]

### Under Company Lock and Key

Because the UTSA may be varied by any state, the level of secrecy required varies from state to state. For

xi See *Ruckelshaus v. Monsanto Co.*, 467 U.S. 986, 1002 (1984).

example, a version of the UTSA adopted by some states contains a provision that reduces the burden of secrecy placed on the owner of a trade secret. Specifically, this version of the UTSA provides that the existence of a trade secret is not negated merely because an employee or other person has acquired the trade secret without express or specific notice that it is a trade secret if, under all the circumstances, the employee or other person knows or has reason to know that the owner intends or expects the secrecy of the type of information comprising the trade secret to be maintained. Although this provision tips the scales in favor of trade secret protection, it should not be viewed as removing the affirmative obligation the UTSA places on one seeking protection of trade secrets. In both states that have and have not modified the UTSA in this manner, the measures taken to secure the information are key to finding whether the information will be protected as a trade secret.

Because trade secret protection is only given to information that is subject to reasonable efforts to maintain secrecy, every person or company that desires to protect its trade secrets under the UTSA should adopt and implement a trade secret protection plan. The specific elements of such a plan will vary depending on the nature of the intellectual property to be protected, as well as the circumstances surrounding its development and use. However, in taking reasonable efforts to protect the secrecy of the information, many different factors are considered. Because no rigid formula exists to determine if reasonable efforts to maintain secrecy are in place, courts look to many of the best practices, discussed below, to determine whether an owner of information made reasonable efforts to protect its secrecy.

## Protection Plans

Memorializing a trade secret protection plan in writing helps to ensure that the business or person is indeed taking reasonable measures to protect the trade secret. The person or company seeking to protect its intellectual property through the use of trade secret law should maintain a written statement of its trade secret security policy. This statement can be written in the form of a policy manual and helps prevent situations in which "unwritten rules" are followed or rules are enforced in a lax manner and then eventually ignored. Moreover, should litigation become necessary, it is easier to persuade a court that the security procedures were indeed a primary concern if they are enumerated in writing. However, if security measures are merely written, but not followed, it may be difficult to prove reasonable efforts to maintain secrecy.[xii]

A trade secret protection plan should include a program for ensuring that employees are made aware of the trade secret status of information and that the employees are periodically reminded of their confidentiality obligations. Discussions between the employer and the employee may be appropriate. Writing an annual conflict of interest letter to remind management-level employees of their responsibilities in keeping information confidential may also suffice. An essential part of this program is making certain that employees are aware of and familiar with the written trade secret protection plan discussed above.

Employees should also be required to sign confidentiality agreements acknowledging that they have access to trade secret information, that they will not disclose or misappropriate that information, and that they will report all disclosures. Finally, "exit interviews" should be conducted for employees leaving the company. This interview provides an opportunity to remind employees of their written obligation not to disclose or misuse any trade secret information, and to extend an open door to discuss any issues or concerns that may arise in connection with their future employment.[xiii]

---

xii See *Lexis-Nexis v. Beer*, 41 F. Supp.2d 950 (D. Minn. 1999).

xiii Compare *Electro-Craft Corp. v. Controlled Motion, Inc.*, 332 N.W.2d 890 (Minn. 1983) (confidentiality agreement signed by employees failed to identify with sufficient particularity what were and were not trade secrets; plaintiff began conducting "exit interviews" ten days after litigation commenced) and *Gordon Employment, Inc. v. Jewel*, 356 N.W.2d 738 (Minn. Ct. App. 1984) (confidentiality never discussed with employees).

In addition to educating employees, reasonable efforts to protect information often include physically restricting access to trade secrets. Trade secret information should be treated differently from nonproprietary information and should, if possible, be physically segregated so that it is not readily accessible. For example, it is not uncommon to restrict visitor access to sales and administrative headquarters. In addition, access to the intellectual property should be restricted to those with a need to know or access the information. Depending on the nature of the intellectual property to be protected, reasonably restricting access to trade secrets may be as simple as segregating the information in separate file drawers, or may require measures as extreme as designating an entirely separate facility to house the intellectual property.[xiv]

If possible under the circumstances, physical security measures should be instituted, including the use of locks on doors, gates, and cabinets containing trade secrets. These physical security steps should be obvious to both employees and third parties who may have occasion to visit the area in which trade secrets are stored.[xv] These types of security measures communicate that an effort is being made to protect the information.

## Strategies for Protecting Trade Secrets

Given the ease with which documents can be reproduced, trade secrets that are reduced to writing should be treated with special care. Documents containing trade secrets should be clearly labeled with shorthand instructions that are consistent with the written trade secret protection plan. For example, documents may be marked "secret" or "confidential."[xvi] Access to these documents should be monitored and all persons allowed access to the documents should be informed of the meaning of the trade secret designation on the document and the relevant provisions of the written trade secret protection plan. This attention to detail should also be followed in arranging for proper destruction of the documents.[xvii]

Like trade secrets that are reduced to writing, trade secrets stored on a computer system are particularly susceptible to theft. Access to a computer system containing trade secrets should be restricted in accordance with the written trade secret protection plan and all physical computer- related items such as discs and printouts should contain the same trade secret legend used to identify documents containing intellectual property.

When allowing third parties, be they members of the public or business associates, access to a facility in which trade secrets are stored or used, care must be taken to ensure that trade secrets are not inadvertently disclosed. Disclosure can occur either passively or actively. **Passive disclosure** might occur by carelessly leaving documents containing trade secrets in open view when business associates from another company visit your facility. **Active disclosure** might occur during a guided tour of the facility when a tour guide reveals the nature of a project or process the company is working on or has recently perfected.[xviii]

---

xiv Id.

xv Id.

xvi See *Gemisys Corp. v. Phoenix American, Inc.*, 186 F.R.D. 551, 558-62 (N.D. Cal. 1999).

xvii *Electro-Craft Corp. v. Controlled Motion, Inc.*, 332 N.W.2d 890 (Minn. 1983) (no technical documents were marked "confidential").

xviii Id. (confidentiality procedures inadequate where, among other things, plaintiff allowed public tour of its plants).

The type of active trade secret disclosure that can occur outside of the facility where trade secrets are housed is through the dissemination of confidential information at trade shows, in magazine articles, in publications, in press releases, or during public speeches. Such disclosures often occur unwittingly because they are made by marketing executives or mid-level managers who are not themselves instrumental in the development of the trade secret and who are often charged with a goal somewhat at odds with maintaining the secrecy of intellectual property—that is, their duty often is to publicly disclose the company's achievements. Similar difficulties might arise when engineers or those responsible for the creation of trade secrets exchange ideas with their colleagues from other companies at professional seminars.[xix] One method of curtailing such disclosures is to insist that all publications, articles, and speeches be reviewed and approved by a "filter" committee prior to dissemination.[xx]

Although the very nature of many businesses requires that a company disclose its trade secrets to prospective buyers, licensees, joint venturers, or other outsiders, this does not mean that a company must surrender all rights to its trade secrets. Rather, when the company enters into a transaction with a third party, it should cautiously monitor the flow of information to the third party and document the nature of the trade secrets exposed and the specific limited use to which they may be put.[xxi] You might consider putting outsiders on notice regarding the need to keep information confidential, and even require the signing of confidentiality agreements. The standard of what constitutes reasonable efforts to maintain secrecy varies substantially depending upon the circumstances and the information that is being protected. However, the different methods of maintaining secrecy discussed above all often help to show that the information in question qualifies as a trade secret, and deserves trade secret protection.

---

xix See e.g. *Mobile Med. Int'l Corp. v. United States*, 95 Fed. Cl. 706, 739 (Fed. Cl. 2010) (finding that although plaintiff may have taken some measures to maintain the secrecy of its trade information, plaintiff's assertions of confidentiality and the steps taken to protect its information were wholly undermined by its publicly displaying a model unit at a trade show).

xx *Gallowhur Chem. Corp. v. Schwerdle*, 37 N.J. Super. 385, 117 A.2d 416, 423, 108 U.S.P.Q. 260 (1955) (information communicated in a public lecture revealed trade secret); *Fishing Concepts, Inc. v. Ross*, 1985 WL 1549 (D. Minn. 1985) (information claimed secret was revealed in article published in advertising magazine).

xxi Id.

# 5.5 Misappropriation of Trade Secrets

**Figure 5.5** (credit: Michael Galpert via flickr / CC BY 2.0)

## Learning Objectives

After completing this section, you will be able to

- Describe the differences between the misappropriation of a trade secret through improper means and disclosure without consent.
- Explain how trade secret owners use direct evidence and circumstantial evidence to prove that a misappropriation of trade secrets has occurred.

The enforcement provisions of the UTSA allow companies and individuals to protect information that qualifies as a trade secret. The protections allowed for by the UTSA are triggered by the actual or threatened "misappropriation" of trade secrets. "Misappropriation" is defined in two ways: (1) acquisition of a trade secret through improper means, or (2) disclosure or use of a trade secret without consent.

## Misappropriation through Improper Means

The first type of misappropriation under the UTSA is acquisition of a trade secret through improper means. Specifically, the UTSA prohibits the "acquisition of a trade secret of another, by a person who knows or has reason to know the trade secret was acquired by improper means."[xxii] "Improper means" includes theft, bribery, misrepresentation, breach or inducement of a breach of a duty to maintain secrecy, or espionage through electronic or other means.[xxiii] In short, the first type of misappropriation is the mere possession of a trade secret that has been acquired through theft or the breach of a duty to maintain the secrecy of the trade secret.

xxii See Unif. Trade Secrets Act § 1(2)(i), U.L.A (1985).

xxiii See Unif. Trade Secrets Act § 1(1), U.L.A (1985).

## Misappropriation through Disclosure

The second type of misappropriation under the UTSA is the disclosure or use of someone else's trade secret without their express or implied consent. Although the statutory definition is somewhat complicated, the UTSA essentially prohibits the disclosure or use of a trade secret that is possessed as a result of theft, breach of a duty to maintain its secrecy, or an accident or mistake on the part of the trade secret owner.[xxiv]

In short, the UTSA prohibits the disclosure or use of a trade secret that is possessed as a result of "improper means" as defined in the preceding paragraph. The rule of thumb is that if you possess, disclose, or use a trade secret that you know or have reason to know is not intended to be revealed to you, beware.

## UTSA's Definition of Misappropriation

The UTSA's definition of misappropriation is rather broad. The protection granted to trade secret owners under the UTSA is further expanded by prohibiting not only the actual, but also the threatened, misappropriation of trade secrets. The distinction between these two types of misappropriation is basically one of timing. The UTSA prohibits the actual disclosure of trade secrets and provides remedies for those whose trade secrets have already been misappropriated. A more difficult question arises, however, with respect to a trade secret owner's rights prior to the actual misappropriation of trade secrets. To address a trade secret owner's legitimate concerns that misappropriation may occur in the future, the UTSA prohibits "threatened" misappropriation.

A trade secret owner may assert legal rights subsequent to any actual unauthorized disclosure or use of trade secrets. In such situations, the wrong has already occurred and the trade secret owner may seek judicial intervention concerning any legal rights that were violated. This is true regardless of whether the misappropriator obtained the secret without the owner's consent, or originally with consent but later used the secret for the misappropriator's own gain.

The burden of proof in an actual misappropriation case is still squarely on the shoulders of the trade secret owner who is alleging that trade secrets have been misappropriated. This burden of proof requires the trade secret owner to demonstrate that he or she was in possession of knowledge or information that was not generally known and was valuable precisely because it was not generally known, and that the knowledge or information was subject to efforts that were reasonable under the circumstances to maintain its secrecy. Depending on the facts and circumstances of a given case, together with the nature of the intellectual property to be protected, proving the elements necessary to make out a trade secret case can be a challenging undertaking. The best way to establish a foundation for successful prosecution of trade secret misappropriation is to follow closely the provisions of a written trade secret protection plan, and take measures to ensure the security of the information as discussed above.

Perhaps the most interesting trade secret cases involve the alleged threatened misappropriation of trade secrets. In these cases, the trade secret owner does not contend that their trade secrets have already been compromised, but rather that unless some action is taken to halt the current progress of events, their trade secrets will be misappropriated at some time in the future. Threatened misappropriation cases often arise when a highly skilled or trained employee who has been exposed to a company's trade secrets leaves the company's employ and goes to work for a competitor. On the one hand, the former employer may well have legitimate concerns about possible disclosure of its trade secrets to a competitor; on the other hand, the employee has a right to choose an employer. Consequently, courts are required to balance these competing interests. The result often depends on the legitimacy of the trade secret owner's concerns of misappropriation and the nature of the evidence that is available to substantiate those concerns.

---

xxiv See Unif. Trade Secrets Act §§ 2(2)(ii)(A)-(C), U.L.A (1985).

When faced with a situation where an employee who has been exposed to trade secrets leaves to work for a new employer, courts typically consider three factors: (1) whether the former employer and the new employer are competitors, (2) whether the employee's new position is comparable to the former position, and (3) the efficacy of steps taken by the new employer to prevent the misappropriation of trade secrets.[xxv]

Mere suspicion that another party may have wrongfully disclosed or used one's trade secrets, in and of itself, does not enable the trade secret owner to assert these rights successfully. Courts will not prohibit the wrongful use or disclosure of trade secrets based upon the mere uneasiness or suspicions of the trade secret owner that some misappropriation may occur. Rather, the trade secret owner is required to demonstrate that the concerns of misappropriation are legitimate. In most situations, this means that the trade secret owner will be required to present evidence, either direct or circumstantial, that misappropriation is likely to occur.

A trade secret owner may present direct or circumstantial evidence to demonstrate that there is an imminent threatened misappropriation of trade secrets. Direct evidence exists when the trade secret owner can demonstrate that action has already been taken, or words have already been spoken, that indicate that misappropriation of trade secrets is going to occur. Common examples of direct evidence supporting a trade secret owner's legitimate concerns of threatened misappropriation are statements made by the former employee or the new employer. Former employees might make statements about the relative lack of weight they give to their former employer's confidentiality policies. Similarly, the new employer might make statements about the purpose of hiring the new employee, why other potential employees were rejected, or the nature of the duties the new employee will be required to perform. Based on evidence of such actions or statements, a court is likely to protect trade secrets by enjoining prospectively their wrongful use or disclosure.

### In the Courtroom

However, in most situations, direct evidence concerning the likelihood of misappropriation does not exist. In such cases, a trade secret owner can present circumstantial evidence to demonstrate that the unauthorized use or disclosure of trade secrets is imminently threatened. Circumstantial evidence demonstrating that imminent misappropriation is likely to occur consists of two types: (1) evidence demonstrating the intent of a party to elicit the wrongful disclosure of the trade secret, and (2) evidence demonstrating that the wrongful disclosure or use of a trade secret is inevitable regardless of any party's intentions.

Evidence demonstrating the intent of the new employer to elicit trade secrets from its new employee takes many forms. Often, a trade secret owner can show that the new employer desires the trade secret and has unsuccessfully attempted to acquire the trade secret information by proper means, either from the trade secret owner, other parties, or independent derivation or reverse engineering.[xxvi] The new employer's intent to misappropriate trade secrets can also be demonstrated by showing that the new employer solicited the trade secret owner's employees and has not made any efforts to solicit employees from the industry in general. Other facts, such as access to a common supplier, access to a former consultant, or failed prior attempts to duplicate technology can also contribute to a circumstantial showing of intent.

Second, in addition to circumstantial evidence demonstrating an intention to elicit improper disclosure of trade secrets, a trade secret owner can show that such disclosure is inevitable by virtue of the particular circumstances of the situation. This showing is most frequently demonstrated by evidence that the work to be performed by the former employee is very similar to the work previously performed for the trade secret owner, and that the former employee will be unable to perform the new job conscientiously without revealing trade secrets previously learned.

---

xxv *Surgidev Corp. v. Eye Technology Inc.*, 648 F. Supp. 661, 695 (D. Minn. 1986), aff'd, 828 F.2d 452 (8th Cir. 1987).

xxvi For example, in *Convolve, Inc. v. Compaq Computer Corp.*, 2006 U.S. Dist. LEXIS 13848, the plaintiffs asserted that the defendants were misappropriating trade secrets in violation of a nondisclosure agreement. As evidence of this violation, the plaintiffs showed that the defendants tried unsuccessfully to reverse engineer the trade secret-protected software. That evidence, interalia, was sufficient to withstand a motion for summary judgment.

Although circumstantial evidence is generally not considered as strong as direct evidence, it is clear that courts will issue injunctions prohibiting the misappropriation of trade secrets based solely on circumstantial evidence that indicates such activity is imminently likely to occur. For example, in *PepsiCo, Inc. v. Redmond* (https://www.openstax.org/l/PepsiVRedmond) , 54 F.3d 1262, the defendant moved from a senior position at PepsiCo to a position at rival Quaker Oats Company (then owner of the Gatorade brand, which is now owned by Pepsi). The court held that it was proper for the district court to conclude that based on the defendant's access to Pepsi's trade secrets, it was inevitable as part of the defendant's new employment that the trade secrets would be relied on. The district court concluded that unless the defendant possessed "an uncanny ability to compartmentalize information," he would necessarily make decisions for the new employer by relying on the trade secrets. This was true even though there was no direct evidence that Redmond disclosed any of Pepsi's trade secrets.

## Act Fast

A trade secret owner who suspects that either actual or threatened misappropriation has occurred or is likely to occur must act promptly to enforce their legal rights. Although the statute of limitations under the UTSA is three years, courts have the power to deny the relief requested by trade secret owners even when an action has been initiated within the statute of limitations period, if the action has not been initiated reasonably promptly. The UTSA assumes that a trade secret owner who suspects misappropriation will move with reasonable alacrity to protect intellectual property, and recognizes that if such action is not taken, then third parties may materially change their positions in a good-faith belief that no trade secret rights have been violated. Under such circumstances, a court may find that the trade secret owner has been estopped from exercising, or waived their right to seek protection under the UTSA. These principles essentially allow the court to find that even though the information that a party seeks to protect meets the requirements of a trade secret, equity demands that the information not be protected as a trade secret because protecting it would harm a third party.[xxvii]

---

xxvii See *Watermark Solid Surface, Inc. v. Sta-Care, Inc.*, 2009 WL 723199 (W.D. Wis. 2009) (discussing waiver of trade secret protection); Christianson v. Colt Industries Operating Corp., 766 F.Supp. 670 (C.D. Ill. 1991) (outlining common equitable defenses in trade secrets cases).

## 5.6 Remedies Available for the Misappropriation of Trade Secrets

**Figure 5.6** (credit: Joe Ravi via Wikimedia Commons / CC BY SA 3.0)

### Learning Objectives

After completing this section, you will be able to

- Describe how injunctions are used to enjoin actual and threatened misappropriations of trade secrets.
- Explain how remedies are awarded under the Uniform Trade Secrets Act.

The UTSA provides a full array of remedies, including **statutory damages**, **injunctive relief**, **attorneys' fees**, and **exemplary damages**.[xxviii] The remedy or remedies will depend on the extent of trade secrets involved, the manner of misappropriation or conversion, and the type of damage sustained by the owner.

### Injunctive Relief

As discussed above, under the UTSA, injunctive relief is available to enjoin actual, as well as threatened, misappropriation. Injunctive relief allows the owner of a trade secret to obtain a court order prohibiting the actual or threatened misappropriation of a trade secret. The ability to enjoin threatened misappropriation is very important because it enables the owner of the trade secret to prevent public disclosure of the trade secret.[xxix] Injunctive relief may take many forms. The scope of an injunction may vary from a broad prohibition on any use of material found to be a trade secret, to a more limited prohibition on the scope of an employee's work with a new employer.[xxx] Both the scope and subject matter of an injunction vary depending upon the specific facts of the case and the nature of the trade secret in question. The UTSA provides that an injunction shall terminate once the trade secret ceases to exist, but may be continued for a reasonable period of time to extinguish any commercial advantage that otherwise would be derived from the misappropriation. This is especially important where, at the time of the action, the information or knowledge is no longer a trade secret. In such a case, the court may still award the owner injunctive relief that is narrowly crafted to deprive the defendant of the benefit of time saved by improper use of the owner's trade secret.[xxxi]

---

xxviii See Unif. Trade Secrets Act §§ 2-5, U.L.A (1985).

xxix *Standard Brands, Inc. v. Zumpe*, 264 F. Supp. 254, 269 (E.D. La. 1967).

xxx See *3M v. Pribyl*, 259 F.3d 587, 598 (7th Cir 2001) (upholding broad injunction on use of material in employee handbook, as overly specific injunctions may invite evasion).

| | |
|---|---|
| Definition | Injunctive relief allows the owner of a trade secret to legally prohibit a former employee, for example, from misappropriating, publicly disclosing, or otherwise profiting from knowledge of the trade secret. |
| Scope | The scope of an injunction varies based on the on the nature of the potential misappropriator's knowledge of the trade secret, and on the potential competitive advantage that knowledge might grant. |
| Duration and Termination | The duration of an injunction is determined based on the amount of time it would take a competitor to reveal the trade secret by proper means. An injunction can be terminated when the trade secret ceases to exist. |
| Permanent Injunctions | To determine the appropriate length of time, courts may rely on the opinions/experience of experts and competitors. They may impose permanent injunctions or rely on other considerations seen as important by the court. |

**Table 5.2** Injunctive Relief

Where the information has not been publicly disclosed, the issue becomes more difficult. The duration of the injunction is often calculated according to the time that would be required for independent development of the information or knowledge that was misappropriated. These "head start" injunctions assume that the information could be properly obtained through reverse engineering or independent development.[xxxii]

To determine what length of time is appropriate, courts may rely on the opinions of experts and the experience of other competitors.[xxxiii] However, a court may also opt to impose a permanent injunction that can later be modified, or in some circumstance rely on other considerations deemed important by the court.[xxxiv]

Courts also exhibit broad flexibility in the nature and duration of relief in cases dealing with former employees. When an injunction is issued in these cases, it usually will not be an outright ban on employment. Rather, it will be a more limited injunction for a more limited duration.[xxxv] Most courts are willing to allow continued employment, but will restrict the employee from working with a particular product line or area of the new employer's business.[xxxvi] However, if the role the employee will assume would inevitably lead to the disclosure of trade secrets, the employment may be prohibited altogether.[xxxvii]

---

xxxi See *Cherne Indus., Inc. v. Grounds & Associates*, 278 N.W.2d 81 (Minn. 1979).

xxxii See, e.g., *Surgidev Corp. v. Eye Technology, Inc.*, 828 F.2d 452, 456-457 (8th Cir. 1987) (affirming 15-month injunction based on the period of time that would be required for independent development of the protected information).

xxxiii See, Restatement (Third) of Unfair Competition Section 44, comment f.

xxxiv See e.g., *General Electric Co. v. Sung*, 843 F. Supp. 776, 780-781 (D. Mass. 1994) (seven-year product injunction, taking into account the willfulness of the misappropriation).

xxxv See, e.g., *Doubleclick v. Henderson*, No. 116914/97 (N.Y. Sup. Ct. Nov. 5, 1997) (granting an injunction restraining two former employees from competing with their former employer for a period of six months).

xxxvi See, *Merck & Co. Inc v. Lyon*, 941 F. Supp. 1443 (M.D.N.C. 1996). See also Allis Chalmers Manf. Co. v. Continental Aviation and Eng. Corp., 255 F. Supp. 645 (E.D. Mich. 1966) (injunction limited to research as to a particular type of pump); but see *Union Carbide Corp. v. UGI Corp.*, 731 F.2d 1186 (5th Cir. 1984) (affirming injunction against use of information in 14 broad areas).

xxxvii *PepsiCo, Inc. v. Redmond*, 54 F.3d 1262, 1272 (7th Cir 1995).

## Damages Awarded

Damages are often awarded in addition to an injunction and are not an exclusive remedy.[xxxviii] For example, in Seagate Tech., LLC v. Western Digital Corp. (https://www.openstax.org/l/SeagateVWD), 834 N.W.2d 555 (Minn. App. 2013), the Minnesota Court of Appeals affirmed a judgment of $630 million in favor of the plaintiffs against the defendants stemming from a trade secret misappropriation dispute. Under the UTSA, damages are measured by the actual loss caused by the misappropriation as well as any resulting unjust enrichment of the misappropriator. Where the amount of actual loss or unjust enrichment cannot be accurately calculated, the UTSA provides that damages may also be measured by the imposition of a reasonable royalty for the misappropriator's unauthorized disclosure or use of the trade secret. Exemplary or punitive damages may be awarded where the court finds that the misappropriation was willful and malicious.[xxxix] For example, in Mattel, Inc. v. MGA Entm't, Inc. (https://www.openstax.org/l/MattelVMGA), 801 F. Supp. 2d 950 (C.D. Cal 2011), Mattel was found to have engaged in a prolonged practice of encouraging employees to use false pretenses to acquire competitive information from the defendant. As a result of this conduct, the jury awarded, and the court affirmed a verdict of $85 million dollars in exemplary damages. A punitive or exemplary award may not exceed twice the amount of the damage award.[xl] However, some states have modified this cap on punitive damages, and allow for punitive damages greater than two times the amount of actual damages.[xli]

**Case Studies**

| Case | Description of Damages |
|---|---|
| *Seagate Tech., LLC v. Western Digital Corp.* (https://www.openstax.org/l/SeagateVWD) | In this case, the Minnesota Court of Appeals affirmed a judgment of $630 million in favor of the plaintiff stemming from a trade secret misappropriation. Under the UTSA, damages are measured by the actual loss caused by the misappropriation and any resulting unjust enrichment of the misappropriator. |
| *Mattel, Inc. v. MGA Entm't. Inc.* (https://www.openstax.org/l/MattelVMGA) | In this case, Mattel was found to have encouraged employees to use false pretenses to acquire competitive information from the defendant. As a result of this conduct, $85 million dollars in exemplary damages was awarded. A punitive or exemplary award may not exceed twice the amount of the damage award.[xlii] However, some states have modified this cap.[xliii] |

**Table 5.3**

In exceptional circumstances, an injunction may entitle the owner of the trade secret to a royalty for the period of time during which the use of the trade secret was prohibited. For example, the Supreme Court of Georgia has affirmed a trial court's reliance on a seldom-used provision of the UTSA to impose a "royalty injunction" instead of an injunction prohibiting the use of the plaintiff's trade secret.[xliv]

---

xxxviii See e.g., *Mikes Train House, Inc. v. Lionel, L.L.C.*, 472 F.3d 398, 413-15 (6th Cir. 2006).

xxxix See, e.g., *Aries Information Sys., Inc. v. Pacific Management Sys. Corp.*, 366 N.W.2d 366 (Minn. Ct. App. 1985).

xl See Unif. Trade Secrets Act § 3(b), U.L.A (1985).

xli *Reingold v. Swiftships, Inc.*, 210 F.3d 320, 323 (5th Cir. 2000).

xlii *Reingold v. Swiftships*, Inc., 210 F.3d 320, 323 (5th Cir. 2000).

xliii See Unif. Trade Secrets Act § 3(b), U.L.A (1985).

xliv See *Electronic Data Systems Corp. v. Heinemann*, 493 S.E.2d 132 (Ga. Sup. Ct. 1997).

A court may also award attorneys' fees to a prevailing party in exceptional circumstances. A bad faith claim of misappropriation, a bad faith resistance to a motion to terminate an injunction, or a finding of willful and malicious appropriation are exceptional circumstances in which an award of attorneys' fees may be appropriate. However, courts are generally disinclined to award attorneys' fees.[xlv] The attorney fee provision is included to dissuade parties from filing malicious misappropriation actions in bad faith, and considered along with the need for exemplary damages.[xlvi]

xlv See, e.g., *Gordon Employment, Inc. v. Jewe1*, 356 N.W.2d 738 (Minn. Ct. App. 1984).

xlvi See Unif. Trade Secrets Act § 4 (comment), U.L.A(1985).

## Assessment Questions

1. Unlike patents and trademarks, the law requires that intellectual property consisting of trade secrets not be publicly disclosed. True or False?
   A. True.
   B. False.

2. Which of the following best describes a trade secret?
   A. Information that many people do not know about how a product like a smartphone is made.
   B. Virtually any information that is of value as a result of not being generally known.
   C. Any information relating to the finances of a publicly held company.

3. Trade secret theft or misappropriation costs the world's richest 40 nations approximately how much of their gross domestic product, or GDP, each year?
   A. 1 to 3 percent.
   B. 4 to 6 percent.
   C. 7 to 10 percent.

4. What are the two main requirements for information to be protectable as a trade secret?
   A. It must be novel and non-obvious.
   B. It must be original and expressed in a tangible form that can be seen or copied.
   C. It must be not generally known by others, and it must have been subject to reasonable efforts to avoid public disclosure.

5. What is one key advantage of trade secret protection versus patent protection?
   A. It protects the information to be kept secret indefinitely.
   B. It prevents others from ever independently deriving the same information.
   C. Both of the above are correct.

6. If you invent faster-than-light travel but believe someone will be able to reverse engineer it by examining your starship, should you patent it or keep it as a trade secret?
   A. Keep it as a trade secret.
   B. Patent it.

7. What did the Supreme Court note in the case of *Bonito Boats v. Thunder Craft Boats*?
   A. One cannot legally misappropriate trade secrets.
   B. Nobody is above the law, not even a trade secret owner.
   C. The holder of a trade secret does not have protection against reverse engineering.

8. If information is protected as a valid trade secret, a competitor can be stopped from using it no matter who he obtained it from. True or False?
   A. True.
   B. False.

9. Trade secret protection is guaranteed by the federal government. True or False?
   A. True.
   B. False.

10. In which country did trade secret law first originate in the early 1800s?
    A. France.
    B. The United States.
    C. England.

11. What impact did the Uniform Trade Secrets Act (UTSA) of 1979 have on trade secret protection in the United States?
    A. It was the first trade secret law binding on every state.
    B. It served as a model that was adopted by 48 of the 50 U.S. states.
    C. It served as a model that was adopted by every state.

12. Which of the following best describes the problem with the current lack of uniform federal protection of trade secrets?
    A. There is no real protection against misappropriation of trade secrets.
    B. The protections against trade secret theft are very uneven.
    C. A federal trade secret law would merely replicate state protections.

13. Which of the following could be considered a trade secret so long as reasonable steps had been taken to prevent its disclosure?
    A. Sales information.
    B. Customer lists.
    C. Manufacturing techniques.
    D. All of the above.

14. Is information not known to the public considered to be a trade secret?
    A. Yes.
    B. No.
    C. It depends.

15. Would a customer list always be considered a trade secret?
    A. It depends on whether the customers want to be identified or not.
    B. To be considered a trade secret, the names of customers must not be available or discernable through public sources.

16. Can a mere idea be considered a trade secret?
    A. No. Just as you cannot patent or copyright a mere idea, you cannot protect a mere idea with a trade secret.
    B. Yes. Under the Uniform Trade Secrets Act, even an idea can sometimes be considered a trade secret.

17. To gain trade secret protection, what must the owner do with confidential information?
    A. Publicize it as widely as possible.
    B. Not disclose it.
    C. Take active steps to keep the information secret.

18. What are the benefits of developing a written trade secret plan?
    A. It serves as a policy manual that prevents situations in which unwritten rules are followed and security procedures are ignored.
    B. In the event of litigation, it can serve as proof that you took active steps to keep the information secret.
    C. Both of these.

**19.** How should companies handle written trade secrets?
   A. Shred them.
   B. Mark them "secret" or "confidential," among other measures taken.
   C. Never store them on a computer.

**20.** Which of these is an example of "passive disclosure" of a trade secret?
   A. Leaving confidential documents lying around for anyone to see.
   B. Inadvertently disseminating information at trade shows or conferences.
   C. Disclosing confidential information in press releases, newspaper articles, or marketing collateral.

**21.** What is one way to guard against the active disclosure of trade secret information?
   A. Prevent employee attendance at trade shows and seminars.
   B. Appoint a trade secret committee to approve publications, speeches, and marketing collateral prior to disclosure.
   C. Avoid meeting with prospective buyers, customers, or licensees.

**22.** Which of the following is NOT an example of misappropriation of a trade secret?
   A. Acquisition of a trade secret through improper means.
   B. Deliberate disclosure of a trade secret by the trade secret owner.
   C. Disclosure of a trade secret without consent.

**23.** The UTSA not only prohibits the actual disclosure or use of a trade secret, it also protects against the "threatened" disclosure of trade secrets. When might a court intervene to stop a "threatened" disclosure before the actual disclosure takes place?
   A. An employee goes to work for another company in a different industry.
   B. An employee caught embezzling is fired and the employer believes the same lack of morals will lead to the fired employee disclosing trade secrets.
   C. An employee goes to work for an arch competitor in a comparable job position.

**24.** The burden of proof in a threatened trade secret misappropriation case lies with whom?
   A. The trade secret owner.
   B. The former employee who leaves to go work for a competitor.
   C. The competitor, who must prove he did no wrong by hiring the ex-employee.

**25.** What remedies does the UTSA provide for the misappropriation of trade secrets? (Choose all that apply.)
   A. Criminal penalties of up to five years for a first offense.
   B. Statutory damages.
   C. Injunctive relief.
   D. Exemplary damages.
   E. Attorneys' fees.

**26.** What remedies were imposed in the case of *Mattel, Inc. v. MGA Entm't, Inc.* in 2013?
   A. An injunction barring a new employer from hiring the former employee of the trade secret owner.
   B. $85 million in exemplary (punitive) damages awarded to the trade secret owner.

# A Glossary

## Chapter 1

- **bargain or contract theory** The premise that people will be encouraged to invent new products and services that benefit society if they are likely to profit by doing so.
- **design patents** A type of patent granted to protect new, original, and non-obvious ornamental designs for articles of manufacture.
- **first office action** A document in which the patent examiner approves, rejects, or requires additional information about the claims and/or other elements of the application.
- **intellectual property** Creations of intellect, such as inventions and artistic works.
- **natural rights theory** The premise that the product of mental labor is by all rights the property of its creator, no less than the product of physical labor is the property of its creator (or of the person who purchases it from that creator).
- **non-obviousness** A patent requirement that ensures that the idea is inventive.
- **non-practicing entities** An entity created by the Founding Fathers to expand the pool of inventors in their then-backward economy to include ordinary citizens without the wealth or resources to commercialize their own inventions.
- **novelty** A patent requirement that ensures that the idea is new.
- **ornamentality** A parent requrement that ensures that the idea is decorative.
- **patent examiner** The person who reviews the patent application to determine if the invention meets the statutory requirements for patentability.
- **patent** An intellectual property right granted by the government of a nation to an inventor that gives them the exclusive right to the invention for up to 20 years, in exchange for disclosing the details of the new technology to society for its ultimate benefit.
- **plant patents** A type of patent to protect new species of plants. The criteria is novelty, distinctiveness, and non-obviousness.
- **utility patents** The most common type of patents, which preclude others from making, using, or selling the invention during the term of the patent, which begins on the grant date and ends 20 years from the filing date (for an average of 17 to 18 years).
- **utility** A patent requirement that ensures that the idea is usable and beneficial.
- **working requirements** Regulations that forced patentees to manufacture products based on their patents within two or three years of issuance or lose their patent rights.

## Chapter 2

- **America Invents Act (AIA)** A 2011 act that substantially revised the nation's patent laws in a number of important ways.
- **Complaint** A legal document filed that sets out why the filing party believes their claim against the defendant is valid.
- **Counterclaims** New charges filed against the plaintiff.
- **covered business methods review** To review patents that claim a method or corresponding apparatus for performing data processing or other operations used in the practice, administration, or management of a financial product or service.
- **doctrine of equivalents** The legal rule that prevents an infringer from copying the essence of the invention, but making insignificant modifications in an effort to avoid infringement.
- **estoppel** Misleading your opponent into believing you would not file suit.
- **laches** Waiting an unreasonable time to make your claim.
- **liability violation** A type of violation in which you do not need to know that you are infringing a patent, or that a patent even exists, to be liable for patent infringement.
- **Markman hearings** Hearings in which parties are permitted to provide their competing arguments in

briefs to the court, usually after discovery is completed, and make an oral argument on their respective positions to the court.

- **post-grant review** A trial proceeding that asks the PTO to take another look at whether the patent is valid, i.e., whether it should have been granted in the first place.
- **royalty** Money by offered the alleged infringer a license to practice your invention.
- **Scheduling Order** A specification of dates by which certain activities must be concluded, issues by the court at, or shortly after, the pretrial conference.
- **stay** A temporary suspention of a case ordered by the court.
- **Summary Judgment** a procedure that obviates a trial where one of the parties can show that its opponent cannot win—as a matter of law.
- **venue** The location for the case.
- **willful** A patent infringement in which the the accused infringer "acted despite an objectively high likelihood that its actions constituted infringement of a valid patent," and the "objectively defined risk . . . was either known or so obvious that it should have been known to the accused infringer."

## Chapter 3

- **Berne Convention** An international agreement to ensure fair and reciprocal copyright protection for member nations.
- **Copyright Act of 1976** An act which extended copyright protection to works performed over cable TV and music performed via digital audio transmission.
- **Creative Commons** A voluntary private sector alternative to traditional copyright that coordinates the creation and consumption of content among a wide variety of individuals and institutions—all without a hint of government intervention.
- **Digital Millennium Copyright Act of 1998 (DMCA)** An act which made it a crime to disseminate technology or services that could circumvent DRM measures used to control access to copyrighted movies, music, and books. It also increased penalties for copyright infringement on the Internet.
- **infringement** A violation of the exclusive rights of its owner of a copyright or any other intellectual property.
- **No Electronic Theft Act of 1997** An act which made it a criminal offense to reproduce or distribute music by electronic means (i.e., over the Internet).
- **Sonny Bono Copyright Term Extension Act** An Act which added an additional 20 years to the term of copyright—extending it for most works to the life of the author plus 70 years after the author is deceased.
- **Statute of Anne** A 1709 copyright statute which stipulated that a copyright could be obtained by anyone, and instead of a perpetual right, the term was limited to 14 years with the right to renew for one additional 14-year term.
- **work for hire** A work prepared by an employee within the scope of their employment, or a work specially ordered or commissioned for use as a contribution to a collective work.

## Chapter 4

- **Arbitrary marks** Real words in common usage that have no descriptive relationship to the product or service being sold.
- **certification marks** Any word, phrase, symbol or design—or a combination of any of these—owned by one party which certifies the goods and services of others when they meet certain standards or requirements.
- **classic fair use** A condition that occurs when a trademark is used in good faith for its primary meaning, and no consumer confusion is likely to occur.
- **collective marks** Any word, phrase, symbol, or design that is owned by a cooperative, association, collective group, or organization and is used by its members to indicate the source of goods or services.
- **descriptive mark** Marks that explicitly describes the purpose, nature, or an attribute of a product or service and is therefore not eligible for trademark registration unless a secondary meaning or association

has been developed in the public's mind through usage.

- **distinctiveness** The fundamental and overriding requirement for a trademark. The requirement for distinctiveness is analogous to the requirement for *novelty* in patent rights and *originality* in copyright.
- **Fanciful marks** Invented words, symbols or devices that have no relation to the good or service being sold and have no meaning other than to distinctly identify the product or service and distinguish it in the minds of consumers from those of any other vendor.
- **generic marks** Simply the common name for the goods and services being sold.
- **nominative fair use** A condition that covers many occasions on which a party other than the trademark owner is using the mark to refer to genuine goods or services.
- **service marks** A mark with the same principle as trademarks except that these words, names, symbols, or devices identify and distinguish the source of a service.
- **similarity** So resembling another name or mark that it will be likely to cause confusion, or to cause mistake, or to deceive.
- **spectrum of distinctiveness** A spectrum of the five basic categories of marks based on how distinct they are. The marks from most to least distinct are: Fanciful, arbitrary, suggestive, descriptive, and generic.
- **Suggestive marks** Marks that suggest or imply a quality or characteristic of the goods and services being sold. They require imagination, insight, or perception on the part of the consumer as to the nature of the article.
- **trademark dilution** The weakening of a famous mark's ability to identify and distinguish goods or services, regardless of competition in the marketplace or the likelihood of confusion.
- **trademark** An intellectual property right granted by a government to an individual, business, or legal entity that creates and uses a distinctive word, name, symbol, or device to distinguish its products or services from those from any other entity in the marketplace.

## Chapter 5

- **active disclosure** A type of disclosure that might occur during a guided tour of the facility when a tour guide reveals the nature of a project or process the company is working on or has recently perfected.
- **exemplary damages** A remedy that is intended to deter the defendant and from engaging in similar conduct.
- **injunctive relief** A remedy that allows the owner of a trade secret to obtain a court order prohibiting the actual or threatened misappropriation of a trade secret.
- **misappropriation** Unauthorized use.
- **passive disclosure** A type of disclosure that might occur by carelessly leaving documents containing trade secrets in open view when business associates from another company visit your facility.
- **statutory damages** A remedy that is stipulated within the statute rather the degree of harm to the plaintiff.
- **trade secret** A law that requires that the intellectual property to be protected not be publicly disclosed.

# Answer Key

## Chapter 1

1. B.
2. A.
3. A. and D.
4. D.
5. C.
6. D.
7. D.
8. B.
9. D.
10. C.
11. C.
12. C.
13. B.
14. A.
15. B.
16. C.
17. D.
18. A. A machine—a tool with moving parts and uses energy.; B. A composition of matter—a synthesized chemical compound or molecule.; C. A process—a way to do something new or a new way to do something old.; D. A manufacture—a part or product produced according to design.
19. A. It's a product—a physical thing.; B. A process—a way to do something new or a new way to do something old.; C. It's also a product—a physical thing.; D. Also a product—a physical thing.
20. B.
21. A.
22. B.
23. B.
24. D.
25. A.
26. B.
27. B.
28. B.
29. B.
30. B.
31. A.
32. C.
33. C.
34. C.
35. B.
36. B.
37. C.
38. A. These are called small entities, and receive a 50% discount in application fees.; B. These are micro-entities, and receive a 75% discount in filing fees.
39. D.
40. B.
41. A.
42. C.
43. B.

44. D.

## Chapter 2

1. C.
2. B.
3. B.
4. A.
5. C.
6. C.
7. D.
8. C.
9. C.
10. A.
11. C.
12. C.
13. C.
14. C.
15. C.
16. B.
17. C.
18. A.
19. B.
20. B.
21. C.
22. D.
23. C.
24. C.

## Chapter 3

1. A.
2. B.
3. A. and C.
4. C.
5. D.
6. A. and C.
7. C.
8. C.
9. C.
10. C.
11. E.
12. B.
13. C.
14. A.
15. B.
16. A. and B.
17. B.
18. C.
19. B.
20. C.

21. B.
22. C.
23. C.
24. A.
25. D.
26. B.
27. A. and B.
28. B.
29. E.
30. B.
31. C.
32. C.
33. E.
34. B.
35. C.
36. B.
37. C.
38. C.
39. B.
40. B.
41. C.
42. B.
43. C.
44. B.
45. B.
46. A.
47. D.
48. A.
49. B.
50. D.
51. C.
52. B.
53. B.
54. E.

## Chapter 4

1. B.
2. C.
3. C.
4. D.
5. A.
6. D.
7. C.
8. B.
9. C.
10. D.
11. D.
12. B.
13. A.

14. C.
15. C.
16. B.
17. A.
18. A.
19. A. Name (Chanel); B. Device (a sound).; C. Device (the distinctive blue color).; D. Device (a sound).
20. C.
21. C.
22. C.
23. B.
24. B.
25. A. Arbitrary. "Apple" is an example of a real word in common usage that has absolutely no relationship to the product or service being sold.; B. Fanciful. "Xerox" is a completely invented word that has no meaning except to indicate the source of a copier manufacturer. Fanciful marks are the strongest type of mark you can have.; C. Suggestive. The word "iPad" suggests or implies a quality or characteristic of the good being sold and is distinctive to its manufacturer (Apple).; D. Suggestive. Again, "Coppertone" suggests the quality or color of the tan you'll get, while indicating which company is selling it.; E. Descriptive. "Windows" is one of the rare marks that describe the nature of a distinctive product (computer software) from a unique manufacturer.
26. C.
27. B.
28. D.
29. D.
30. A.
31. B.
32. D.
33. D.
34. B.
35. A.
36. A.
37. B.

## Chapter 5

1. A.
2. B.
3. A.
4. C.
5. A.
6. B.
7. C.
8. B.
9. B.
10. C.
11. B.
12. B.
13. D.
14. C.
15. B.
16. A.

**17**. C.
**18**. C.
**19**. B.
**20**. A.
**21**. B.
**22**. B.
**23**. C.
**24**. A.
**25**. B.
**26**. B.

# Index

Made in United States
Cleveland, OH
05 November 2026

47675526R00108